Your Baby and Toddler Problems Solved

Gina Ford

Vermilion
LONDON

1 3 5 7 9 10 8 6 4 2

Vermilion, an imprint of Ebury Publishing,
20 Vauxhall Bridge Road,
London SW1V 2SA

Vermilion is part of the Penguin Random House group of companies
whose addresses can be found at global.penguinrandomhouse.com

Copyright © Gina Ford, 2016

Gina Ford has asserted her right to be identified as the author of this
Work in accordance with the Copyright, Designs and Patents Act 1988

First published in the United Kingdom by Vermilion in 2016

www.penguin.co.uk

A CIP catalogue record for this book is available from the British Library

ISBN 9781785040344

Printed and bound in Great Britain by Clays Ltd, St Ives PLC

MIX
Paper from
responsible sources
FSC
www.fsc.org
FSC® C018179

Penguin Random House is committed to a
sustainable future for our business, our readers
and our planet. This book is made from Forest
Stewardship Council® certified paper.

Contents

Acknowledgements

I would like to say a very special thank you to all the parents who have shared their parenting experiences with me. Your trust and faith in me and the constant support and feedback you have given me over the years has enabled me to learn so much about the sleeping and feeding habits of babies and young children, and make this book possible.

I would also like to express my thanks and gratitude to Imogen Fortes for her constant source of great ideas and helpful suggestions – you were completely invaluable in helping to pull this book together.

A special debt of thanks to my agent Emma Todd, my publisher at Ebury Susanna Abbott, my Editor Morwenna Loughman, Emma Owen for all your help throughout the editorial process, Julia Kellaway, Sarah Bennie and everyone else at Random House. I shall be eternally grateful for your never-ending support.

And, finally, a huge thank you for the wonderful support given to me while writing this book by Kate Brian, the website editor, Alison Jermyn, Christel Davidson, Rory Jenkins and the rest of the team at Contentedbaby.com

Introduction

When you become parents to a newborn baby, you are entering a wonderfully exciting world, but the first few months are often quite daunting. Parents may feel unprepared for the overwhelming change to their lives that a new baby can bring. It will be an enriching experience, but initially you may feel anxious about caring for the tiny new baby who is entirely dependent on you.

Over the years I have worked with many thousands of parents, and helped to find solutions to the challenges they are having with their babies and their toddlers. My first book, *The Contented Little Baby Book* (published in 1999), was based on my experiences of working with over 300 babies and their families, and since then I have communicated with thousands of parents through my consultancy work and the Contented Baby website, www.contentedbaby.com, which I set up to help parents who felt isolated as they navigated their way through those early months. Through this direct contact, I have become familiar with the most common problems new parents experience. I know how tired and anxious mums and dads can become, desperately seeking immediate solutions to their problems – and they don't want to search hard for the answers.

With that in mind, I decided to write a problem-solving guide, to provide parents with the answers to the questions they most frequently seek. This book addresses the most common problems I come across for parents who need straightforward easy-to-access solutions.

I have divided the chapters up by age in order to focus on the range of issues that can arise at different stages of your baby's development. Each chapter will begin with a brief explanation of what parents might expect at that age, highlighting some of the areas where concerns can arise. I will then outline and explore some of the most common problems I encounter in my consultations – giving a brief explanation of the problem as you may experience it and then providing the different solutions that can be used to address it.

Within each chapter problems are grouped under 'feeding', 'sleeping' and 'general' problems. What I have found, however, is that all too often a parent comes to me with a sleeping problem that is actually a feeding problem – diet can have a huge impact on sleep – or will come to me with a feeding problem that is caused by overtiredness, which makes feeding difficult. This isn't just true for babies; with older children too, eating the wrong type of food can lead to behavioural problems. It's surprising how rarely the overlap between these issues is acknowledged, with so much of the advice offered today being focused on one specific area rather than looking at the bigger picture. I would therefore encourage you to read both sections as what you think is a feeding problem may in fact be caused by something to do with your baby's sleep.

When parents come to me for consultations, I always aim to get as broad a picture as possible of their baby's routine, sleep and feeding patterns so that I can see where the links in the chain may be weak or broken, and work out which issues need addressing. I have drawn on all the latest research in the field of childcare, in order to ensure that my conclusions take account of the most recent theories and developments.

You will discover that some of the same problems crop up more than once in the book as you progress from month to month. This is because, as your baby grows and develops, the reasons he may be feeding fussily or waking several times in the night will change so I have tried to take account of what is happening at his age.

Whether you have a specific problem that you are hoping to solve, or just wish to learn more generally about the issues that can arise at different stages of your baby's development, I hope that you will find much of interest in the pages ahead. I firmly believe that many of the challenges parents face are best addressed in a holistic way, and that this will help ensure that you have a happy and contented baby or toddler.

Gina

PART 1

Understanding the Basics

1

The Contented Little Baby Philosophy and Routines

I remember my first babysitting assignment with a six-month-old baby. I arrived at the house around 6.45pm and the baby had just been put to bed. I heard a loud wailing from the nursery upstairs, but was assured by the mother that little Joseph would soon settle within 10 minutes. True to his mother's word within eight minutes Joseph was fast asleep and remained so until the parents arrived home around 11pm.

When I first started caring for babies nearly 40 years ago, strict four-hourly feeding routines with a bedtime around 6.30/7pm was the norm/fashion and this was the approach that was adopted by the majority of parents. Never in a million years did any of those parents I worked for ever think that what they were doing was uncaring. They believed that being a good parent wasn't just about loving their baby, but ensuring that their baby was well fed and slept soundly, so that long-term sleeping and feeding problems were avoided.

Fast forward 10 years and attitudes to parenting changed, as approaches like baby-led and attachment parenting became the norm/fashion. Out went the strict four-hourly routines, regular feeds and early bedtimes and in came babies feeding every two hours around the clock, watching the 10 o'clock news and sleeping with their parents. Over the next 10 years I worked as a maternity nurse with many different families, some still following the strict four-hourly feeding routines and many more following the more relaxed baby-led approach. Working with so many different families gave me an incredible insight into the different strategies on child rearing. I could see benefits and pitfalls in both approaches and my instinct told me that there had to be a middle ground: an approach somewhere in between the strict old-fashioned four-hourly feeding routines where a baby would not be fed before the scheduled time, regardless of whether they were hungry or not, to the other extreme where the least whimper from a baby, irrespective of what they really needed, prompted a reaction of feeding them.

As the popularity of baby-led parenting increased, so did the use of the famous 'controlled crying' method of sleep training. After months and months of feeding two hourly around the clock and babies rarely sleeping more than a two-hour stretch at a time, a huge number of sleep deprived parents would resort to sleep training their baby using the controlled crying method. I was convinced that there must be another way of getting babies to sleep through the night, without having to endure the crying that is inevitable with controlled crying.

This belief led me to taking copious notes for all the babies that I worked with. I charted their sleeping and feeding patterns, some following the baby-led approach and others the strict four-hourly routine approach. Little by little I adapted things from these two parenting methods, combining what I believed to be the best from each and eliminating what I believed to be the negatives. What evolved over those years is what is now known as the Contented Little Baby (CLB) routines. Unlike the four-hourly routines, the nine different routines that I devised for the first year of a baby's life could be adapted to meet the needs of a baby so that they never had to cry to be fed or because they were tired and needed to be put down. The CLB routines are based upon a baby's natural feeding and sleeping rhythms – you feed your baby and put him to sleep at certain times, thereby ensuring that his feeding and sleep are in sync with each other so that he is never too tired to feed and always takes a full feed so that he does not wake up from a nap early because he is hungry. Most importantly, the routines can be adapted to suit the individual needs of each baby; from extensive experience, I know that all babies are different.

In the time since this book was published, I have communicated with thousands of parents as a result of my consultancy work and through the Contented Baby website, www.contentedbaby.com. This regular and direct contact has enabled me to obtain useful feedback from parents on the CLB philosophy. The CLB routines and my core philosophy remain the same, but my advice has been expanded in response to this valuable feedback, and adapted to today's circumstances.

Why follow a routine?

Many years have passed since I first typed the four words, 'Why follow a routine?' Little did I know then the controversy those four simple words would create. But here I am, years later, explaining again why I think routine is important. I must stress that my views have not changed one little bit from when I wrote my first book. I personally believe that the majority of babies thrive and are happier in a routine. But I certainly realise and respect that following a routine is not a choice for all parents. The CLB routines will most certainly benefit both you and your baby and they are followed successfully by hundreds of thousands of parents around the world. But follow your own instinct as a parent as to what works best for you and your baby; the advice in this book is for all parents, regardless of whether they follow a routine or not.

Do I need to be following the CLB routines to benefit from this book?

Not at all – the advice in this book is for all parents, regardless of whether they follow a routine or not. There are, however, certain aspects of my philosophy and the way I structure the timings of a baby's day, particularly with regard to sleep, that it would be beneficial to understand so that you can appreciate the logic behind the solutions to the problems or so that when I use terms such as 'morning nap' or 'lunchtime nap' you will understand what I mean.

In *The New Contented Little Baby Book* my advice on sleeping is based on a day which runs from 7am to 7pm. The routine within that day is made up of blocks of sleep and awake time based around the baby's feeding and sleeping needs. By ensuring in the early days that a baby is awake no later than 7am, the timing of this day will allow you to fit in enough feeds, along with short blocks of awake and asleep time, before his 7pm bedtime so that a natural pattern of night-time feeding will also emerge. It will mean that a young baby is only waking and feeding twice in the night between 7pm and 7am. As the baby is always well fed and settled by 7pm, it means that he will sleep his first block of sleep in the night soundly for three to four hours. When he does wake he is ready to take a full feed and then settle back to sleep for his second block of sleep in the night, before waking in the middle of the night for another feed and then settling back to sleep for his third block of sleep.

As the baby grows the second block of sleep will become longer and longer until he is sleeping one shorter block of sleep from 7pm to 10/11pm and one longer block of sleep from a late feed around 10/11pm to nearer 7am in the morning.

By six to seven months most babies who are fully weaned will be ready to drop the late feed and then they will sleep one long block of sleep of 11 to 12 hours, from around 7pm to 6/7am.

Even if you have not been following my CLB routines and starting your day at 7am, the advice in this book can still be adapted and used to help resolve any problems that you may be having. While the individual sleeping and feeding needs of babies do vary from baby to baby, the table opposite will give you an approximate guide as to how much sleep your baby needs during his first year, broken up into night-time sleep and daytime sleep. I hope it will become a useful reference as your baby grows.

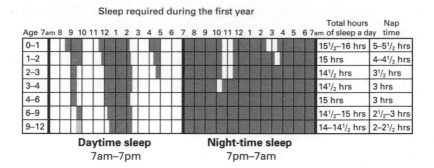

Sleep required during the first year

Age	7am 8 9 10 11 12 1 2 3 4 5 6 7 8 9 10 11 12 1 2 3 4 5 6 7am	Total hours of sleep a day	Nap time
0–1		15$^{1}/_{2}$–16 hrs	5–5$^{1}/_{2}$ hrs
1–2		15 hrs	4–4$^{1}/_{2}$ hrs
2–3		14$^{1}/_{2}$ hrs	3$^{1}/_{2}$ hrs
3–4		14$^{1}/_{2}$ hrs	3 hrs
4–6		15 hrs	3 hrs
6–9		14$^{1}/_{2}$–15 hrs	2$^{1}/_{2}$–3 hrs
9–12		14–14$^{1}/_{2}$ hrs	2–2$^{1}/_{2}$ hrs

Daytime sleep   **Night-time sleep**
7am–7pm   7pm–7am

I should also stress that, depending on your family's schedule, a 7am start might not be the most appropriate for you. I know many parents who adapt the timings of their day (and my routines) to suit an 8am to 8pm or 6am to 6pm day, according to their circumstances, so I hope you will do the same if this applies to you.

Understanding your baby's sleep and how much he needs is one of your most valuable tools in helping you to resolve problems, which is why the whole of the following chapter is devoted to sleep. I'd encourage you to read that chapter before you embark on any kind of problem-solving as I believe it will really help you to understand where things might be going wrong.

Preparing to resolve problems

Careful planning is the key to resolving problems as quickly as possible. While the advice and case studies in this book are here to help you, they alone will not resolve a problem if you do not also have a clearly written down plan of how you are going to approach it. When you are faced with trying to resolve problems a lack of sleep can blur one day into another and sometimes it is very difficult to remember what the main issues or action points are. By writing down a plan that both you and your partner are agreed upon, you will be much more likely to succeed in resolving it than if you try to deal with it as it is happening.

Timing is also critical. I usually advise parents to try, if possible, to start any form of troubleshooting on a Friday and even better if it can be done on a bank holiday weekend, where you have an extra day to get the plan going. I am not suggesting that your problems will be totally resolved in a weekend, but having three clear days to get your troubleshooting plan in operation, will certainly give you the best chance of a long-term resolution to the problem. Similarly, at weekends there will more likely be two of you at home, or the opportunity to call on another carer, which can provide extra help and support.

Below is a list of helpful tips you can use to prepare your action plan:

- Write down what you think is the main problem.

- List any additional issues that you think are connected to the problem, such as a partner working very long hours and not being around to help.

- Keep a detailed feeding, sleeping and behaviour diary for at least a week before commencing the troubleshooting.

- Discuss with your partner, child carer or nursery any points that they think are relevant to the problem.

- Once you have made a list of all the relevant points, discuss a plan of action with your partner and how you are going to approach it. Write down your plan of action. It's very easy to keep deviating when you're sleep deprived, but the key to resolving problems is to be consistent and writing a plan down will help you stick to it as you can easily refer back to it.

- If your problem-solving involves any form of sleep training (see pages 356–72) agree in advance whether one of you or both of you are going to deal with the night wakings.

- Agree a date that you are going to start the troubleshooting and ensure that you keep the first three days clear of any special family occasions, visitors and lengthy outings.

With most problems I'm trying to solve, once you get through the first few days you're well on your way. Problem-solving can of course be hard, but try to remind yourself that the reason you're doing this is to build a firm foundation. Any energy you put into problem-solving now will be so useful further down the line and prevent something becoming a long-term or bigger problem.

2

Understanding
Your Baby's Sleep

Sleep is probably one of the most misunderstood and confusing aspects of parenthood. The misconception is that for the first few weeks all a baby will do is feed and sleep. While many do, some newborns can be tense, fretful and difficult to settle and this can be very worrying for new parents. Please take heart – sleep problems in the early days need not be a reflection of your baby's future sleep habits. However, in order to understand the background to many of the problems in this book and how to solve them, I feel it is important to have an understanding of a baby's sleep patterns and how much sleep they need.

While the amount of sleep that individual babies need does vary and constantly changes as they grow, having a better understanding of sleep means you will be much more able to determine whether your baby or toddler has, or is possibly developing, a long-term sleep problem.

Above all, before attempting any form of routine or sleep training it is very important that you have a basic understanding of the different stages of sleep that babies and young children experience. Like adults, babies and children drift in and out of different stages of sleep and parents who do not fully understand these different phases often disturb what is a natural progression of the different sleep cycles.

When a baby stirs during a light stage of sleep, he will, if allowed and not needing a feed, usually return to a deeper stage of sleep. Parents who assume that these stirrings are caused by hunger and rush to the baby too quickly to try and get him back to sleep, often create long-term sleep association problems without realising what they are doing. Filmed research shows that all babies come into a light sleep several times a night, some even waking up fully for short spells. When the wakings are not due to genuine hunger, the research shows that the babies who have learned to self-settle will get themselves back to sleep fairly quickly. Babies who have been rocked, patted or fed to get them to sleep are unable to settle themselves back to sleep without the attentions that they associate with going to sleep.

Once the wrong sleep associations are created it will be very difficult for a baby to sleep a longer stretch. A baby who is always rocked, fed or given a dummy to get to sleep will be much more likely to continue to wake several times a night, long after the age when he needs a feed to get him through the night. Because he will naturally come into a light sleep several times a night, he will more than likely need the same comfort to get him back to sleep at each cycle.

Sleep Cycles

Sleep is divided into Rapid Eye Movement (REM) sleep, usually referred to as light sleep, and non-REM sleep, usually referred to as deep sleep. A newborn baby goes straight into REM sleep when he first goes to sleep. During this light sleep his breathing becomes irregular, his body may twitch or jerk, his eyelids will flicker and his eyes appear to roll. He may even smile or frown during this cycle. This sleep is often described as active sleep because a baby uses more oxygen and energy than during non-REM sleep. A baby who has gone full term will spend 50 per cent of his sleep cycle in REM sleep. A premature baby will spend 80 per cent in REM. The rest of the sleep cycle is spent in non-REM sleep.

During non-REM sleep the baby's breathing will be slow and regular. There are no eye movements and only the occasional twitch or jerk of the body. This calm sleep cycle is often described as quiet sleep. It allows the baby's mind and body to recharge, enabling him to cope with his next awake period. Research also shows us that this deep sleep is essential for the healthy development of a baby's mental and physical growth.

Dr Richard Ferber is widely recognised as America's leading authority in the field of children's sleep problems. His book *Solve Your Child's Sleep Problems* explains every aspect of children's sleep in great detail, as well as how problems evolve and how parents can resolve them. Dr Ferber says that non-REM sleep is well developed at birth but has not evolved into the four distinct stages experienced by older children and adults. It is not until the second month that a sequence of non-REM sleep stages begins to develop. When a baby of three months is ready to sleep, he first enters Stage One of non-REM – a drowsy sleep – then quickly passes into Stage Two – a light sleep – before reaching Stages Three and Four – very deep sleep. A whole cycle lasts around 40 minutes in babies and for toddlers it is around 60 minutes.

I have observed that it is between the ages of eight and 12 weeks that many parents begin to experience problems with their baby's daytime sleep, as the different stages of non-REM sleep begin to develop. These more distinct stages of light and deep sleep can sometimes result in a baby waking up 30–40 minutes into his middle-of-the-day nap and having difficulty getting back to sleep, although I have found that is most common in babies who are being assisted to sleep and have not learned how to self-settle.

If your baby is used to self-settling and starts to wake up 30–40 minutes into his lunchtime nap, provided you know he is well fed, then I would recommend that you allow him a short period of fussing to see if he will settle himself back to sleep. Usually I find that babies who are capable of self-settling will go back to sleep within 10–20 minutes. However, a baby who is used to being assisted to sleep is unlikely to return to sleep without your help and even babies who are self-settling at all of their other sleep times, will sometimes have difficulty self-settling at their lunchtime nap. The following tips can help get your baby through his first sleep cycle at the lunchtime nap.

● Offer your baby a top-up feed just prior to his lunchtime nap.

● Five minutes before your baby comes into his light sleep, stay close by his bed so that when he does come into his light sleep you can quickly shush him and stop his arms from thrashing around, which in turn stops him waking up fully.

- If he wakes fully and is getting upset, pick him up and offer him a feed to see if you can get him sleepy enough to settle him back into his bed again.

In the short term the important aim at this point is to get your baby back to sleep whichever way you can, so that he wakes up refreshed and happy to cope with social activities in the afternoon. In the long term, however, it is best if you help teach your baby to self-settle, so that he eventually learns to self-settle when he comes into his light sleep cycles during his lunchtime nap. If at this age you do not teach your baby to self-settle, you could find that he starts to wake in the evening 30–40 minutes after he has gone to sleep, and then increasingly start to wake up more often during the night when he comes into his light sleep cycle. Through my consultancy I often have to deal with young babies who are not capable of sleeping longer than one sleep cycle and need to be assisted back to sleep several times during the night.

If you find that despite all of your efforts your baby does not settle back to sleep at his lunchtime nap, you will then have to offer him two shorter naps in the afternoon: the first one probably being 1–1½ hours from the time he woke up from his lunchtime nap and the second usually another 1–1½ hours after that. The length of the naps will depend on how old your baby is, but a general guideline is to split what is left of his daily sleep allowance between the two shorter naps.

Daytime Sleep

Allowing too much sleep during the day can result in middle-of-the-night wakings or in difficulty settling your baby in the evening. But allowing too little sleep can often result in worse problems. Many parents make the mistake of allowing their baby or toddler little or no sleep during the day in the belief that he will sleep better at night. In my experience this rarely works, as the baby or toddler usually becomes so overtired and irritable that he is difficult to settle in the evening and is much more likely to wake in the night. Research confirms what I have always believed. Poor quality daytime sleep can affect not only the baby's mental development but also his ability to sleep well at night. Dr Marc Weissbluth, a leading researcher, paediatrician and founder of the Sleep Disorders Center, Children's Memorial Hospital, Chicago, and the Northwestern Children's Practice, has conducted extensive research into the nap patterns of more than 200 children. In his book *Healthy Sleep Habits, Happy Child* he says that: 'Napping is one of the health habits that sets the stage for good overall sleep.' He explains that a nap offers the baby or child a break from stimuli and allows it to recharge for further activity. Several other experts are in agreement that naps are essential to a baby's brain development and to helping establish long-term healthy sleep patterns. John Herman, PhD, infant sleep expert and associate professor of psychology and psychiatry at the University of Texas, says: 'If activities are being scheduled to the detriment of sleep, it's a mistake. Parents should remember that everything else in a baby's life should come after sleeping and eating.' Charles Schaefer, PhD, an American professor of psychology, supports this research and says: 'Naps structure the day, shape both the baby's and the mother's moods and offer the only opportunity for Mom to relax or accomplish a few tasks.' There is further evidence to support my view of the importance of daytime sleep being established at the right time. The best time for the longest nap of the day is between 12 noon and 2pm as this coincides with a baby's natural dip in alertness. A nap at this time will be deeper and more refreshing than a nap that starts later in the day.

Although babies and toddlers do vary in the amount of sleep they require, it is important that you have a clear understanding of how much sleep they need. The following summary of daytime sleep is a guide to how much sleep your baby or toddler needs and the best times for sleep to happen.

Summary of daytime sleep

Morning nap

During the first week or two most newborns will only manage to stay awake for an hour or so at a time and most of this time is taken up with feeding and changing. Between the second to fourth week they will usually be managing to stay awake properly for one to one and a half hours, although some very wakeful babies may manage to stay awake for up to two hours. The important thing to remember during the very early days is never to let your baby stay awake longer than two hours. If a baby stays awake longer than two hours he will often become overtired and fight sleep when you try to put him down for a nap. Overtiredness is one of the main causes of very young babies not settling well at nap times, and care should be taken that this does not happen.

Generally speaking, a baby under one month of age is usually ready for a nap one and a half hours after the time he wakes in the morning; some sleepy babies may only manage to stay awake for up to one hour. By the time babies reach two months, providing they're sleeping well at night, it is likely that they will manage to stay awake nearer to two hours before needing their morning nap. A typical pattern may be that when they first wake in the morning, they will stay awake for a full two hours, then after they have their first nap of the day they may only manage to stay awake for one and a half hours. Again the important thing is to watch for your baby's cues (see box overleaf) as to when he is sleepy and ensure that he is well fed and settled in his bed before he becomes overtired.

By the time they reach six months, the majority of babies can stay awake for between two and two and a half hours provided they're sleeping well in the night. If you are starting your day at 7am, babies should be woken from their morning nap no later than 10am if you want them to sleep for a longer time at midday, even if this means they have a short morning nap of only 20 minutes.

Between nine and 12 months most babies will cut right back on their morning nap, cutting it out altogether somewhere between 12 and 15 months. If you notice your baby starting to cut back on his lunchtime nap or waking earlier in the morning, this is a sign that he may need to cut the morning nap out. Some babies, if they're not sleeping well at night or at their lunchtime nap, may need to drop the morning nap sooner, sometime between nine and 12 months.

Signs your baby is ready to sleep

Below are the most obvious signs that your baby is getting tired and ready to sleep. Although he may not be quite ready to sleep the minute you notice any of the following signs, you should take your baby to his bed and have some quiet time: allow 10–20 minutes of quiet time with babies under six months and 5–10 minutes with older babies. With quiet time it is best to hold your baby in the crook of your arm as opposed to over your shoulder or across your chest, that way he will not suddenly miss the pressure of your body when laid in his bed. The minute his eyes start to get heavy and you notice that they are more closed than open, you should settle him in his bed, before he gets into a deep sleep. It is important that your baby is sleepy but aware that he is going into his bed. It is also important that you allow him a short period of fussing. If you find that the fussing starts to escalate into crying you should try shushing and patting him in his bed rather than immediately picking him up. With very young babies who do not settle within 10–20 minutes, it is possible that hunger is the cause and they should be offered a feed and then resettled using the same procedure as above.

● He starts to yawn – not just once but two or three times

● His eyes start to open and close quite rapidly

● He pulls his head to one side as if trying to root for a feed

- His body becomes tense; some babies also arch their back

- He starts grizzling or crying very suddenly

- Older babies may pull at their ears or start to suck their fingers.

Lunchtime/middle-of-the-day nap

A baby under one month is usually ready for this nap one to one and a half hours after the time he wakes from his morning nap, but by the time he reaches two months he can usually make it to two hours. Ideally, this should be the longest nap of the day, as research shows that a nap between 12 noon and 2pm is deeper and more refreshing than a later nap, because it coincides with the baby's natural dip in alertness.

Depending on how well the baby has slept at his morning nap, this nap usually lasts between two and two and a half hours reducing to around two hours by six months. At around one year this may be cut back to one and a half hours if the baby is still having a full 45-minute nap in the morning, although it may lengthen again to two hours if the morning nap is cut right back or dropped altogether. At one year the length of the lunchtime nap is determined by how well the baby is sleeping at night. Some babies who are sleeping 12 hours at night will continue to need two hours' sleep at lunchtime, while some babies, if they are waking earlier in the morning, will need to have their lunchtime nap cut back. The majority of babies will continue to need a nap in the middle of the day until they are at least two years of age with the length of the nap again depending on how well they're sleeping at night. Babies who are starting to wake earlier or starting to wake in the night may need to have their lunchtime nap cut down or cut out altogether. This can happen anywhere between 18 months and three years of age, depending on the child's individual needs.

Late afternoon nap

If a baby sleeps well at the two earlier naps of the day, this should be the shortest of the three naps. A baby under eight weeks usually needs between 30 minutes and one hour. By the time they reach 12 weeks the majority of babies who have slept well at lunchtime will only need a very short nap of 10–20 minutes, in order to revive them enough for the bath and bedtime routine. This nap is usually dropped by the age of four months provided they're sleeping well at their lunchtime nap. If a baby is having less than two hours at lunchtime, they may continue to need 10–15 minutes in the late afternoon until nearer nine months of age. Allowing a baby to have too much sleep later in the day is often the reason a baby does not settle well at his bedtime. The total amount of daily sleep your baby or toddler has between 7am and 7pm (depending on when you start your day) will play a big part in how well he sleeps at night. The timing of the sleep is also important if overtiredness is to be avoided. Listed below is an approximate guide to the number of hours of daily nap time a baby or toddler needs.

- Birth to four weeks – 5 hours

- Four to eight weeks – 4 to 4½ hours

- Eight to 12 weeks – 3½ hours

- Three to six months – 3 hours

- Six to 12 months – 2½ to 3 hours

- 12 to 15 months – 2½ hours

- 15 to 18 months – 2 to 2½ hours

- 18 to 24 months – 2 hours

- Two to two and a half years – 1 to 2 hours

- Two and a half to three years – 0 to 1 hour

How to Sleep

Through all my experience of working with children I have come to the conclusion that the key to ensuring good sleeping habits is teaching your baby or child to go to sleep in his cot/bed unassisted. Establishing the right sleep associations from an early age is vital if you wish to avoid long-term sleep problems.

Sleep associations

If you constantly cuddle, rock, feed or use a dummy to get your baby to sleep, it is what he will come to associate with falling asleep. This does not often create a problem during the first few weeks, but once the baby develops and starts to come into a light sleep every 30–40 minutes, a real problem can evolve. In my experience babies who depend on their parents to help them get to sleep will, at around eight to 12 weeks, start to wake up increasingly in the night. Babies who were often feeding only once in the night end up feeding every couple of hours; others will not settle unless cuddled or rocked.

If your baby is under eight weeks, this problem can be avoided by ensuring that you allow enough time to settle your baby at sleep times. Make a note of how long your baby can stay awake before he falls asleep then make sure that you allow a 10- or 15-minute wind down period before he goes to sleep. If he has fed earlier and is unsettled but you are sure he is not hungry or windy, give him a cuddle or the dummy, but make sure that he is settled in his cot before he falls asleep and without the dummy. If he has just had a feed and is falling asleep on the breast or bottle, try to rouse him slightly before you put him into the cot so that he is aware that he is going to bed. Provided he has been well fed and winded and is ready to sleep, he should drift off to sleep within five to 10 minutes, although I have had a few babies who would fuss and fret for up to 20 minutes before settling off to sleep.

If your baby is under eight weeks and not settling well despite looking sleepy, it is important that you look closely at his feeding. In my experience the cause is usually one of two things: the baby is still hungry or the baby was too sleepy during the feed and has not fed properly (see box below). With an older baby or toddler who doesn't know how to go to sleep unassisted, eliminating the wrong sleep associations will be more difficult and some form of sleep training (see Chapter 10) will probably be needed if persistent night-time wakings are to be resolved and a healthy sleeping pattern established. Establishing healthy sleeping habits also depends on several other factors. Getting the feeding right and ensuring that your baby or toddler's physical, mental and emotional needs are being met also have a huge influence on how well he sleeps.

Is your baby feeding or sleeping on the breast?

If you allow your baby to feed with his eyes closed or half asleep, two things can happen: firstly, he won't feed properly and will still be hungry or show signs of hunger again very soon after his feed. Secondly, the feed time will actually amount to a little catnap, which will have a knock-on effect on his sleep later in the day. By catnapping, he will have added to his sleep quota for the day and therefore may not go down properly for his next sleep. This prevents you trying to establish proper nap times and can therefore cause more longer-term problems.

The bedtime routine

The majority of experts agree that a good bedtime routine is important for young babies and children. However, there is much disagreement over the age at which parents should start a bedtime routine and what it should consist of. Somewhere between the age of six weeks and three months seems to be the time that most experts think you can start to establish regular times for a bath, feed and then settling the baby in his bed.

My own view is that the sooner a bedtime routine is established, the less likely the parents are to encounter problems trying to settle their baby. When I worked as a maternity nurse I established a routine in the very early days, usually around the fifth day, when the mother's milk came in. I believe that this is one of the reasons I rarely had to deal with a crying baby in the evening. Of course there are times in the early days when a young baby will not immediately fall asleep, but if you are consistent in how you try to settle him, a pattern should emerge where he settles quickly and easily, between 6.30 and 7pm. This will have a knock-on effect on what happens later and in the middle of the night. A baby who feeds and settles well in the early evening and sleeps until his next feed is due is much more likely to feed well at the last feed of the night, which should come at around 10 or 11pm.

This is particularly true of breastfed babies, as the time the baby sleeps in the evening allows the mother to have a meal and a good rest, which will help ensure that she has time to produce enough milk for a good feed last thing at night. A baby who has a good last feed is much more likely only to wake up once in the night and then settle quickly, because again the mother will have had sufficient rest to produce enough milk for a full feed.

Regardless of whether he is bottle-fed or breastfed, if a baby gets into the habit of catnapping in the early evening, he will more than likely get into the habit of feeding little and often. When the parents attempt to offer him a late feed before they go to bed, it is very unlikely that he will take a full feed, particularly if he has fed within the last couple of hours. He will therefore be much more likely to wake up around 1am looking for a feed, then again at 5am. A pattern of two feeds a night is very quickly established, and for a breastfeeding mother this can have dire consequences, as tiredness sets in and the milk supply is greatly reduced. If you wish to avoid a pattern of unsettled evenings and excessive waking in the middle of the night, I would strongly advise that you establish a routine as soon as possible.

Bath time

I am aware that many experts advise that it is not necessary to bathe your baby every day and that a top and tail will suffice in the early days. I believe that babies are no different from us adults and that a warm bath and a gentle massage is a wonderful way of unwinding and relaxing in the evening. Research also shows that babies who are bathed and massaged in the evening tend to sleep better than those that aren't.

PART 2
The First Year

3

The First Month
(Birth to Four Weeks)

The first four weeks of your baby's life can feel overwhelming, and new parents are often anxious and uncertain about how best to look after their newborn. The focus at this stage is really on the basics: sleeping, feeding and changing your baby's nappy. It often feels as if this takes up all your day at first and there is little time left for anything else. Although your baby's needs may initially seem all-consuming, you will gradually become more confident and adept.

In the very early days, you may still be recovering from the birth, particularly if you had a difficult labour or a Caesarean section, and you should not underestimate what an impact this can have. You may experience the 'baby blues' at this time, or you may feel totally elated. I always recommend trying to enjoy a 'baby moon' in the first few weeks where you spend time getting to know your baby with your partner, and try to limit visitors which can help you to become more confident about caring for your baby as well as giving you time to recover physically.

Newborn babies need to feed a lot as their tummies are tiny; most will feed anything from eight to 12 times a day and some even more. And in the early days, your baby may need his nappy changing as many as 12 times a day, but this will gradually reduce.

The other concern for parents at this stage is their baby's sleeping pattern and if you don't have any kind of routine for your baby, you may find that you are being woken up throughout the night not just in the very early days, but throughout the first few months. Establishing a sleep pattern will help to ensure that everyone in the family gets the sleep that they need.

Young babies can go through an unsettled period around the age of three to six weeks when they go through a growth spurt and may cry more than usual. If your baby is crying a lot you will want to make sure that you have eliminated the possible causes, which may be hunger, tiredness, overtiredness, wind or colic. Sometimes babies are just bored, as they do need some stimulation when they are awake.

The first month is a time of rapid development for your baby, as he begins to respond more to you and to his environment. A newborn baby has quite limited vision and his eyes are light sensitive. He has little head control, and you will need to support his head and neck when you pick him up. As he grows and develops, his vision and hearing improve so that he can see and hear you more clearly.

CASE STUDY: Beatrice, aged four weeks

Problem: Colic/wind and excessive crying

Cause: Overfeeding

Beatrice, who weighed 2.7kg (6lb) at birth, was put on to a strict four-hourly feeding routine (not a CLB routine) within a week of being born. For the first three weeks she fed and slept well, waking only once in the night after her 10pm feed. Between the third and fourth week, Beatrice started to become more unsettled, sometimes screaming long before feeds were due. Because Christina, her mother was sticking to a strict four-hourly feeding plan, Beatrice would often scream from the time she woke up until the time she was due a feed. Then when offered a feed, she would only drink around 120ml (4oz) feed before coming very upset. She would scream and bring her legs up to her chest as if in pain. It could take Christina up to an hour to get Beatrice to take a 150ml (5oz) feed.

Beatrice, who had previously always settled well at 6.30pm, would often cry on and off (regardless of how her parents tried to calm her) for two hours before she eventually fell asleep. Christina had read that colic usually started around three weeks, and was convinced that this was the problem with Beatrice. She contacted me when Beatrice was four weeks. At that point she was being fed 150ml (5oz) at around 2/3am, and then at 6am, 10am and 2pm. At 6pm Christina had increased her feed to 210ml (7oz), in the belief that Beatrice may also be unsettled in the evening because she was hungry. She would then take a dream feed of 120ml (4oz) at 10pm. Her daily milk intake was around 900ml (30oz) a day.

The first thing that I noticed was Beatrice, who now weighed 4.3kg (9lb 8oz), had put on well over 1.5kg (3lb) in weight since birth. Her feeding and sleeping routine looked like this:

2/3am	150ml (5oz)
5.45am	awake
6am	150ml (5oz)
7am	asleep
9am	awake
10am	150ml (5oz)
10.30am	asleep
1pm	awake
2pm	150ml (5oz)
2.30pm	asleep
4pm	awake
6pm	180ml (6oz) over a period of two hours
9pm	would fall asleep exhausted after two to three hours of intermittent crying
10pm	120ml (4oz) – dream feed

Although all babies are individuals and their feeding needs can vary, the guidelines of 75ml (2½ oz) of formula milk per pound of the baby body weight over a 24-hour period meant that Beatrice should have been taking 720ml (24oz) per day. The fact that Beatrice was taking 180ml (6oz) more each day, along with her weight gain of more than 10oz (280g) each week, and her tummy was very hard and distended at the time, led me to believe that overfeeding was the main cause of the excessive crying periods.

The problem was also exacerbated by the times of the feeds. For the first three weeks when Beatrice was fed at 6am, she was put back to bed to sleep until the next feed at 10am. By the time she reached three weeks, she was starting to naturally cut back on her daytime sleep and had started waking up earlier and earlier after the 6am feed and was now waking up regularly at 9am. Christina, who was determined to keep her in a strict four-hourly feeding pattern, would not feed her until 10am. This caused two problems – a baby as young as four weeks, even if not quite ready for a feed, will automatically look for a feed when they wake, and secondly, babies of this age usually start to get tired after being awake for an hour and a half. I believe that Beatrice, who had been awake from 9am, would be getting tired halfway through her feed and would want to go to sleep the minute she felt full. This usually occurred once she had taken 120ml (4oz), which is much nearer the recommended amount for her weight than the 150ml (5oz) that her mother was making her take.

The rest of the nap times, along with the large feeds, had a knock-on effect of Beatrice not settling at bedtime and crying excessively. Because Beatrice was awake from 4pm in the afternoon, trying to feed her two hours after she had woken up meant that she was very overtired for the 6pm feed. I believe that this, along with constantly offering too much milk at that time, caused much of the distress and any possible pain she may have been experiencing.

I suggested that Christina alter the sleeping times during the day and, apart from the bedtime feed and late feed, she should try to offer no more than 120ml (4oz) a feed, aiming for a daily total of between 720ml (24oz) to 800ml (27oz) of milk. At no time should Beatrice be made to feed more than she needs. If for some reason she took a lot less than the recommended amounts, she could be topped up with a small amount prior to her morning or lunchtime nap. Below is an example of the suggested times and amounts for feeding and sleeping.

2/3am	120ml (4oz)
6am	120ml (4oz)
6.15am	settle back to sleep
7am	awake
7.30am	30–60ml (1–2oz) top-up before 8am (not to be forced)
10.30am	120ml (4oz)
11.30am	sleep
2pm	120ml (4oz)
3.30/4pm	sleep
5pm	90–120ml (3–4oz) – only as much as baby needs to keep her calm for bath
5.45pm	bath
6.15pm	30–60ml (1–2oz) – top-up feed
6.30pm	settle in cot no later than 6.45pm
10pm	120ml (4oz)

During the first week of following the new feeding and sleeping times, Beatrice continued to wake up between 2 and 3am, and then at 6am, and take a 120ml (4oz) feed at both of these times. Sometimes she would not take a top-up feed at 7.30/8am and Christina would have to feed her early at 10am, and then top her up prior to her lunchtime nap, otherwise she found Beatrice would only sleep for an hour and a half at lunchtime.

Christina saw an almost instant change to Beatrice's feeding and sleeping during the day, with little or no crying, but it did take a further week to get the settling at bedtime sorted out. Although Beatrice did not cry with the same intensity, and Christina was convinced she was not in the same pain as she used to be, it was still taking over an hour of shushing and patting for her to fall asleep. I suggested that Christina should try to push her afternoon nap closer to 4pm, so that it was reduced by 30 minutes, and allow her to sleep no more than one hour. She should also ensure that Beatrice was in bed no later than 6.45pm.

By the time Beatrice was seven weeks old, she was settling well in the evening and at all nap times. I advised Christina that when Beatrice went through a growth spurt, she should first increase the 6/7am feed by 30ml (1oz) then the next feed she should increase should be the 10/11am feed by another 30ml. The third feed to increase would be the split feed at bedtime. If Beatrice was not settling at the late feed or started to wake up earlier in the night, she should also increase that feed by 30ml. By increasing the feeds in this order it would ensure that Beatrice did not need to have the middle-of-the-night feed increased when she went through a growth spurt. I also advised that a small top-up feed before the lunchtime nap was fine if she found that Beatrice was not sleeping the full two hours at lunchtime.

There are many reasons why a baby cries excessively in the evening; in Beatrice's case it was being overfed and becoming overtired. Babies who are underfed or overtired can also display the same behaviour as Beatrice was. With very young babies it is important to look at their weight gain if they are crying excessively in the evening. A regular weight gain of 8 to 10 ounces each week, could be a sign of overfeeding, and a weight gain of less than 5 ounces a week is often a sign that a baby is being underfed.

Feeding

One of the issues mothers most often contact me about during the first few months is feeding, as breastfeeding is not always as easy to establish as they may have expected.

Breastfeeding is the best option if it is possible, but if you are still experiencing problems despite seeking professional help and support, you should not feel guilty about bottle-feeding your baby as many thousands of formula-fed babies are growing up perfectly healthily.

The key to successful breastfeeding is to ensure that the baby is latched on properly, as poor positioning can lead to cracked or sore nipples and make it difficult for the baby to feed properly.

If you are having problems with this, it is important to seek help from a professional early on.

What to expect

After the birth I advise that babies should be offered a feed every three hours around the clock until a mother's milk comes in. The three hours is calculated from the beginning of one feed to the beginning of the next. However, if a baby is demanding a feed long before three hours have passed, he should of course be fed, and also offered both breasts at each feed, if he still remains unsettled.

I believe that feeding a baby three-hourly will help build up the milk supply much faster, and if a baby is fed enough during the day, he will be much more likely by the second week to begin to sleep for longer periods between feeds in the night.

With babies who are being bottle-fed, provided they take a full feed, they may manage to go slightly longer between feeds. To work out how much a full feed would be for your baby you should calculate that he would need 70ml (2½oz) of milk for each pound of his body weight; a baby weighing around 3.2kg (7lb) would need approximately 500ml (17½oz) a day. This is only a guideline; hungrier babies may need an extra ounce at some feeds. If your baby is one of these try to ensure that you structure your feeds so he is taking the bigger feeds at the evening feed and last feed of the day, to encourage your baby to sleep longer through the night.

During the third week babies go through a growth spurt, so it is important to offer your baby longer on the breast if you are breastfeeding, and if needed adding some top-up feeds before naps, to ensure that your baby sleeps well at nap times. With formula-fed babies you should add an extra ounce of milk if he is draining his bottles.

What to aim for

By the second week, provided a baby has regained his birth weight, it should be possible to establish a pattern of three-hourly feeding during the day and four-hourly feeding at night. If you manage to fit in enough feeds between 6/7am and 10/11pm, your baby should manage to sleep around four hours between feeds in the night. By the end of the first month your baby's feeding should look something like the following, provided he is taking full feeds at his daytime feeds: 6/7am, 10/10.30am, 2/2.30pm, 5/6.15pm, 10/10.30pm and one feed somewhere between 2am and 4am.

Obviously, if you are starting your day later – at 8am – then the feeding times would move on by approximately an hour.

Feeding Problems

Fussy feeding

Most newborns will take to the breast or bottle quickly and easily. However, there are babies who will fuss and fret within minutes of starting a feed.

- If your baby becomes tense at feed times try to avoid having visitors then as it will be hard to keep things very calm and quiet if you are having to make conversation.

- Try to give the feed in a calm, quiet room without stimuli such as the telephone.

- Prepare everything you need for the feed in advance and make sure that you have eaten, had enough water to drink and are well rested.

- When your baby wakes for his feed, do not change his nappy as this may cause him to cry.

- Make sure you are comfortable before you start feeding.

- Do not try to latch the baby on to the breast or put the bottle in his mouth if he is crying. Hold him firmly in the feeding position and calm him down with gentle patting on the back.

- Try holding a dummy in his mouth. Once he has calmed down and has sucked steadily for a few minutes, then quickly ease the dummy out and offer him the breast or bottle.

Sleepy feeding

In the early days, I say that babies who are breastfed and take a full feed should manage to go three hours between feeds (though some formula-fed babies may manage to go slightly longer between some of their feeds). This time is calculated from the beginning of a feed to the beginning of the next feed. As he grows and the amount he drinks increases, your baby should manage to extend the time he goes between feeds to between three to three and a half hours during the day and nearer to four hours during the night. Eventually, regardless of whether they are breastfed or formula-fed, most babies will start to extend the length of time they sleep in the night, until they are sleeping through from the late feed at around 10/11pm. However, as I have said, this is all dependent on the baby taking full feeds at each feed.

There can be many reasons why a baby may not take a full feed, but one of the main ones is when a baby is a 'sleepy feeder'. This is very common, especially in the early days, but it can continue for several months if the baby gets into the habit of snacking, which is what happens with sleepy feeders. Sleepy feeders will either feed for a short spell then fall asleep on the breast, only to wake within the hour looking for another feed, or from the beginning of the feed they will doze on and off with their eyes shut while feeding. Because they have not been feeding efficiently, they will again be looking for a further feed within an hour or so. Although this problem is more common among breastfed babies, it can also become a problem with bottle-fed babies.

Here are the tips and techniques I have learned over the years for how to get a sleepy baby to feed well.

- Make sure that your baby is fully awake before starting a feed: changing his nappy and wiping his face and hands with a damp facecloth will help with this.

- During the day feed him in a bright room and place a changing mat on the floor right next to the chair in which you are feeding.

- Try to wear a cool, short-sleeved T-shirt or blouse, as opposed to a warm, woolly, long-sleeved sweater, which would give him the feeling of being enclosed in a blanket while feeding.

- Undo the legs of his bodysuit, so that his legs are fully exposed to the air. If your baby is very sleepy strip him down to his vest.

- With breastfed babies, massage their feet during the feed, stroke their face and with your forefinger and middle finger gently press upwards on their chin when they stop sucking.

- With bottle-fed babies who stop sucking during the feed, moving the teat around in their mouth will often get them sucking again. I also found that holding the bottle around the neck with my thumb, forefinger and middle finger, rather than halfway down the bottle meant that I could use my remaining fingers to gently press upwards on their chin to get them feeding again.

- If in spite of doing all of the above your baby is still either falling asleep during his feed or feeding for more than a minute or so with their eyes closed, I would gently remove them from the breast or bottle and place them flat on the changing mat for a minute or so. Sometimes I would have to do this several times during a feed, but I found that the perseverance was worth it – within a week or so the baby had learned to stay awake well during feeds and also happily for a short spell after feeds. This in turn meant that they took a full feed and would then sleep much better and longer for both daytime naps and night-time sleep.

Breastfed baby not settling in the evening

As babies reach four weeks of age, some start being difficult to settle. They may go down sleepy and seem ready for sleep, but within 10 minutes have woken again.

- It is most likely that a breastfed baby of this age is hungry. By offering him the breast again as soon as it becomes apparent to you that he is not going to settle, you should help prevent him becoming distressed. Rather than trying to settle him by rocking him or offering him a dummy, offer him the breast that you fed him on at his last feed.

- Babies of this age can also get very sleepy early evening, and keep falling asleep on the breast, but that does not mean that they are full. You may have to pick him up two or three times during the settling period and each time he should be offered the breast. If he then settles for the evening you will know that hunger was the main cause of the problem.

- If he still doesn't settle despite being offered the breast several times, it could be that your milk supply is low at this time of the day (see below). In that case it would be worth offering a bottle of expressed milk after his bath to see if that helps him settle any better (see page 47 for when to express for this feed).

- If despite increasing the milk your baby continues to be unsettled in the evening you should consider bringing his bedtime forward so that he is actually in bed slightly earlier. Next to hunger, overtiredness is one of the main causes of babies not settling in the evening. An earlier bedtime should ensure that he is not going down overtired and, along with more milk, should help him fall into a relaxed sleep more easily.

Wind

All babies take a certain amount of wind while feeding – bottle-fed babies more so than breastfed ones. Given the opportunity, most babies bring up their wind easily. If you suspect that your baby's crying is caused by wind, check that you are allowing enough time between feeds.

- A breastfed baby needs around at least three hours to digest a full feed, and a formula-fed baby should be allowed three and a half to four hours. This time is always from the beginning of one feed to the beginning of the next feed.

- I would also suggest that you keep a close eye on your baby's weight gain. If his weight gain is in excess of 240–300g (8–10oz) a week and he appears to be suffering from wind pains, it could be that he is overfeeding, particularly if he weighs over 3.6kg (8lb) and is feeding two or three times in the night.

Expressing

I believe that expressing milk in the early days plays a huge part in determining how successful a mother will be in breastfeeding while following a routine. I am convinced that one of the main reasons the majority of the mothers I work with are so successful at breastfeeding is because I encourage the use of an electric expressing machine in the very early days.

The simple reason for this is that breast milk is produced on a supply and demand basis. During the very early days, most babies will empty the first breast and some may take a small amount from the second breast. Very few will empty both breasts at this stage. By the end of the second week, the milk production balances out and most mothers are producing exactly the amount their baby is demanding. Some time during the third and fourth week, the baby goes through a growth spurt and demands more milk. This is where a problem often sets in if you are attempting to put your baby into a routine and have followed the current advice of not expressing before six weeks.

In order to meet the increased demand for more food, you would more than likely have to go back to feeding two- or three-hourly and often twice in the night. This feeding pattern is repeated each time the baby goes through a growth spurt and often results in the baby being continually fed just prior to sleep time. This can create the problem of the wrong sleep association, making it even more difficult to get the baby back into the routine. Mothers who express the extra milk they produce in the very early days will always be producing more than their baby needs. When their baby goes through a growth spurt, the routine stays intact, because simply expressing less milk at the early morning feeds can immediately satisfy any increased appetite. Expressing from the very early days can also help avoid the problem of a low milk supply. However, if your baby is over one month and you already have the problem of a low milk supply, by following my plan for increasing your milk supply (see page 51), you should see a big improvement within six days.

If you decide some time between one and four weeks to introduce a bottle of either expressed milk or formula at the late feed, you will be able to hand over feeding responsibility to your partner. This means that you will be able to get to bed early if you are feeling exhausted from night feeding. I advise in my routines that you express some milk at this time or that you feed the baby. If the baby takes a bottle, then you can express between 9.30–10pm and then go to bed. Expressing milk at this time is important to keep the supply up and ensure you have plenty for the later feed.

If you have previously experienced difficulties with expressing, do not be disheartened. The following guidelines should help make it easier:

● The best time to express is in the morning as the breasts are usually fuller. Expressing will also be easier if done at the beginning of a feed. Express one breast just prior to feeding your baby, or feed your baby from one breast, then express from the second breast before offering him the remainder of his feed. Some mothers actually find that expressing is easier when done while they are feeding the baby on the other breast. It is also important to note that expressing at the beginning of a feed allows slightly longer for that breast to make more milk for the next feed.

- In the early days, you will need to allow at least 15 minutes to express 60–90ml (2–3oz) at the morning feeds, and up to 30 minutes at the evening expressing times. Try to keep expressing times quiet and relaxed. The more you practise, the easier it will become. I usually find that, by the end of the first month, the majority of my mothers can easily express 60–90ml (2–3oz) within 10 minutes at the 9.30pm expressing when using a double pumping system.

- An electrical, heavy-duty pumping machine, the type used in hospitals, is by far the best way to express milk in the early days. The suction of these machines is designed to simulate a baby's sucking rhythm, encouraging the milk flow. If you are expressing both breasts at 9.30pm, it is also worthwhile investing in an attachment that enables both breasts to be expressed at once, therefore reducing the time spent expressing.

- Sometimes, the let-down is slower in the evening when the breasts are producing less milk; a relaxing warm bath or shower will often help encourage the milk to flow more easily. Also, gently massaging the breasts before and during expressing will help.

- Some mothers find that it is helpful to have a picture of their baby close by for them to look at, while others find it better to watch a favourite television programme, or to chat to their partners or husbands. Experiment with different approaches to see which one works best for you.

Low milk supply

Not producing enough milk, especially later in the day, is a very common problem for breastfeeding mothers and one of the major reasons breastfeeding can go wrong. I believe that hunger is why so many babies are fretful and difficult to settle in the evening and if the problem of a low milk supply is not resolved in the early days, then a pattern soon emerges of the baby needing to feed on and off all evening to try and satisfy his needs. Mothers are advised that this constant feeding is normal and the best way to increase their milk supply, but in my experience it usually has the opposite effect. Because the amount of milk the breasts produce is dictated by the amount of milk the baby drinks, these frequent feeds signal the breasts to produce milk little and often. These small feeds will rarely satisfy the baby, leaving him hungry and irritable. I also believe that the stress involved in frequently feeding a very hungry, irritable and often overtired baby can cause many mothers to become so exhausted that their milk supply is reduced even further. Exhaustion and a low milk supply go hand in hand. I am convinced that by expressing a small amount of milk during the early weeks of breastfeeding, when the breasts are producing more milk than the baby needs, the mother can help avoid the problem of a low milk supply. For more about expressing see the box on page 47.

If your baby is under one month of age and not settling in the evening, it is possible the cause is a low milk supply. Expressing at the times suggested in the plan below should help increase your milk supply (you will just need to adjust the times accordingly if you start your day later or earlier).

If your baby is over one month and not settling in the evening or after daytime feeds, the following six-day plan will quickly help to increase your milk supply. The temporary introduction of top-up feeds will ensure that your baby is not subjected to hours of irritability and anxiety caused by hunger, which is what usually happens when mothers resort to demand-feeding to increase their milk supply.

Plan for increased milk supply

Days one to three

6.45am

- Express 30ml (1oz) from each breast.

- Baby should be awake, and feeding no later than 7am, regardless of how often he fed in the night.

- He should be offered up to 20–25 minutes on the fullest breast, then up to 10–15 minutes on the second breast.

- Do not feed after 7.45am. He should now stay awake for up to two hours.

8.30/ 9am

- If your baby has been awake since 6.30/7am he should be ready for a nap around now. If he has not been settling well for his nap, offer him up to 5–10 minutes on the breast from which he last fed then put him down for a nap.

10am

- Baby needs to be fully awake now, regardless of how long he slept.

- He should be given up to 20–25 minutes from the breast he last fed on.

- Express 60ml (2oz) from the second breast, then offer him up to 10–20 minutes on the same breast.

11.45am

- He should be given the 60ml (2oz) that you expressed to ensure that he does not wake up hungry during his midday nap. It is important that you have a good lunch and a rest before the next feed.

2pm

- Baby should be awake and feeding no later than 2pm, regardless of how long he has slept.

- Give him up to 20–25 minutes from the breast he last fed on while you drink a glass of water. Express 60ml (2oz) from the second breast, then offer up to 10–20 minutes on the same breast.

4pm

● Baby will need a short nap depending on his age.

5pm

● Baby needs to be fully awake and feeding no later than 5pm.

● Give up to 15–20 minutes from both breasts.

6.15pm

● Baby should be offered a top-up feed of expressed milk from the bottle. A baby under 3.6kg (8lb) in weight will probably settle with 60–90ml (2–3oz); bigger babies may need 120–150ml (4–5oz).

● Once your baby is settled, it is important that you have a good meal and a rest.

8pm

● Express from both breasts.

10pm

● It is important that you again express from both breasts at this time, as the amount you get will be a good indicator of how much milk you are producing.

10.30pm

● Arrange for your partner or another family member to give this feed to the baby so you can have an early night.

● Baby should be awake and feeding no later than 10.30pm. He can be given a full feed of either formula or expressed milk from a bottle. Refer to the box below for details of the amounts to give.

How much milk does a formula-fed baby need?

Until a baby is weaned the general guidelines are that a baby needs 2.5oz (70 ml) of formula per pound of his body weight to drink each day. For example, a baby weighing 12lb would need around 30oz (800 ml) of milk a day, some may take an ounce or so more, others an ounce or so less. If a baby is feeding six times a day, he could take approximately 5oz (140 ml) per feed, although the amount that he drinks at each feed can often vary slightly and it is important to aim to get him to have his biggest milk feeds first thing in the morning and at bedtime.

Once a baby begins solids the amount he drinks will gradually reduce and by the time he reaches seven months, if he is eating three full solids meals a day, he may only be on three to four milk feeds a day. The minimum amount that a baby who is fully weaned on to solids needs per day is around 20oz (560 ml).

If you are giving your baby expressed milk from a bottle, the above guidelines can be used as to how much to offer him at a feed, but because breast milk is digested differently to formula milk, you may find that your baby cannot go quite as long between feeds as a baby being given a bottle of formula milk.

Please note that the amounts given are guidelines and should you have any concerns about the amount your baby is drinking, you should discuss these with your health visitor.

In the night

A baby who has had a full feed from the bottle at 10.30pm should manage to get up to 2–2.30am. He should then be offered 20–25 minutes from the first breast, then possibly 10–15 minutes from the second. In order to avoid a second waking in the night at 5am, it is very important that he feeds from both breasts. If your baby fed well at 10.30pm and wakes earlier than 2am, the cause may not be hunger. Other reasons which may be causing him to wake earlier include:

● Kicking off the covers may be the cause of your baby waking earlier than 2am. A baby under six weeks who wakes up thrashing around may still need to be fully swaddled. A baby over six weeks may benefit from being half swaddled under the arms in a thin cotton sheet. With all babies, it is important to ensure that the top sheet is tucked in well, down the sides and at the bottom of the cot. For more on swaddling, see pages 85 and 123.

● The baby should be fully awake at the 10.30pm feed. With a baby who is waking up before 2am, it may be worthwhile keeping him awake longer, and offering him some more milk just before you settle him at around 11.15pm.

Day four

By day four, your breasts should be feeling fuller in the morning and the following alterations should be made to the above plan:

● If your baby is sleeping well between 9am and 9.45am, reduce the time on the breast at 9am to five minutes.

- The top-up at 11.45am can be reduced by 30ml (1oz) if he is sleeping well at lunchtime, or shows signs of not feeding so well at the 2pm feed.

- The expressing at the 2pm feed should be dropped, which should mean that your breasts are fuller by the 5pm feed.

- If you feel your breasts are fuller at 5pm, make sure your baby empties the first breast completely before putting him on to the second breast. If he has not emptied the second breast before his bath, he should be offered it again after the bath, and before he is given a top-up.

- The 8pm expressing should be dropped and the 10pm expressing brought forward to 9.30pm. It is important that both breasts are completely emptied at the 9.30pm expressing.

Day five
- Dropping the 2pm and 8pm expressing on the fourth day should result in your breasts being very engorged on the morning of the fifth day; it is very important that the extra milk is totally emptied at the first feed in the morning to avoid your breasts becoming uncomfortable.

- At the 7am feed the baby should be offered up to 20–25 minutes on the fullest breast, then up to 10–15 minutes on the second breast, after you have expressed. The amount you express will depend on the weight of your baby. It is important that you take just the right amount so that enough is left for your baby to get a full feed. If you managed to express a minimum of 120ml (4oz) at the 10pm feed, you should manage to express the following amounts:

(a) Baby weighing 3.6–4.5kg (8–10lb) – express 120ml (4oz)

(b) Baby weighing 4.5–5.4kg (10–12lb) – express 90ml (3oz)

(c) Baby weighing over 5.4kg (12lb) – express 60ml (2oz)

Day six

By the sixth day, your milk supply should have increased enough for you to drop all top-up feeds, and your baby should manage to go longer between daytime feeds. I would advise that you continue to express milk early on in the day, which will ensure that you will be able to satisfy your baby's increased appetite during his next growth spurt. I would also suggest that you continue with one bottle of either expressed or formula milk at the 10/10.30pm feed until your baby is weaned on to solids at six months. This will allow the late feed to be given by your husband or partner, enabling you to get to bed earlier after you have expressed, which, in turn, will make it easier for you to cope with the middle-of-the-night feed.

Feeding several times a night

I believe that by the end of the second week a baby who weighed 3.1kg (7lb) or more at birth should really only need one feed between midnight and 6am. This is provided, of course, that he is feeding well at all of his daytime feeds and gets a full feed at the late feed between 10 and 11pm. If he feeds well at every feed, is gaining a good amount of weight each week and is sleeping well at all of his other sleep times, a baby may not be getting enough milk at the 10–11pm feed and this can cause him to wake. (Please note that feeding times and amounts for a premature baby or a very tiny baby are different and medical advice should be sought on how best to deal with these special circumstances.)

In my experience, regardless of whether they are breastfed or bottle-fed, a baby who continues to feed two or three times in the night will eventually begin to cut back on his daytime feeds. A vicious circle soon emerges, where the baby cuts back so much on his daytime feeds that he ends up genuinely needing to feed in the night so that his daily nutritional needs can be met.

With bottle-fed babies it is easier to avoid a pattern of excessive night-time feeding evolving by monitoring the amounts they are getting during the day.

Excessive night feeding is considered normal for breastfed babies and is actually encouraged by many breastfeeding advisors. Mothers are advised to have their baby sleep with them, so that he can feed on and off throughout the night. Much emphasis is placed on the fact that the hormone prolactin, which is necessary for making breast milk, is produced more at night. The theory is that mothers who are feeding their babies more in the night than in the day, are much more likely to sustain a good milk supply. This advice obviously works for some mothers, but breastfeeding statistics prove that it clearly doesn't for many others as so many give up in the first month. I believe that exhaustion caused by so many night-time feeds is one of the main reasons why many mothers give up breastfeeding in the very early days.

In my experience from working with hundreds of breastfeeding mothers and advising thousands more, I have found that a good stretch of sleep in the night results in the breasts producing more milk. A full and satisfying feed in the middle of the night will ensure that the baby settles back to sleep quickly until the morning, and signals the breasts to make more milk. The guidelines below explain how excessive night-time feeding can be avoided.

● If a low milk supply at the last feed is the problem, it can easily be solved by ensuring your baby has fed from both breasts at the late feed, then is offered a top-up of expressed milk from a bottle. Expressing a small amount of milk from the breasts before the morning feed will provide you with the milk for this top-up. If you decide to replace the late feed with a full bottle of expressed milk, then you should ensure that you express from both breasts an hour or so before the baby's late feed is due.

● Many women are concerned that introducing a bottle too early may reduce their baby's desire to take the breast. Nearly all of the babies I helped care for were offered one bottle a day as a matter of course and I cannot recall any of them having nipple confusion or refusing the breast. Offering a full bottle of expressed milk at the late feed also has the advantage that the father can give the feed and enable the mother to get to bed slightly earlier.

● If after one week of giving your baby a full feed at this time there is no improvement, and your baby is still waking up several times a night or more, it is more likely that there is a problem with his sleeping than his feeding. I would suggest that you continue to offer the top-up feed or bottle of expressed milk, but refer to page 89 for reasons other than hunger why your baby is waking up so much in the night.

Tongue tie

Tongue tie is a condition in which the tissue that attaches a baby's tongue to the floor of his mouth is too short. It restricts the baby's tongue movement and can make it difficult for him to feed. Your paediatrician or midwife will check for tongue tie after your baby is born or during their first routine check but it is difficult to spot and can sometimes be missed. If your baby has mild tongue tie you may not experience any problems; however, in more serious cases it can affect breastfeeding for both you and your baby:

- your baby may have difficulty latching on

- he may slide off your breast while feeding

- he may not be gaining the amount of weight he should

- you may suffer sore nipples, ulcers or bleeding

If you are experiencing difficulties with breastfeeding, it is a good idea to rule out tongue tie as a cause so do ask your GP, midwife or health visitor to do a check.

Tongue tie can also cause problems in bottle-fed babies so if you are having problems with feeding your baby, the signs to look for are:

- your baby having difficulty latching on to the teat properly which results in poor sucking

- milk leaking out of the side of the baby's mouth while feeding

If a baby can't latch on to the teat of the bottle properly, he will be inclined to swallow more air while feeding, resulting in him becoming very windy.

Tongue tie is treated with a simple operation in which the doctor will snip the base of the baby's tongue. If your baby is still very young he may not feel anything at all – the operation is generally performed without anaesthetic though in some cases a local anaesthetic will numb the area; he may even sleep through it. Older babies may need general anaesthetic and the procedure is slightly more complex so ask your GP to explain it to you fully.

CASE STUDY: Tess, aged one month

Problem: Tongue tie

After weeks of misery desperately trying to breastfeed her baby Tess with little success, a lactation consultant came to visit Tess's mother when Tess was five weeks old. The consultant diagnosed Tess as having tongue tie – not straightforward tongue tie where the tongue is fused very obviously to the floor of the mouth, but posterior tongue tie which is difficult to spot. This explained why despite trying so hard, Tess's mother didn't seem to have enough milk and was in constant pain when feeding. Tess's tongue tie interfered with her ability to stimulate the breast properly, so her mother wasn't producing enough milk and, despite all her efforts, Tess would never be able to suck properly and feed well until the tongue tie was looked into.

On the consultant's advice, her parents decided to have Tess's tongue freed so they took her to see a paediatric surgeon whose area of specialisation was posterior tongue tie. He carried out the procedure to snip her tongue successfully.

After the procedure, things settled down. Tess was all smiles the next day and had healed very well. Her feeding was better and Tess's mother had much more milk, leaky breasts and engorgement in the morning. The hard work had paid off.

Baby not going longer between feeds

In the very early days a newborn baby can need to feed little and often, sometimes up to 12 times a day or even more. But by the second week if they are feeding properly at each feed, they should start to manage to go a little longer between feeds. Although all babies are different in their feeding needs, I find that during the day if fed well most babies can manage to go three hours between feeds. It is important to calculate that time from the beginning of a feed to the beginning of the next feed, which would mean an approximate gap of a couple of hours or just slightly more between feeds. However, if you find that your baby is not managing to go even two hours between feeds during the day, you should look at the following list of possible causes.

- Check the position of your baby as you feed. With both breastfed and bottle-fed babies I have often found the cause of them not drinking enough to go longer between feeds is because the baby is being fed in an almost laying, flat position – it causes their tummies to start to feel full before they've taken a full feed.

- Sleepy feeding is another possible cause. It is important that you ensure your baby is properly awake while feeding. If you allow them to sleepy feed with their eyes closed they are unlikely to feed well enough to last two hours until their next feed (see page 43 for how to resolve this problem).

- Sometimes in the early days some babies need a short break during the feed in order for them to take enough to go two hours. For example, if you feed your baby at 7am and he falls asleep one and a half to two hours later, only to wake up after 30 minutes looking for food, it would be worth offering a split feed. Allow the baby to drink as much as he wants at 7am, ensuring that he is feeding efficiently and not dozing on the breast. Then encourage him to have a good kick on his play mat and just prior to 8am offer him the rest of his feed. As long as the top-up is within the hour of the baby starting to feed, then the habit of snacking can be avoided and your baby will then be more likely to go longer between feeds. Similarly when your baby feeds at 10am you could split the feed and offer a top-up at 10.50am.

- In the early days babies tend to look for food the minute they wake, even if they are not quite ready to feed. Check that your baby is not looking to feed simply because he has not slept for long enough and is waking early from his nap (see page 99 for more on this problem). Kicking off his covers is another reason a baby would wake up earlier and then look for food the minute they wake even if they are not hungry, so ensuring that he is well tucked in is an important factor in helping establish regular feed times (see page 84 for guidance on tucking your baby in).

Colic

Babies under three months can suffer from excessive crying, which can be seen as colic. A 'colicky' baby is usually described as being in great pain, screaming as he brings his knees up to his tummy, which is often distended and noisy. Although a baby can suffer from colic at any time of the day, the most common time seems to be between 6pm and midnight. The crying spells can last for several hours and colic can make life miserable for the baby and the parents. Experts are divided as to what causes colic but the majority agrees that there is no magical cure. You can buy over-the-counter medications but most parents with a baby suffering from severe colic say they are of little help. Parents resort to endless feeding, rocking, patting, driving the baby round the block – most of which bring little or no relief. As parents of a colicky baby will confirm, it usually disappears by four months of age, but by that time the baby has learned all the wrong sleep associations.

I get contacted by thousands of parents, asking me what I did when the babies I cared for suffered from colic. The honest answer is that not one of the babies I looked after ever had it. Babies with colic share one thing in common: they are all being fed on demand. While demand feeding suits some families, I am convinced that by structuring a baby's feeding and sleeping from day one and following a routine that ensures your baby is never allowed to be left hungry, overtired or overstimulated colic will not occur. My advice to parents with a colicky baby is always the same: follow a good routine. Below is some short-term advice for how to cope with the excessive evening crying associated with colic, but in the long term I would advise switching to a routine. For detailed day-by-day routines for your baby's age, please see *The New Contented Little Baby Book*. Parents that do adopt a routine tell me that their baby's colic usually disappears overnight.

If your baby is crying for hours every evening and showing some of the signs of colic outlined above, it could be for one or more of the reasons below. By eliminating these causes and following a routine appropriate to your baby's age, you should find that his excessive crying is greatly reduced.

● Many breastfed babies are very unsettled in the evening because their mother's milk supply is low. I would strongly advise that you try topping up your baby with a bottle of expressed or formula milk after each of the evening feeds. If things improve, it will be clear that a low milk supply is the problem. Try to increase your milk supply by expressing to ensure that a low milk supply does not become a long-term problem and cause you to give up breastfeeding. For more on expressing and low milk supply turn to pages 47–54.

● With a baby of between one and three months of age who was feeding excessively in the night and consistently putting on more than the recommended weight gain each week, I would recommend that you discuss with your health visitor the possibility of using the core night method on page 352 to reduce the number of feeds in the night.

● With a baby who has developed the wrong sleep associations as a result of the colic, I use the crying down method (see page 347) to get him back to being able to settle himself, and within three or four nights they are going down happily and sleeping well until the late feed. Because they have slept well and have gone a full four hours since their last feed, they feed well at the late feed and last for an even longer spell in the night.

This method, along with the routines, will encourage a baby who has suffered from colic and developed the wrong sleep associations to sleep through the night, normally within a couple of weeks.

Reflux – arching back when feeding

Sometimes a baby displaying all the symptoms of colic (see above) actually has a condition called reflux. It is normal for babies to bring up a small amount of milk after a feed and this is known as 'posseting' (see page 103). All babies experience a small amount of reflux at some point in their first year as the muscle at the lower end of the oesophagus, which keeps milk in their stomach, has not developed properly yet, and this is normal. However, excessive posseting is one of the symptoms of gastro oesophageal reflux disease (GORD), a more long-term and more serious form of reflux. In this condition the muscle preventing the food coming back up from the stomach is too weak and stomach acid rises back up along with the milk, causing a very painful burning sensation in the oesophagus.

If your baby is arching his back during feeding, refusing to feed and crying, posseting excessively or coughing a lot at night, he may be suffering from reflux. In some cases babies with reflux won't actually sick up the milk, and suffer from what the medical profession call 'silent reflux'. These babies can often be misdiagnosed as having colic. They can be very difficult to feed, constantly arching their backs and screaming during a feed. They also tend to get very irritable when laid flat, and no amount of cuddling or rocking will calm them when they are like this.

If your baby displays any of these symptoms, insist that your doctor does a reflux test. I have seen too many cases of babies being diagnosed as having colic, when in fact they were suffering from reflux, despite not being sick. If you think that your baby is suffering from reflux, it is essential that you do not allow anyone to dismiss the pains as colic. Reflux is very stressful for the baby and parents, and it is essential that you get ongoing advice and support from your GP.

If you feel that you are not getting the help you need, do not be frightened to ask for a second opinion. If reflux is not the problem, you will at least have eliminated it as a possible cause. If it is the problem, with the help of the right medication, your baby will have been saved months of misery from the pain it can cause.

The other thing that I would recommend is that you put your baby in loose clothing at all times. While, of course, trendy little jeans and leggings look adorable, I do think that any clothing with a waistband can cause discomfort to babies after they have fed.

It is recommended that babies with reflux are fed little and often and kept upright for at least 30 minutes after feeding. While keeping a baby upright after feeding for 30 minutes can certainly help with reflux, it can sometimes lead to other problems. For example, if your baby is ready to sleep fairly soon after he is fed, it is almost inevitable that he will fall asleep on your shoulder. A problem can then arise whereby he wakes up immediately or very soon after you transfer him to his bed and then you have to spend a considerable time trying to resettle an upset, possibly overtired baby.

To avoid a sleep association problem developing because your baby is falling asleep on you, I would recommend that you try to structure your baby's feeding so that whenever possible he is not ready for a sleep immediately after he feeds. The following feeding and sleeping schedule for a baby under six months will ensure that for most of the time he is not due to sleep immediately after feeding. Obviously, you may need to adjust the timings to suit your baby's needs, but following a plan like this, or similar, will help ensure that settling problems are less likely to ensue.

7am	awake and feeding
7.30am	holding upright
8am	social time
8.30/9am	nap
10am	awake
10.15/10.30am	feeding
11am	holding time
11.30am	short play and cuddle time
11.45am	nap time
2pm	awake time
2.15/2.30pm	feeding
3pm	holding time
4/4.30pm	nap time
5pm	split feed
5.30pm	holding time
6pm	bath
6.15pm	small settling bedtime feed
6.30pm	holding time
6.45pm	settling time

7pm	sleep time
10pm	awake and feeding
10.30pm	holding time
11.15pm	offer remainder of feed
11.30pm	settling time

During the night I would recommend that you follow the same approach as for the late feed. I usually find that because babies are more sleepy at the middle-of-the-night feed, they are more relaxed and can be settled back to sleep with less holding time.

I find that once a baby is on the correct medication I can actually reduce the time they are kept upright to between 10 and 15 minutes. Instead of holding them upright I also find that positioning cushions under your left arm, then holding the baby on a pillow at a 30/40° angle while feeding and for 10 to 15 minutes after being burped, work well and are not so tiring for you as holding your baby fully upright. If you have a chair with a 30° angle that keeps your baby's back totally straight, it may be worthwhile trying it out, to see if it works as well as holding your baby upright. Car seats and most regular baby seats do not work as they do not allow the baby's body to remain straight enough, therefore these should be avoided.

Some babies with reflux may need medication for several months until the muscles tighten up. Fortunately, the majority of babies outgrow the condition by the time they reach one year. If your baby is diagnosed with reflux it is worth taking a look at the reflux section on my website, www.contentedbaby.com. Here you will find more case studies, plus lots of advice and tips on how to survive those early months with a reflux baby.

CASE STUDY: Alice, aged six weeks

Problem: Constant screaming and fussy feeding

Cause: Silent reflux

Alice was four weeks old when I went to help care for her. I had helped look after her elder brother, then aged two, for six weeks when he was born. He had been a model baby and had gone into the routine from day one. He slept through the night at six weeks and had continued to so ever since; he had always been a good feeder and a very easy baby. I felt confident that their mother would only need me for four weeks with the second baby, as she has always shown an excellent understanding of sleep rhythms, the importance of the right sleep associations and the correct structuring of feeds.

It therefore came as a bit of a shock when I arrived to find that Alice was not quite in 'the routine'. Her sleeping pattern was fine, she settled well at 7pm, I woke her at 10pm, she then fed well and would sleep until 5am then feed and settle back to sleep quickly until 7am. Her lunchtime nap was also good. The problem was when she was awake during the day, she would not be put down on her play mat, or settled in her chair for even five or ten minutes. Her mother would have to carry her the whole of her awake time.

After several days of helping care for Alice, I could see why she had to be held the whole time as the minute she was put down on her play mat or in her bouncy chair, she would scream hysterically. Her mother was becoming increasingly worried about how she was going to cope in the long term with a very active toddler and a baby who refused to be put down for even two or three minutes.

I suggested to her mother that it was possible that Alice was suffering from silent reflux, and that she should have Alice checked over by her GP. The doctor totally dismissed the possibility of reflux as Alice was not bringing up any milk after feeds, and was sleeping well at night. He was of the opinion that Alice's behaviour was typical of many babies of her age, and that in time she would calm down and the excessive crying would stop.

A week later Alice's behaviour was getting even worse and I advised her mother that she should phone the surgery and demand a referral to a paediatrician. After a consultation with him, like the doctor, he was also adamant that Alice did not have reflux and suggested that we were spoiling her and that we should be stricter about leaving her in her chair or on the play mat.

Over the two weeks that followed, despite very small feeds at 6.15pm and 10pm Alice would continue to sleep well at night. However, the days got worse and she screamed and screamed and screamed. Things came to a head when she started to arch her back the minute we tried to feed her. It could take over an hour to get her to drink just a couple of ounces.

We arranged to see the paediatrician for the second time, as I was convinced that Alice did have silent reflux. He was still adamant that it was not reflux as she wasn't being sick. A further two weeks went past with Alice's behaviour getting worse and worse, and either her mother or I had to hold her virtually the whole of her waking time.

A third visit was booked to the paediatrician. This time Alice's father accompanied us, and was insistent that a test be done to rule out reflux. The result came back positive; Alice had very severe silent reflux. She was prescribed medications and within a very short time, the intense crying had stopped, and she would happily spend short spells on the play mat looking at her toys. Her feeding also got easier.

The sad thing about Alice is that as a very small baby, she must have suffered a lot of pain. All too often babies are dismissed as being difficult or having colic, when in fact they are suffering from reflux. If your baby shows signs of behaviour similar to Alice, even if he is not bringing up milk, please do be insistent that you get a paediatrician. Reflux causes a huge amount of distress to young babies, and if your baby is crying a lot and showing all of the signs of reflux, it is important the possibility is ruled out.

Sleep

During the first month, babies need approximately 16–18 hours' sleep a day, divided into some short and some longer sleeps. In his first week, your baby will need to sleep for about five and a half hours during the daytime (7am to 7pm) and by the end of his first month this should be around five hours.

Babies don't sleep through the night right away, and it will happen at different ages for different babies, but in my experience most babies in a routine will start to sleep through from the 10pm feed until 6 or 7am when they are somewhere between the ages of eight and 12 weeks.

Babies under the age of six weeks usually get tired after an hour of being awake and although they may not need to sleep at that point they do need some quieter time. Babies should not usually stay awake for more than two hours during the first three months as they can get overtired. If a baby is too tired, he will not be able to drift off to sleep naturally and babies who are very overtired often fight sleep. Once they get into this state it can be really difficult to get them to settle.

Understandably Sudden Infant Death Syndrome (SIDS) is a cause of concern for many parents. To help reduce the chance of SIDS it is recommended that babies are put to sleep in a separate cot or Moses basket in the same room as parents or caregivers for the first six months, during the day as well as the night. On their website, the Lullaby Trust (the organisation that promotes expert advice on safer baby sleep and raises awareness on sudden infant death) states that 'a large study of evidence from across Europe found that the risk of sudden infant death was significantly reduced when the infant slept in the same room, but not the same bed, as the parent'.

The position in which you put your baby down to sleep each night is also one of the most protective actions you can take to ensure your baby is sleeping as safely as possible. There is substantial evidence from round the world to show that sleeping your baby on their back (known as the supine position) at the beginning of every sleep or nap significantly reduces the risk of SIDS (while sleeping a baby on their front or side greatly increases the risk). The best way to make sure your baby sleeps on their back is to do it from day one, and to keep putting them to sleep on their backs at every day- and night-time sleep. If your baby has rolled on to his tummy, you should turn him on to his back again. Only once your baby can roll from back to front and back again on their own (for more on this see page 161), can they be left to find their own position.

Babies are also at risk of SIDS if they become too hot. It is therefore important to make sure that the room your baby is sleeping in is neither too hot or too cold. The recommended room temperature is between 16–20°C, with light bedding tucked in very securely or a lightweight well-fitting baby sleep bag. Adults find it difficult to judge the temperature in the room, so use a room thermometer.

For more detailed advice on SIDS and how to help reduce its risks I would advise you visit the Lullaby Trust's website: www. lullabytrust.org.uk

What to expect

During the first couple of weeks the majority of babies will be fed and only manage to stay awake for a short spell before needing to sleep. By the third week they will start to show signs of being able to stay awake for slightly longer after daytime feeds. All babies are different; some may only manage to stay fully awake for an hour, while others will manage to stay awake for an hour and a half or slightly longer. It is important that babies of this age are never allowed to stay awake longer than two hours, as they would be at risk of becoming very overtired and then would be very difficult to settle to sleep.

What to aim for

How your baby sleeps at night will depend very much on what happens during the day. As already mentioned in the feeding section, a small baby needs to feed little and often during the early days.

- If your baby is allowed to sleep for long stretches between feeds during the day, he will be more likely to wake more during the night needing to be fed.

- Waking and feeding your baby every three hours during the first month will mean that he will be much more likely to go his longer stretch in the night.

- To ensure that this longer stretch is between 11pm and 6/7am, it is important that he sleeps well in the early evening. Many parents think keeping their baby awake for most of the evening will help them sleep longer in the night. I have rarely found this to be the case. More often than not, the baby is fretful and irritable and needs to be fed on and off during the evening, then is so exhausted by 10pm that he only takes a small feed, waking again a couple of hours later. Because breast milk is produced on a supply and demand basis, a pattern of feeding every couple of hours can soon evolve.

● A baby whose daytime feeds and sleeps have been structured, and who feeds well at 6pm and settles to sleep well between 7 and 10pm will wake up refreshed and ready to take a full feed that will help him to sleep a longer stretch in the middle of the night.

CASE STUDY: Milly, aged four weeks

Problem: Unsettled evenings

Cause: Possibly colic, probably hunger

I was contacted by Milly's parents when she was nearly four weeks old. They had tried to follow the Contented Little Baby routines from the very early days, but with little success. Milly would rarely settle for naps at the times the routines suggested and would cry and feed on and off all evening. She would eventually settle at 11pm, but only after her mother had topped her up with formula. Her parents were convinced that she was suffering from colic, as she would bring her legs up and scream as if in terrible pain when she cried. This would go on all evening, no matter how many times her mother put her to the breast.

When I enquired about her weight gain, her parents were unsure as they had not had her weighed for nearly two weeks, although she had regained her birth weight by the time she was two weeks old. I advised them to get her weighed and call me back once they had an accurate weight. They called back the following day to say that Milly had only put on 7oz in the last two weeks. This confirmed what I had suspected, that the reason Milly was so unsettled, particularly in the early evening, was hunger and not colic. When I took more details from her parents it also transpired that while they had followed the Contented Little Baby routines to the letter where the sleeping and feeding were concerned, Laura, Milly's mother, had not expressed at the times suggested in the book. This meant that when Milly went through a growth spurt at three weeks, she did not get the extra milk she required. The reason why it is so important to express during the early days of following the Contented Little Baby routines is to ensure that the mother always produces more milk than the baby actually requires. This means that when a baby goes through a growth spurt, the mother can express slightly less at the first feed of the day, so ensuring that there is extra milk to satisfy the baby's increased needs.

As this did not happen with Milly, I advised her mother that she would have to top her up before the first two naps of the day to ensure that she got the extra milk she needed. The extra stimulation of emptying the breasts would help increase the milk supply and hopefully we would be able to get back to the original routine within a few days. I also suggested that Laura offer Milly a small top-up of formula after the bath, as I was sure that her milk supply was very low then.

Within a couple of days the screaming and fretfulness had stopped. However, Milly would still get upset when put in her cot. She would feed well and look sleepy but the minute she was put in the cot she would wake up screaming, only to fall asleep the minute she was picked up and held in either of her parents' arms. I explained that while we had resolved the feeding issue, Milly had probably also learned the wrong sleep associations, having got used to being held for much of her sleep time.

I suggested that they should try the crying down method to see if Milly would settle at nap times and in the evening. Her parents were not totally convinced that the problem was a wrong sleep association and were sure that she was still suffering some sort of physical pain which prevented her from settling to sleep.

I was very concerned that the constant handling from one parent to the other was creating a long-term problem, but could understand that they did not want their very young baby to be left to cry.

I therefore suggested that if Milly had to be held during naps or in the evening, it should be done consistently and by only one parent. For the next three days I advised them not even to attempt to put Milly in her cot at nap times or early evening. Instead, one or the other should lie in a quiet, dark room with Milly and cuddle her throughout the whole of the sleep time. It was important that the same person was with her during the allocated sleep time and that she was not handed back and forth or walked around from room to room.

As I had predicted, Milly slept soundly in one or the other of her parents' arms at each allocated sleep time.

After one week of this, her parents were also convinced that Milly was neither hungry nor in pain and were confident about trying the crying down method described on page 347.

The first evening, Milly cried for 10 minutes before her parents checked her, then fell asleep after a further 10 minutes of intermittent crying. Her nap times followed much the same pattern. Within a week the crying decreased and Milly was happy to settle in her cot, sleepy but awake.

During this time, Laura had also been following my plan for increased milk supply, and within a further week, Milly was having all of her feeds from the breast during the day, without a top-up. Her parents continued to give her a full formula feed at 10pm. On the occasions when Laura had had a hectic day and felt her milk supply might be low at 6.15pm, she would top Milly up with the milk she had expressed at 10pm the previous evening.

Transferring your baby to the big cot

Most baby books advise that in the early days a cot is not necessary, as babies are happier in a Moses basket or small crib. While this may seem a more practical solution when moving your baby from room to room with you, I am not convinced babies are happier or sleep better in these. Because of current guidelines that babies should not be put in their own room to sleep until they are six months (this includes the evening sleep time between 7 and 10pm), I recommend that parents buy a multi-purpose pram in which babies can be put down to sleep in the evening. There are many different brands offering models designed for this purpose – three-in-one prams which are suitable for birth right up until the toddler years. They have a lightweight, detachable carry cot for a baby to lie in up until six months and a pushchair seat for your growing baby and toddler which can be put in various positions. It is a better option to have a pram with a firm mattress made up for him in your living area that he will use for the duration of this period than having to buy an additional piece of equipment. And as his cot will most likely be in your bedroom, I would advise that from day one there is no reason why your baby can't be put in his big cot after the late feed.

Choosing a cot

When choosing a cot, it is important to remember that it will be your baby's bed for at least two or three years and should therefore be sturdy enough to withstand a bouncing toddler. Even very young babies will eventually move around their cot. I would suggest choosing a design with flat spars instead of round ones, as pressing the head against a round spar could be quite painful for a young baby. Cot bumpers are not advised for babies, as they can end up sleeping with their heads pressed up against the bumpers, and because body heat escapes through the top of the head, blocking it off increases the risk of overheating. This is thought to be a contributing factor in cot death. You can, however, now buy breathable mesh cot liners, which reduce the risk of suffocation.

Other points to bear in mind when choosing cots are:

● All cots have a low base level, which is of course necessary as your baby grows and needs to be prevented from climbing out of his cot. However, lowering a tiny baby down into a very low-level cot can be difficult. Newborn and young babies also need a lot of attention when you're settling them – you've got to tuck your baby in and he may need to be stroked. All this becomes difficult for you physically if your baby is low down and you've got to bend over for extended periods. Having a cot you can adjust makes things much easier.

- Drop-sides should be easy to put up and down without making a noise. Test several times.

- The cot should be large enough to accommodate a three-year-old child comfortably.

- All cots must comply with the recommendations set out by the British Standards Institute, Number BS1753. Spars must be no less than 2.5cm (1in) apart and no more than 6cm (2½in) in width. When the mattress is at its lowest position, the maximum distance between that and the cot top should be no more than 65cm (26in). There should be a gap of no more than 4cm (1½in) around the edge of the mattress.

- Babies should always sleep on a firm, flat, waterproof mattress in good condition, so buy the best possible mattress that you can afford. I have found that foam mattresses tend to sink in the middle within a few months. The type I have found to give the best support for growing babies is a 'natural cotton spring interior' type. All mattresses must comply with Safety Standards Numbers BS1877 and BS7177.

Bedding for the cot

Everything should be 100 per cent white cotton so that it can be washed on a hot wash along with the baby's night clothes. Due to the risk of overheating or smothering, pillows, quilts and duvets are not recommended for babies under one year old. If you want a pretty matching top cover for your baby's cot, make sure it is 100 per cent cotton and not quilted with a nylon filling. For parents who are handy with a sewing machine, a considerable amount of money can be saved by making flat sheets and draw sheets out of a large cotton double-bed sheet.

Making up the cot

(a) Remove mattress and lay a sheet and blanket lengthways across the base of the cot.

(b) Replace mattress and cover with bottom sheet.

(c) Place sheet over baby and tuck in at least 15cm (6in) at the other side. Push a small, rolled-up towel down either side between the cot mattress and spars to stop the baby kicking the sheet off.

Note that the cot should be kept as clear as possible and the following items should not be placed inside as they can increase the risk of accidents:

- pillows or duvets

- soft toys

- loose bedding, comforters and muslins

- products to keep a baby in one sleeping position such as wedges or straps.

The Moro reflex and swaddling your baby

For several weeks after birth many babies will twitch and startle when they drift in and out of sleep, sometimes so much that they wake themselves up. Some babies will go through this twitching stage when drifting off to sleep. This reaction is called the Moro reflex and is often very strong in the early days. These sudden jerky movements can be very upsetting to a baby as he does not realise that the sensations he is feeling are being caused by his own body movements. I believe that nearly all babies benefit from being swaddled in the first few weeks, which will help prevent this provided it is done properly.

The following guidelines should help ensure that your baby is swaddled correctly, which will help him feel more secure and – provided he is well fed – help him sleep more soundly until his next feed is due.

The choice of swaddling blanket is important – it needs to ensure that your baby is wrapped securely but does not become overheated. When I worked as a maternity nurse I used to make my own swaddling blankets. They were very basic, but they did the trick.

To make two swaddling blankets all you need is 2m (6ft) of stretch cotton T-shirt fabric, available from any department store or haberdashery shop. The fabric is usually 1.25m (4ft) wide, which may seem enormous the first week or two, but does allow for growth. Cut the fabric into two lengths and make a hem of 2cm along the bottom and up both sides, then fold down a double hem of 4cm (2in) at the top. It is important that the hem that goes around the baby's neck is deep and secure.

Because the swaddling blanket is rectangular as opposed to square it allows extra fabric to go around the back of the baby, making the swaddle more secure. One of the reasons babies get out of a square swaddle is that once the first arm has been tucked in and the fabric tucked under the baby's back, there is not usually enough fabric to take right under the baby's back once the second arm has been tucked in.

I used to get my clients to practise on a large teddy. Once you have done it 20 or so times with a teddy, it becomes easier to get it right with your baby in the shortest time possible. One of the reasons that so many babies cry when they are being swaddled is because of the time it takes, not because they actually dislike being swaddled. Another reason many babies get upset when they are being swaddled is that parents pull their arms down by their sides to wrap them. Most babies hate this, as they feel more secure with their arms across their chests. I always swaddled my babies kimono-style, which involves making little pockets within the swaddle so that the blanket is wrapped around their arms before being taken across the chest and the excess blanket tucked around the back. The basic steps for contented baby swaddling are:

- Lay the swaddling blanket on a large flat surface such as your bed or the floor and position your baby so that he is more to the right side of the blanket than the left, but ensure that there is enough blanket to the right for it to be able to stretch across his body and around his back. You should also ensure that the top of the blanket is slightly higher than the back of his neck.

- Take the top corner of the right-hand side of the blanket and pull it up and away from your baby's neck.

- Take your baby's left hand in your right hand, pointing it outwards from his body, then with your left hand draw the right-hand side of the swaddle blanket across your baby's chest. Gently tug it downwards so that the 4cm (2in) border is sitting firmly around your baby's neck.

- The baby's left hand and your right hand will now be under the swaddle material. Place your free hand on top of your baby's chest, which is now covered by a layer of swaddle material. Then, using your right hand, bring your baby's left hand across his chest, so that it is as if you have made a sleeve. Tuck the excess blanket around his back and under his bottom (think kimono).

- Repeat the same procedure with your baby's right hand. Hold it up and outwards in your left hand, then with your right hand bring the remainder of the swaddling blanket across his chest. Take the arm wrapped in the blanket across his chest, tucking the excess under his back and bottom. This swaddle ensures that your baby cannot wriggle free. He feels secure because he has his hands across his chest, but he can also move them around within the little pockets that you have created.

- Once you have established regular feeding times and sleep times you should start to get your baby used to being half swaddled. Start off by leaving the second arm out. Once he is happily sleeping with one arm out then you should progress to half swaddling him so that both his arms are out.

- It is very important that you get your baby used to being half swaddled by the time he is two months old so that he is not at risk of overheating. It is also important at all times during the swaddling period to adjust the layers of clothing and bedding in accordance with the room temperature. For more help with swaddling, including a demonstration by video, you can refer to the Contented Baby website: www.contentedbaby.com

Sleep Problems

Moving around the big cot

Once your baby is having some time in his cot, you need to keep him securely tucked in so that he doesn't move around – you don't want him rolling on to his tummy, getting his arms in a muddle or banging his head on the top of the cot or the spars, all of which will cause him to wake or worse, cause him pain or put him in danger.

- In the early weeks, the key is to ensure that the cot is made up properly, with enough of the top sheet and blanket being tucked right in under the mattress (please see description on page 83).

- However, in the second month the problem of your baby moving around is likely to happen when he is unswaddled. When that happens I would recommend that he is put in a lightweight sleeping bag, but that you put a thin cotton sheet across the baby and tuck him in as described on page 84.

- When the baby is sleeping in the pram, if he is kicking off his covers and waking himself up, you should put a sheet lengthways across the pram, which will ensure he can't kick his covers off. There should be at least 20cm (8in) on each side to tuck under the mattress.

Baby is unsettled in the evening

The three main reasons very young babies do not settle in the evening are hunger, overtiredness or too much sleep during the day. A baby will sometimes sleep all morning, because they are not sleeping well between 7pm and 7am. A vicious circle is soon established and can be difficult to break.

- To eliminate the possible cause of hunger and overtiredness, often an earlier bath/bedtime routine and a top-up milk feed is all that is needed to solve this problem. For a couple of nights, do not feed your baby at 5pm, instead try and stretch him out until after the bath. Start the bath at 5.30pm and then feed at 6pm. This will ensure that your baby has a really big feed after the bath.

- However, if your baby is still unsettled for a few nights you may have to assist him to sleep following the technique described on page 350. Do not worry about creating the wrong sleep association as resolving the unsettled evenings is the important thing at this stage. Once your baby has slept well for several nights between 7 and 10pm, you may have to allow a short crying down period (see page 347) when you go back to settling him in the cot.

- Once your baby starts to sleep better between 7 and 10pm, you will then find it easier to keep him awake more in the mornings, which in turn would have a knock-on effect of him sleeping better in the evening.

- I would also suggest that in the morning when your baby gets tired at 8.30am you do not put him in the cot, instead allow him a short nap in the bouncy chair of 20–30 minutes, then give a further short nap at around 10.30/10.45am of around 15 minutes. This would make a total nap time of no more than 45 minutes, reducing the amount of morning sleep considerably. He will then hopefully manage to stay awake until 12.15/12.30pm, when he can nap for two hours.

Important points to note:

● Do offer him more milk if your baby does not settle within 10 minutes in the evening. A breastfed baby may need a second top-up of expressed milk.

● Do remember to gradually reduce the amount of daytime sleep and revert back to your original routine once your baby is settling well between 7 and 10pm. When he is settling well between 7 and 10pm it is really important that you have him awake properly at 10pm for the late feed, otherwise you could get another wakeful slot in the middle of the night. I would suggest that you try a split feed at 10/11.15pm once your baby is sleeping well in the evening.

Settling a baby of up to six weeks

The following guidelines will be of help when trying to settle a small baby at bedtime.

● In order for a small baby to settle well in the evening it is very important that he takes a full feed prior to going to bed, is well winded and has been awake enough throughout the day and is ready to sleep.

● Babies under six weeks can usually stay awake for between one and two hours at a time.

● A baby who has only been awake a total of four hours between 7am and 7pm may not settle as quickly as a baby who has had a lot more sleep because the latter has had too much daytime sleep.

- Keep the bedtime routine calm and quiet; once the bath is over, do not allow lots of visitors in the nursery as this can overstimulate your baby.

- Keep the lights dim and avoid lots of talking and eye contact during the last feed. Make sure that he is well winded before you attempt to settle him in his cot.

- Always settle your baby in his cot before he falls asleep. If he has become sleepy on the breast or bottle, rouse him slightly before putting him in the cot. It is important to help your baby to learn self-soothing techniques from an early age.

- I would advise that you use the same holding positions each time. By using the same technique your baby will soon start to associate it with falling asleep. Many babies get very distressed when they suddenly go from the warmth of their parent's chest and arms to being on their back, alone in the cot. The settling technique described below will help make the transition from your arms to the cot much easier for your baby.

  - Holding your baby across your chest will help him feel calm and secure and also prevent him from thrashing his arms and legs around if he is fretful.

- Once he is calm and his breathing is steady you should move him to the crook of your arm, but continue to hold his hands across his chest.

- After a minute or two you can let go of one of his hands, a minute or two later let go of the second. If he remains relaxed and sleepy you can now gently lower him into his cot. The aim is to have his whole body in a relaxed sleepy state but settled in his cot before he actually goes to sleep.

- Make sure that he is tucked in very securely, as babies under six weeks still have a strong Moro reflex and get very upset when they thrash their arms and legs around. Some younger or smaller babies may benefit from swaddling (see page 85). Try to allow your baby five to 10 minutes to settle himself to sleep. If he is getting very upset, pick him up and offer him more milk. Hunger is one of the main causes of young babies not settling in the evening, particularly breastfed babies. Resettle him in his cot again and leave him a further five or 10 minutes. If he is still very unsettled, repeat the same procedure. You may find that for a week or so you have to resettle him several times before he eventually falls asleep. The key is to be consistent and keep settling him until he does go to sleep. With some babies it can take up to a couple of weeks or more to perfect the settling process in the evening.

- The important thing is to be consistent and persistent. In the long term this will be much more reassuring to your baby than to keep changing your tactic at bedtime. Do not be tempted to take him downstairs into his daytime environment, as this will confuse him even more.

● Keep a diary of what your baby takes at each feed during the day and how long he is awake, then if he is unsettled you may be able to trace why from your notes.

● If, after several nights, you find that it is taking many attempts to settle him and you are convinced that he is well fed and winded and has been awake enough and is ready to sleep, try sitting or lying quietly with him in the darkened room for a few nights. If you find that he will fall asleep in your arms happily for over an hour or more but gets upset when put in the cot, it may be that he has already learned some of the wrong sleep associations. You will then have to decide whether you are going to continue to establish the wrong sleep associations by assisting him to sleep or use the crying down method (see page 347) to help him learn how to settle himself to sleep.

Crying immediately when put down to sleep

Listening to a baby cry is extremely distressing, particularly if you are a new parent. When I wrote my first book *The Contented Little Baby Book*, in 1999 I said that I would be horrified if the babies that I cared for cried for even an hour a day. But in that book and in subsequent books I do recommend a method called 'crying down' as a way of helping babies who are fighting sleep. Sadly this method has often been confused with 'controlled crying', which is a sleep training technique used for babies over six months who have a serious sleep problem and are unable to settle themselves to sleep without assistance and are usually waking up several times a night.

I do recommend that if a baby who is well fed and ready to sleep is fighting sleep then crying down can be used so that he learns to settle himself to sleep. A baby who doesn't learn to self-settle is more than likely to take increasingly longer to settle in the evening and will often continue to wake up several times a night for many months. Please refer to pages 346–55 to understand the importance of self-settling.

If your baby is over two weeks old, weighed over 3.1kg (7lb) at birth, has regained his birth weight and putting on a good amount of weight each week, then you should consider allowing him to cry down if he is taking a long time to settle in the evening. A baby who takes a long time to settle in the evening and needs to be constantly picked up and calmed down, will soon become overtired and will often fight sleep for hours before falling asleep through sheer exhaustion.

The one concern that many parents have when I advise trying crying down is how do they know if their baby is not in pain or genuinely hungry when they are crying. Before attempting crying down I recommend that parents use the 'assisting to sleep' method described on page 350. If you do this for three nights and your baby sleeps at least a couple of hours before becoming unsettled, I think you can be reassured that his previous unsettled evenings were not due to colic pain or hunger. This being the case you can then try the crying down method so that your baby learns to settle himself to sleep. Remember, self-settling is a skill that the majority of babies have to learn and until your baby does learn to self-settle you will more than likely go on to have more and more unsettled evenings and disrupted sleep.

Overtiredness

Overtiredness is usually a result of overstimulation or missing the baby's cue for sleep (see pages 22–3). A baby who is allowed to become overtired reaches a stage where he is unable to drift off to sleep naturally, and the more tired he becomes, the more he fights sleep. Although overtiredness can happen at any age during the first year, it is particularly common among babies under the age of three months. Once a baby becomes overtired it can be very difficult to get them to sleep and when they do, they will often awake crying very shortly after they have fallen asleep.

● It is important to ensure that your baby isn't allowed to stay awake too long between naps and prior to bedtime, if overtiredness is to be avoided. During the first few months babies who are allowed to stay awake for longer than two hours at a time are more prone to overtiredness. All babies are different; some may only stay awake for an hour before being ready to sleep, others may manage to stay awake slightly longer. The important thing is to take note on how long your baby stayed awake happily, on the occasions that he settled to sleep easily and quickly. Once you have established how long he can stay awake, then aim to start winding him down 15/20 minutes in advance of that time, so that you do not miss his put down time and overtiredness is avoided.

- If overtiredness does set in (see the box below for the main signs) it is important to calm your baby down before you attempt to settle him in his bed. If he is very young, try swaddling him securely so that he cannot thrash around. Once swaddled gently pat and shush him until he calms down. If he is used to a dummy, try soothing him with that. Once he is calm try offering him a feed and when he gets sleepy, try settling him in his bed again. Some overtired babies will settle better if they are allowed some crying down time. For how crying down works, turn to page 347.

- Sometimes an overtired baby who has calmed down will get a second wind and become very awake, so it is important not to try to settle him in his bed until he looks sleepy. It is better just to sit quietly with him until he does show signs of being sleepy before attempting to settle him.

- With older babies who are too big to swaddle, holding them closely and firmly in a quiet room with some gentle music will often help them calm down. And again like the younger baby it is always worth offering them a feed, to help get them calm and sleepy. Once he looks as if he is about to sleep you should settle him in his cot and allow him a short spell of fussing or crying down time.

Signs your baby is overtired

- He will get fussy and often turn his head to the side as if rooting for a feed

- He will start to yawn several times

- He may have bouts of hiccups or sneezing

- He goes very quickly from fussing to inconsolable crying

- He arches his back or / and pulls up his legs up as if in pain

- Older babies tend to give more obvious signs such as rubbing their eyes or pulling their ears

Short daytime naps

For the first month your baby should happily sleep for one to two hours at nap times without interruption, ideally with one of the naps being a longer nap of two to two and a half hours. Mothers find this time invaluable – it's a little time for themselves – and therefore it can be very distressing if your baby won't sleep for long enough. There are several reasons your baby may not be sleeping enough at his nap times, the first is because he is hungry. The other reasons relate to his natural sleep cycles (for more on this see page 17) – the baby will come into his light sleep after 30 or 40 minutes, wake himself up and then not return to sleep. Below are the main reasons I find that babies are not napping for the full two hours. You may need to try a few of the suggested solutions before you can assess what is causing your baby to wake early.

● The main cause of short naps in the early days is hunger. During the day a baby of this age can normally manage to stay awake for one hour to one hour and a half before needing a nap. Once he is asleep he should sleep until the next feed, if he has fed well. In the early days, regardless of whether they are breast- or bottle-fed, some babies will initially feed very well, then pull themselves off the breast or bottle, giving off all the signals that they are full. If you find your baby is doing this, but then not sleeping well at nap time, it could be a sign that he is not taking a big enough feed. Until he is capable of taking a full feed in one go, I would advise that you offer a top-up feed just prior to nap times. Once he has been sleeping consistently well at his naps for at least a week, you can gradually bring the top-up feed back by five minutes each day, until he is actually being topped up within 40 minutes of having his main feed.

● Your baby may be doing a lot of sleepy feeding on the breast and, while he may seem to take a full feed, he may wake up early from his daytime naps because he has been catnapping while sleeping on the breast or bottle earlier. I think it is really important, especially with daytime feeds, that you encourage your baby to stay properly awake while feeding. You can do this by having his play mat or changing mat right by the chair in which you are feeding him. Each time he shows signs of closing his eyes while feeding, pop him on the mat for a couple of minutes until he is fully awake. By doing this consistently at all daytime feeds your baby will quickly learn to stay fully awake while feeding.

● If a baby becomes overtired (see page 98) either physically or mentally, he may become irritable and stressed and fight sleep, not settle to sleep easily and then wake up early. Many babies do not give off an obvious signal of tiredness and are allowed to stay awake for too long a period between daytime naps. Others are kept up too late in the evening by their parents in the hope that they will sleep better during the night. In both cases the baby becomes overtired. A baby's natural sleep cycle will affect how long he sleeps. As your baby's sleep cycle develops into more distinct stages of light and deep sleep, he will often find it more difficult to settle back to sleep after the 30–40-minute sleep cycle. Although his body clock may need more sleep, particularly in the middle of the day, he will often find it difficult to get himself back to sleep. As the day progresses, the baby gets more and more irritable, and by late afternoon he is often very overtired and fights sleep even more. Parents, desperate to help their child get some much-needed sleep, often resort to feeding, rocking or giving the dummy and a double problem of overtiredness and the wrong sleep associations is quickly established. First you will need to address the wrong sleep associations, by following the 'assisting to sleep' technique on page 350. By doing this and then following the other guidelines in this section on how to lengthen his nap times you should also prevent him becoming overtired.

● He may have been overstimulated just prior to his nap. Overstimulation before sleep time can cause real problems, and several cuddles or too much noise around him all add up and can leave your baby fretful and difficult to settle, preventing him from sleeping well. Please do not feel guilty about restricting the handling during the first few months, especially prior to sleep times. Start to calm things down 20–30 minutes before the nap, avoiding lots of talking and eye contact and then allow 10 minutes to gently soothe and settle your baby. This will become a signal to him that it is quiet time and help prepare him for sleep.

- Light might be another reason your baby is waking from his naps early. Again, he might sleep for one sleep cycle but then won't be able to go back into a second because he is sensitive to the daylight. As guidelines now state that your baby should always sleep in the same room as you, you could buy blackout shades for your pram or travel cot, which will rule out this problem.

- If your baby has a strong Moro reflex (see page 85), he may be getting out of his swaddle and therefore waking himself up. Make sure your baby is swaddled correctly and securely – see my guide on page 85. If you're struggling with swaddling there are zip-up and Velcro swaddle garments available to buy, which will keep your baby secure. Even if he is swaddled you will still need a thin cotton sheet tucked across him otherwise his legs can thrash about and he may wake himself. Remember that it is very important that you get your baby used to being half swaddled by the time he is two months old so that he is not at risk of overheating. It is also important at all times during the swaddling period to adjust the layers of clothing and bedding in accordance with the room temperature.

- Finally, make sure your baby is not in any physical discomfort. Adults can adjust their pillows and bedding to make themselves comfortable, but of course babies can't, so do check that mattress protectors, sheets and blankets are smooth and not crumpled. Also try to make sure that the clothes you dress your baby or toddler in for bed are 100 per cent cotton. Polyester fabric does not allow the skin to breathe, and wool can be itchy or bring some babies out in a rash, while loose threads and labels that stick out can cause irritation and pose a safety risk.

General Problems

Hiccups

Hiccups are very normal among tiny babies, and very few get distressed by them.

- Hiccups often happen after a feed. If it has been a night-time feed and your baby is due to go down for a sleep, it is advisable to go ahead and put him down regardless. If you wait until the hiccups are finished, there is a bigger chance of him falling asleep in your arms, which is something to be avoided as he will develop the wrong sleep associations.

- If your baby is one of the rare ones who gets upset by their hiccups, then try giving him the recommended dose of gripe water, which can sometimes help.

Posseting

It is very common for some babies to bring up a small amount of milk while being burped or after a feed. It is called posseting, and for most babies it does not create a problem. However, babies who bring up a lot of milk get hungry and may need to feed again. If your baby is regularly gaining more than 240g (8oz) of weight each week it could be that he is drinking too much.

- With a bottle-fed baby the problem is easily solved as you are able to see how much the baby is drinking and therefore slightly reduce the amount at the feeds during which he appears to posset more.

- It is more difficult to tell how much a breastfed baby is drinking. But by keeping a note of which feeds cause more posseting, and reducing the time on the breast at those feeds, the posseting may be reduced.

- If your baby is posseting excessively and not gaining weight it could be that he is suffering from a condition called 'reflux' (see page 66). With babies who are inclined to bring up milk, it is important to keep them as upright as possible after a feed, and special care should be taken when burping.

Any baby bringing up an entire feed twice in a row should be seen by a doctor immediately.

4

Two to Three Months
(Five to 12 Weeks)

By the second month both you and your baby will have got a grasp of the basics – feeding, bathing, etc. You will be starting to feel more confident at looking after him, so the next challenge is for you to start getting out and about more, to enjoy some time out of the house, and to start building up your social life as a family – with your partner, if he or she is part of it. Life will have changed dramatically and adjusting to this change – this new little person in your life – takes time. On a practical note, it is very normal to feel nervous about leaving the safe cocoon of the home, where you are likely to have spent most of the past month, and you may feel daunted by going out. It's important to have time to yourself though and do some things that will make you feel more relaxed around other people with your baby. If you're planning a trip to the shops and are worried about feeding in public, simply feed before leaving; don't try and push yourself to do things that might make you, and therefore your baby, anxious.

Your baby's sleep will no doubt be a cause of concern as he grows and you may still be dealing with early morning waking or feeding more than once in the night. Hopefully this chapter will help address any problems of that kind. Young babies can go through an unsettled period between the ages of three to six weeks when they may cry more than usual. If your baby is crying a lot you will want to make sure that you have eliminated the possible causes which may be hunger, tiredness, overtiredness, wind or colic. Sometimes babies are just bored, as they do need some stimulation when they are awake.

Babies who cry a lot, particularly during the evening, are often said to be suffering from colic which is a common problem for babies during the first three months (see page 64). It can be very upsetting as your baby may scream for hours at a time, and may seem to be in considerable discomfort. In my experience, babies who are settled into a routine with structured feeding and sleeping patterns do not suffer from colic, which is most common among babies who are fed on demand, but a colicky baby can be very upsetting and there is advice on pages 64–6 on what to do if you think your baby is suffering from colic.

Breast milk is produced on a supply and demand basis, and your baby will go through periods of rapid growth when he may suddenly need far more milk. These growth spurts are common at around six weeks and then again at around nine weeks. At these times, you may find that you need to start feeding your baby more. I recommend learning to express milk from early on so that you are producing more than your baby needs and can stay ahead when he needs more (see page 47).

Your baby will make noises and may begin to smile during his second month. He will put his fingers in his mouth and begin to kick his legs and will be grasping hold of things by the end of the third month. Parents are often worried about how their baby is developing, comparing him with others of a similar age and wondering whether he is doing all that he should. In reality, all babies develop at different speeds, and how quickly he can do things during his first three months is not an indicator of his development for the rest of his life.

Your baby will start to develop his own character by the end of the first three months. He will recognise familiar faces and places and will respond to you with gurgles and smiles, using his body movements and expressions to demonstrate his feelings. You will find that you have changed too during this time, and have become more confident as a parent, and more aware of your baby's needs.

Feeding

What to expect

During the second month your baby usually starts to establish a more regular feeding pattern of around five or six feeds during the day, and if he gets most of his milk intake during these hours (roughly 6am–11pm) he will be able to sleep for longer at night. He should be steadily gaining weight now, at a rate of around 170–240g (6–8oz) each week. As your baby grows he will be capable of taking bigger feeds and therefore going longer between feeds.

By the end of the third month, if you are breastfeeding you may find your baby is feeding more efficiently but you should still let him guide you as to how long he spends on the breast. As long as he is gaining weight and managing to go for three or four hours between feeds, he should be getting all the milk that he needs.

What to aim for

Provided feeds are structured properly during the day and they are having at least five to six feeds between 6am and midnight, the majority of babies will manage to go the longer stretch in the night cutting out the 2/3am feed and sleeping to somewhere between 5 and 7am from a late feed.

In the CLB routines I always recommend to start the day at 7am, as I feel this gives parents the best opportunity to fit in the right number of feeds and for the baby to have naps at times that can fit around other children and family life.

By the end of three months a typical day should look similar to that outlined below. Obviously, if your baby is starting his day earlier or later, you can adjust the times accordingly, but aim for the same distance between feeds and naps, so that your baby is getting the right number of feeds and that his sleep is working in conjunction with his feeds.

7am	awake and feeding
9am	nap (no longer than 45 minutes)
10.45/11am	feed

12 noon	nap (no longer than 2¼ hours)
2.30pm	feed
4.30pm	nap (may need 15 minutes if he slept less at previous nap)
5.45pm	bath and bedtime routine
10/10.30pm	late feed

Feeding Problems

Overfeeding

If your baby is gaining more than 240–285g (8–10oz) per week you should discuss his weight gain with a health visitor as you may be overfeeding him. Most breastfed babies should be gaining 140–200g (5–7oz) per week; with formula-fed babies it can be slightly more – 180–240g (6–8oz) per week.

● Overfeeding is a more common problem among babies who are formula-fed. In my opinion the reason for this is that some babies take the bottle of formula so quickly that their natural sucking instincts are not satisfied and they end up screaming when the bottle is removed by their mothers. Some mothers interpret this as a cry of hunger and give them more formula. This can quickly turn into a pattern of overfeeding and your baby gaining more weight than he should each week. If the problem is allowed to continue, you can quickly reach a situation where milk alone will not satisfy your baby's appetite yet he is too young to be given solids.

● Overfeeding is generally only a problem in breastfed babies when mothers use breastfeeding as a comfort to calm their baby. If your baby is over six weeks and still waking twice in the night (between midnight and 6/7am) to feed and is putting on too much weight each week, I would suggest that you discuss the possibility of using the core night method (outlined on page 352) with your health visitor to eliminate one of the night feeds.

Fussy feeding (breastfed baby)

In the second month, the reasons a breastfed baby is fussy at feed times can change from the first month. One of the main causes of fussy feeding in the second month is hunger. Usually around the sixth week a baby will go through a second growth spurt (the first being at around three weeks) and if you have not been expressing any of the extra milk you were producing in the first few weeks, then you may find that your supply may not be enough to meet his needs. If this is the case, your baby will feed for around five to 10 minutes then your milk supply will run low and your baby will stop feeding and fuss. He will have to work harder to get as much milk as he'd like, or as quickly, so he will become frustrated, unable to get the amount of milk he needs to satisfy his appetite. He will also start to demand feeds sooner than usual and often wake up more in the night demanding to be fed.

● One of the reasons I recommend expressing in the early days is to avoid the problem of fussy feeding when a baby goes through a growth spurt. If you have been expressing extra milk in the morning, by now you will be overproducing milk, so when he goes through a growth spurt you will have enough to supply the increase in his appetite. Now is therefore the time to decrease the amount you express by an ounce or so, to give your baby more from the breast and ensure that his increased appetite is satisfied.

● If you have not been expressing it will mean that during the growth spurt you will have to accept that your baby may be a little fussier on the breast and need to feed more often for several days, even up to a week, until he is through the growth spurt. If the fussiness and extra feeding continues for longer than a few days, it could mean that your milk supply is very low. If a very low milk supply is the problem, I would advise following my plan for increasing it, which you will find on page 51.

● Once you have used the plan to increase your milk supply, continue to express a small amount in the morning to ensure that when your baby goes through his next growth spurt, you can simply decrease the amount of milk you are expressing by an ounce, which will then ensure that your baby's increased appetite is being met immediately.

- After you have followed the plan to increase your milk supply, you should be producing more milk than your baby needs. To ensure that your baby continues to get enough milk I would on the first day after the plan express any extra milk at the first two feeds of the morning once you have fed your baby and know that he is fully satisfied. The quantity you express will give you a rough idea about how much extra milk you are producing. Moving forward, if you continue to express after feeding, I would recommend that at both morning feeds, you offer your baby the first breast, then before offering him the second, you express the extra quantity estimated above from the second breast, before putting him on that breast. Although all mothers are different in how much they can express I find that the majority can comfortably express around 90ml (3oz) at the morning feeds at this age and still meet their baby's needs.

- The reason for expressing before feeding is that when you put your baby on the second breast, the fore milk will have been expressed, so he will reach the hind milk much quicker. Not only will this satisfy his appetite more quickly, but as the baby is always more efficient at extracting milk from the breast than a pump is, it will ensure that the breast is being fully stimulated to produce more milk.

- Another cause of fussy feeding is that your baby may be 'snacking' and using the breast to comfort himself. This will lead to a cycle of your breasts not producing enough at each feed and your baby receiving only fore milk, which will not fully satisfy him and therefore make him unsettled between feeds. In order to take enough of both fore and hind milk he must empty one side before being offered the second breast. If he begins to fuss, don't assume that it is hunger and offer him the breast again. Provided he is winded and content, let him have some kicking time on the floor or time to sit in his bouncy chair. If he is not happy to go on his play mat or in the chair, try to distract him with some toys for a short spell to see if the fussiness will pass.

● Although you may not want to use a dummy excessively, using it during waking times to pacify a baby who likes to suck can really help. If your baby is feeding fast he will need some 'sucking time' and a dummy will provide that. Begin to offer him a dummy to suck on after his feed at 7–7.45am. Before putting him down for his nap at 9am, offer him the other breast so he will settle well to sleep.

Refusal to take the bottle

In *The New Contented Little Baby Book* I recommend that if you wish to ensure that your breastfed baby will happily take a bottle of expressed milk, that you introduce a bottle around the second week. I am aware that many experts recommend that a bottle is not introduced until six weeks so as not to interfere with establishing a good milk supply, but having cared for over 300 babies, the majority of whom were introduced to a bottle within the first couple of weeks, I have honestly never experienced a mother who has introduced a bottle having problems establishing a good milk supply; whereas I certainly have had to advise a huge number of mothers who have delayed introducing a bottle to then find that their baby will refuse it.

An enormous amount of patience and perseverance is needed when a baby is refusing the bottle and all you can do is to keep offering it to him at one feed every day until he will eventually accept it happily. This can often take weeks, therefore it is important that you do not miss a day when you try at one feed at least.

Waking up too soon for the late feed

A baby will sometimes wake too soon for his late feed and if you do not resolve this problem early on, you could end up with your baby waking up twice in the night after midnight. In order to ensure that the longest time he sleeps is after his late feed, it is important that he sleeps well from 7pm until the late feed. Below are the main reasons he could be waking too soon for the late feed.

- The first cause is possibly genuine hunger, in which case it would be worth increasing his feed after his bath. If your baby is breastfed try encouraging him to feed longer on the second breast. If this doesn't help it could be that your milk supply is low, therefore it would be worth offering 30–60ml (1–2oz) of expressed milk after he has fed from the second breast. If your baby is bottle-fed I would recommend you increase the feed by 30ml (1oz).

- He may be waking early because he has come out of his swaddle or kicked his covers off and if this happens it would be a good idea to re-swaddle him to try to get him back to sleep.

- If your baby doesn't settle back to sleep quickly, it is more likely that hunger is the cause. If this is the case then he should be fed, though of course feeding a baby earlier than 10pm could put him off taking a full feed at the late feed, which could result in him waking earlier in the middle of the night. There are two options to deal with this:

  - The first is to give the baby a quick, short feed and settle him back to sleep, then move the 10pm feed to nearer 11.30pm/12am.
  - The second option is to offer a split feed. Offer the baby as much as he will take at 9pm, then keep him fully awake for an hour (taking care not to overstimulate him). To encourage the baby to stay awake for a short spell between the split feed I would normally allow him a little kick on his play mat. While it is fine to talk and interact with your baby, try not to stimulate him too much with a lot of talking. I used to find that parents who overstimulated their babies too much at this feed, would end up with the baby waking up even earlier in the night, which of course defeats the whole purpose of splitting the feed and having the baby awake a bit longer. At 10pm offer him a top-up feed and settle him back to bed around 10.30pm. The split feed and having him awake a bit longer should help prevent him waking much earlier than he usually does in the night.

Refusing the late feed

Some babies don't like being woken for their late feed, or don't wake at all, and will only take a small amount of milk or refuse it altogether. Although babies may be reluctant to take milk at this feed I do not recommend dropping it, however small, until after solids have been introduced. Many babies have a growth spurt between the third and fourth month and it would be hard for a baby to get enough milk during this spurt if he is only taking four feeds a day. This feed is not usually dropped until solids are being given twice in the day as milk is still an important source of nutrition for your baby, so until then it is important to try and resolve the problem.

● One reason your baby is refusing to feed is that he may not be hungry, the main cause being that he is having too big a feed after the bath. If this is the case, it would be worth gradually reducing the time your baby is on the breast by a minute every couple of nights until he starts to take a full feed at the late feed. With bottle-fed babies, I would recommend reducing the amount of formula by 15ml (½oz) every couple of nights. You have to be careful, however, that you do not reduce the feed after the bath so much that your baby then wakes a lot earlier for his late feed, hence my advice of reducing it by a tiny amount every couple of nights.

● If your baby does not want to wake, many mothers find it is possible to 'dream feed' their babies. This means picking them up from their cots at 10pm but not fully waking them. The feed is given to the baby while it's in a sleepy state.

Feeding twice in the night

If your baby has taken full feeds throughout the day and has taken a full feed at 11pm, at this age he should not still be hungry during the night, so if he is waking more than once in the night, there is likely to be another reason.

- With a baby under six months of age the Moro reflex can still be very strong, and when they come into a light sleep they can often wake fully and find it difficult to settle back to sleep if they have kicked their covers off. You may find it difficult to get your baby to settle again without feeding. If you use a 0.5-tog sleeping bag, this will enable you to also use a thin top cotton sheet to tuck him in well and prevent him thrashing around, without causing concern that he could overheat. Place the cotton sheet lengthways across the cot, and tuck at least 15cm (6in) of the sheet well under the mattress, then push a rolled-up towel down either side, between the mattress and the spars of the cot (see page 84).

- For babies who wake more than once for a feed during the night, it is worth considering a split feed at the late feed. Rather than letting your baby sleep until 11pm in the evening, I would suggest that you begin to wake him at 10pm. As soon as he is well awake offer him a feed. Offer him as much of a milk feed as he will take, then let him have a period of 20–30 minutes of quiet play under his baby gym. This can be in a room which is quite light and has some background noise. Between 11/11.15pm you should take him to his room, change his nappy and then offer him as much as he will take of the breast or a fresh bottle. Ensure that he is burped and tucked in really well following the instructions above. By having him awake longer at the last feed, and offering him a split feed he should start to sleep longer and more soundly in the night. When offering a split feed at the late feed most formula-fed babies will take an ounce more over the two feeds than they would if they were having one full bottle-feed. With breastfed babies they will normally spend longer on the second breast than they would if they were having one feed. When he does wake in the night it is important that you offer him a big enough feed so that he settles back to sleep quickly, and sleeps through until 7am.

● It would also be advisable to look at the amount of daytime sleep your baby is having. If his nights have become unsettled he probably needs more sleep during the day than is recommended for his age. It is not worth cutting back his middle-of-the-night feed if it results in him being more unsettled in the night and needing to sleep more during the day. Once he goes back to sleeping longer and better in the night, you should aim to gradually reduce the amount of sleep that he is having at his morning nap. Try keeping him awake five minutes longer every few days until he is going down nearer to 9am. Once a shorter nap is established at 9am, you can gradually cut back the late afternoon nap. Once he is taking a shorter nap in the morning and later afternoon, you should be able to cut back the time he is awake at 10pm. Again do this gradually reducing the time he is awake by five to

10 minutes every few nights, so that he continues to sleep well throughout the night.

● Finally, do remember to keep increasing your baby's feeds during the day. If you are unsure as to exactly how much your baby needs to drink for his age and weight you should discuss this with your health visitor or GP.

Sleep

By two to three months the daytime sleep should be divided into three separate naps in the morning, at lunchtime and in the afternoon. This is important as the way that your baby sleeps at night will depend on what happens during the day.

What to expect

By the second month the majority of babies need around four and a half hours of daytime sleep; by the end of the second month, your baby's daytime sleep should be reduced to around four hours; and by the end of the third month his daytime sleep should be reduced to around three to three and a half hours. This will hopefully now be divided between two shorter and one longer nap. As the amount of daytime sleep decreases, the length of time they sleep in the night should increase. By the end of three months many babies are capable of sleeping one longer spell in the night of between six to eight hours.

What to aim for

Following a good daytime routine of sleeping and feeding should very quickly help reduce any excessive night-time feeding to one feed in the night and encourage a baby to go a longer spell from his last feed.

- I have found that all babies, even those that are demand-fed, will usually show signs of managing to go one longer spell between feeds by the time they reach four to six weeks of age. To ensure that the longer spell comes after midnight you should aim to have your baby awake and start his day somewhere between 6 and 8am, which will allow you enough time to fit in at least five feeds before midnight.

- Along with ensuring he has at least five full feeds during this time, structuring his daytime sleep will also help him sleep a longer spell in the middle of the night.

- By keeping the morning nap shorter and the middle-of-the-day nap longer, your baby will be ready to settle between 6 and 8pm in the evening. Ensuring he has a good bath and bedtime routine at this time will also help him sleep longer from the late feed.

- The majority of babies who are only feeding once in the night at one month gradually push themselves right through the night, dropping the middle-of-the-night feed as soon as they are physically capable.

Sleep Problems

Morning nap too short

At two months your baby should be having a nap of around one hour in the morning and by the end of three months this will have reduced to a maximum of 45 minutes. If your baby is sleeping for much less than this, it will alter his routine for the whole day ahead so the problem needs to be addressed.

- The main reason that very young babies wake up too early from their morning nap is because they are hungry, so a good preventative measure is to offer your baby a small top-up feed prior to his nap to ensure that he sleeps for long enough.

- If he still continues to wake early, it is worth trying to get his routine back on track by offering a short catnap of 10–15 minutes after the 10/10.30am feed. This will mean that the lunchtime nap will probably push on by 10–15 minutes, with the baby going down slightly later. To keep his sleep total on track for the rest of the day, you should still wake the baby up from his lunchtime nap at his usual time.

Waking too early from the lunchtime nap

Between two and three months most babies will need a lunchtime nap of between two and two and a half hours, depending on their age. However, it is not uncommon for babies to wake having only slept for 35–45 minutes after being put down. To prevent babies getting overtired later on in the afternoon, many parents will put their babies down for an hour or so after their 2pm feed. This is fine for a few days but you may find that in a few weeks' time it is not so easy to settle your baby at 7pm if they have had a longer sleep later in the afternoon. To avoid a late bedtime, it is best to keep trying to settle your baby for a longer lunchtime nap at noon. To do this:

● Try bringing the baby's mid-morning feed forward by half an hour and topping him up just prior to his lunchtime nap. If you find that doesn't work or he refuses to take a top-up you could try offering him a small dream feed (see page 115) five minutes prior to him coming into his light sleep.

● When you place him back in his cot, gently hold both his hands across his chest with your hands until he goes back into a deeper sleep – this should help him sleep for another sleep cycle. Getting him to settle himself back to sleep can take a while but it will, in the long term, help avoid the possibility of him becoming unsettled in the evening, which could happen if he continues to have a longer sleep later in the day.

Early morning waking

In my experience all babies and children come into a light sleep between 5 and 6am. During the first few weeks, a baby who is waking and feeding between 2 and 2.30am may wake again between 5 and 6am and genuinely need to feed. This is not a problem provided they will settle back to sleep for a further hour or so after this feed, but many do not.

However, one of the main reasons that babies do not settle back to sleep is that, because it is so near to morning, parents tend to treat the feed like a daytime feed and the baby becomes overstimulated.

- I have always treated any waking before 7am like a night-time waking. If the baby needed feeding I would do so quickly and quietly with the use of only a small socket night light and without talking. I would always settle the baby back to sleep until 7–7.30am, even if this meant they were only going back to sleep for 10–15 minutes. Whenever possible I would try to avoid a nappy change as this usually wakes the baby too much.

- Once a baby is waking and feeding between 3 and 4am, waking at 6am is not usually related to hunger. This is the one and only time I would advise parents to help their baby return to sleep. At this stage the most important thing is to get him back to sleep quickly, even if it means cuddling and offering him a dummy to make sure he sleeps until 7am.

- With babies between two and four months who are sleeping through most of the night, too small a feed at 10pm is often the cause of early waking and the baby should be offered more at that feed. Breastfed babies may need to be offered a top-up of expressed or formula milk from a bottle if they are emptying both breasts at this feed.

● Next to hunger, light filtering around the side of curtains, above a curtain pole, under a gap in the door or on account of a night light is a cause of early waking. Research shows that the chemicals in the brain work differently in the dark, preparing it for sleep. In my experience, even the smallest chink of light can be enough to wake a baby fully when he comes into a light sleep between 5 and 6am. Check that there is nothing that could be allowing light to come in once the sun rises.

Unhappy if not swaddled

During the second month, it is important to get your baby used to sleeping unswaddled so as to prevent the dangers that may occur through overheating. Use the following method to get him used to being half swaddled, before removing the swaddle completely.

● Start with the nap he has at around 8.45/9am and swaddle him as usual, but leave one arm free. If you can, remember to alternate the arm that is left out each morning. As this is a short nap, he should not be too disturbed. After a few days of this, begin to do the same thing at 7pm as well, while continuing to swaddle him fully for the night after his 10.30pm feed.

● After a few days, once he is used to one arm being left out at the shorter naps, use the same method of swaddling through the night, leaving alternate arms free.

- Once your baby is happy having alternate arms free, you can then start to half swaddle him with both arms out. I would recommend starting with the morning nap and late afternoon nap. When he is sleeping well at these naps with both arms out I would then recommend leaving both arms out during the lunchtime nap and in the evening.

- Finally, once he is sleeping happily at all of his daytime sleeps and in the evening with both arms out you can start to half swaddle him from the late feed. You may find that when you do this, he starts to stir or wake up at random times in the night. Try to reassure him back to sleep with a gentle stroke or pat and shushing, before picking him up. It can take several nights for a baby to get used to sleeping half swaddled, so while he may need some reassurance, do not assume that he needs feeding if he wakes up earlier than he has been.

5

Four to Six Months
(17 to 26 Weeks)

Once your baby reaches this stage of development, you will have become more accustomed to looking after him and more confident in your parenting skills. This is a time of rapid development, physically and mentally, and your baby may have growth spurts. When your baby has one of these growth spurts, he may need extra feeding. Usually by four months, a baby should be on five milk feeds a day, but when he is in the middle of a growth spurt this may not be enough and you may need to offer an extra feed, re-introducing a 5pm feed.

Weaning, or introducing solids, isn't recommended until the end of this phase – at six months. Some babies start to be very discontented towards the end of this period, even if they are offered extra milk, and you may feel that your baby would benefit from early weaning. You should always ensure that you discuss this with your family doctor or health visitor before starting (for more on this see page 144).

Many mothers return to work at some point during this stage, and if you are planning to do this and you are breastfeeding, you will probably be looking to replace some of your breast feeds with bottles of expressed milk or formula.

If you wish to replace the breast feeds with a bottle of expressed milk I would recommend that you have a plan in place for a couple of weeks before you actually return to work. You will need to decide when you are going to express the milk needed for the bottle feeds that will replace your breast feeds. As your baby will still be on a late feed at this age, you will have to look at expressing the milk you need at work. If you are replacing the 10am and 2pm feeds, then if possible you should look to express around those times at work, to ensure that your milk supply does not reduce.

If you are replacing the breast feeds with formula you should drop the breast feeds one at a time, and I recommend allowing about a week for each feed – which means it will take five weeks to slowly switch all feeds and get your baby used to bottle-feeding. I would advise that you have your new feeding plan in place for at least two weeks before you return to work, so that you are confident it is working well before you actually start work. You should consider offering your baby expressed milk from a bottle during the run-up to replacing breast feeds with formula feeds, as once he is happy to take the expressed milk from a bottle, it will make it easier to replace the expressed milk with formula milk, as opposed to attempting to go straight from a breast feed to a bottle of formula milk.

Early morning waking is sometimes a problem with babies of this age and you want to make sure that it isn't the cold causing your baby to wake. Sometimes as babies become more active, they kick off their covers during the night and get cold. Therefore until he is six months and able to sleep without being tucked in, ensure that his covers are tucked in well enough under the mattress so that he is not able to kick them off.

It is important to stick to regular nap times, but you may need to do some adjusting at this stage. Babies who are sleeping well at night and having a middle-of-the-day nap for around two hours, somewhere between 12.30pm and 3pm, usually manage to get through the afternoon without a further nap. However, if your baby sleeps for less than two hours at lunchtime he may need a brief nap between 4 and 5pm to ensure he doesn't get overtired by the time you get to his bath and bedtime routine. How long you give him will depend on how long he slept at lunchtime. For example if he slept only an hour at lunchtime I would recommend he be given around 30–40 minutes at the late afternoon nap, any more than this and he may not settle at bedtime. If he slept one and a half hours at lunchtime, then a short nap of 15–20 minutes should get him through to bedtime without becoming overtired.

As he grows more physically active there is a greater danger of your baby becoming overtired in the afternoon if he regularly cuts back on his lunchtime nap. If this happens you can try reducing the morning nap to see if that will help him sleep longer at the lunchtime nap.

This is a time of great change for your baby as his concentration grows and he becomes stimulated by all that he can hear and see around him. He will be able to support his own head, and he may like being propped up in a sitting position so that he can feel a part of whatever is going on. Some babies will begin to sit unaided by the end of this time, but usually just for a few minutes. Your baby will also begin to roll over by the end of this stage. He may be keen to push himself up on his legs although he will not yet be mobile. Your baby may be able to wave, and will show you a whole range of emotions. Parents are often endlessly amazed at the way that babies of this age seem to be able to do something new every day.

Your baby's hand-to-eye coordination will be developing rapidly and this means you need to be careful as he will reach out and grasp for things, whether that may be your earrings, glasses or necklace. And although babies are often able to grasp quite well, they may not have learnt how to let go properly – and this can be a problem if it's your hair or earring that your baby has grabbed hold of!

Your baby's first teeth may start to appear when he is somewhere between five and seven months, although it is important to remember that this will be different for each child; some babies are even born with a tooth showing, while others don't get their first teeth until they are about a year old. The signs of teething can include slightly swollen-looking gums and a baby who wants to gnaw on things. Teething can be painful for babies and he may be irritable or drool a little, and he may get a rash around his mouth and chin. Contrary to popular belief, though, teething does not cause fevers or tummy upsets.

Once your baby has teeth, you will need to start cleaning them. Initially you can do this by wrapping a piece of gauze around your finger and gently rubbing your baby's tooth with a little baby toothpaste. Once he has more than one tooth, you can move on to a soft baby toothbrush.

The upcoming period is one of great change as you move towards weaning your baby, which will mean new routines for you both.

Feeding

What to expect

Once they reach four months, most babies are capable of sleeping right through the night from the late feed until 6 or 7am. However, if your baby is solely breastfed, you may need to offer him an early morning feed at 5 or 6am if he isn't getting enough at the 10/11pm feed to last him through until he wakes for his day. If your baby starts waking in the night when he is totally breastfed and refusing to settle without a feed, you may want to try topping him up after the late feed with expressed breast milk or formula to see if this helps him to settle. If your baby is waking between 5 and 6am it is important to treat that feed like a night feed with the minimum of talking or eye contact, so that he settles back to sleep quickly. It can be very tempting when a baby wakes around 6am just to start the day, but the problem with settling for a 6am start at this age, is that as he grows older that start of the day could become 5.30am or even earlier. If you aim for a 7am start, then should he start to wake around 6.30am, it is more acceptable.

Some larger babies may be taking five full milk feeds a day and are not able to sleep right through the night, because milk alone is no longer satisfying their hunger. If you feel your baby is perhaps ready to be weaned early then you should discuss this with your health visitor. If you decide that you do not want to wean before the recommended age of six months for introducing solids, then you will have to accept that your baby may need to go back to having a feed in the night again.

What to aim for

Until your baby is weaned it is important to keep offering him the late feed. Some babies at this stage often become very difficult to rouse at the late feed and when they do feed, will often only take a very small amount of milk. While it can be tempting to try dropping this feed and seeing how long your baby goes, I would not recommend doing this. Certainly some babies will actually sleep 12 hours to nearer 6/7am, but in my experience this can only last a week or two and they then start to wake up around 4/5am genuinely hungry. Having dropped the late feed, it can be very difficult to reintroduce it and you could actually end up feeding your baby early in the morning for several weeks until he is established on solids.

The only time I would recommend dropping the late feed before solids are introduced is if a baby is being fed at the late feed and then still waking up in the middle of the night looking for a feed. When this happens I would recommend dropping the feed so that the baby is not feeding twice in the 12-hour night.

In the CLB routines I always recommend to start the day at 7am, as I feel that gives parents the best opportunity to fit in the right number of feeds and have naps at times that can fit around other children and family life.

Between four and six months a baby on the CLB routine would look something like the following. Obviously, if your baby is starting his day earlier or later, you can adjust the times accordingly, but aim for the same distance between feeds and naps, so that your baby is getting the right number of feeds and that his sleep is working in conjunction with his feeds.

7am	awake and feeding
9am	nap (no longer than 45 minutes)
11am	feed
12 noon	nap (no longer than 2¼ hours)
2.15/3pm	feed
4.30pm	nap (may need 15 minutes if he slept less at previous nap)
5.45pm	bath and bedtime routine
10/10.30pm	late feed

Feeding Problems

Fussy feeding

Being fussy at a feed is a common problem at this age, and there are a number of reasons why your baby may suddenly start fussing or refusing the bottle at feed times. In the worst cases this can be very distressing with babies shaking their heads or kicking their legs and getting very upset.

● Sometimes a baby who is taking too large a feed at the late feed will get fussy with his morning bottle. Obviously if your baby is sleeping well at night and sleeping through to nearer 7am, you do not wish to disrupt this pattern and end up with him waking up earlier by reducing the late feed too much. To try and resolve this, first you can gradually reduce the late feed by 15ml (½oz) every three nights, until he is waking up hungrier for his first feed of the day. However, you will only want to carry on doing this if he continues to sleep through to nearer 7am. If you find that taking less at the late feed is resulting in him waking up earlier, I would recommend that you continue to give him the bigger feed and accept that he will not take a full feed at the first feed of the day. And because he is not taking a big feed at his first feed of the day, he will more than likely become hungrier a bit earlier for the second feed of the day. It is fine to feed him a bit earlier, but in order to ensure he has a good lunchtime nap I would recommend that you offer him a top-up feed prior to this nap.

When offering a top-up before the lunchtime nap, you will probably find that your baby drinks less and fusses at the mid-afternoon feed. If this is the case I would advise that you accept that your baby only needs a smaller feed at this feed and do not be tempted to push the mid-afternoon feed later. If you push the mid-afternoon feed later, it could impact on his bedtime feed becoming smaller, which could result in him either not settling so well in the evening, or waking earlier for the late feed. If either of these situations arises they could affect how long he sleeps in the night. It is more important that he takes a bigger feed after the bath than in the middle of the afternoon.

- Another reason a baby of this age often will start to get fussy with feeds is because solids have been introduced. It is really important that if you start weaning before six months that you do not increase solids so rapidly that it reduces your baby's appetite for his milk. Until the age of six months, milk should be the main source of nutrition for your baby. If your baby is being offered solids in the morning, it is important that he is offered the majority of his milk feed before being offered the solids.

- Finally, he may be beginning to show symptoms of teething. A baby whose gums are sore will know that sucking may hurt them further and so become upset when they know a bottle is going to be offered. You could try putting some teething gel on his gums about 20 minutes before his feed is due and also offer it to him at a cooler temperature than usual as this will be more soothing.

Refusing the late feed

Sometimes a baby will refuse the late feed altogether and get very upset when you try to feed him. When this happens you have little option but to drop it, as it is pointless trying to feed your baby if he is getting so upset.

If your baby does drop the late feed it is doubtful that he will sleep through to 6/7am without a feed, therefore when he does wake in the night, he will need to be offered a big enough feed to get him through to 6/7am. This is particularly so if he wakes up at 2 or 3am. Do not think that feeding him a big feed at this time is a regression; remember if he has gone from 6.30pm to 2/3am he has gone eight or nine hours, which is around the same amount of time that he would go if he were taking a feed at the late feed. Restricting a feed in the middle of the night with a baby who has dropped the late feed can often result in him waking again around 5/6am. Therefore it is better for him to have one good feed at 2/3am and sleep through to 7am. He will eventually start to sleep later and later in the night and when this happens you may find that when he is sleeping to around 5/6am, he is fussy with his 7am feed. When this happens do not try to force him to feed when he wakes – allow him to drink what he wants and just accept that he will need to have his second feed of the morning earlier. Again if he has this feed earlier, I would always recommend a top-up before his lunchtime nap so that he sleeps well then.

It may be that your baby is simply being fussy about his late feed and reducing the amount he will take then. This is fine as long as your baby continues to sleep through to nearer 7am. However, if the reduced late feed is resulting in early morning waking, I would recommend that you still try to encourage a bigger late feed. To do this, you should gradually cut back on the feed after the bath. Gradually decrease the amount he takes by 15ml (½oz) every three days until he is taking a bigger feed at the late feed and sleeping through to nearer 7am again. This will of course only work if he continues to sleep to nearer 10pm before waking for this feed. If he starts to wake up earlier in the evening, then you will have to go back to giving him more at the feed after the bath. Even if your baby does reduce his late feed to just a couple of ounces, I would continue to offer it to him, as he will go through another growth spurt until he is fully weaned and may suddenly need to increase this feed again.

Night-time waking

Middle-of-the-night or early wakings are a problem I encounter all too commonly at this age. Although guidelines do not recommend weaning until six months, some parents are advised to wean early to encourage their babies to sleep. In my experience weaning too early to encourage better sleep rarely works and can have disastrous and even dangerous consequences. It can increase the risk of a baby developing allergies and can damage his digestive system. Do not be pressurised into weaning early just to get your baby sleeping through the night.

Many parents think their baby is ready to be weaned because he is waking two or three times a night and wanting to feed. In fact the reason the majority of babies over eight weeks are waking in the night hungry is not because they are ready for solids but because they are not getting full milk feeds during the day.

- A full milk feed is either a formula feed of 240ml (8oz) or a feed from both breasts. If your baby is under four months and feeding more than once in the middle of the night, it is unlikely that he is taking five full feeds between 7am and 11pm.

- If this is the case, it would be advisable to use the core night method (see page 352) to reduce his night-time wakings and feedings. This should help improve his daytime feeding and in turn reduce his night-time wakings and feedings.

• Remember when bottle-feeding that your baby may not take exactly the same amount at every feed. The important thing is to try and structure feeds so he is taking the bigger ones, just prior to his lunchtime nap and the bedtime feed after the bath.

• If your baby is under six months and is showing signs that his appetite is no longer satisfied by four to five full milk feeds a day, it would be advisable to discuss with your health visitor whether solids should be introduced early. For more about whether to wean early, see page 144.

CASE STUDY: Jack, aged five months

Problem: Weaned baby refusing daytime milk feeds

Cause: Introducing certain foods too early

By five months baby Jack was on four full formula feeds a day, and a small amount of solids at 11am and 5pm. He was also sleeping well from 7pm to around 6.30am every night. At around six months, Jack suddenly woke up at 2am. Myra tried to settle him with a cuddle and some cool, boiled water but he could not be consoled. Myra was concerned that he might genuinely be hungry as he had only taken 150ml (5oz) at his 6pm feed, so she decided to offer him a small 120ml (4oz) feed. Jack drank this quickly but still refused to settle back to sleep until he was given a further 120ml of formula. He then settled back to sleep very quickly and had to be woken at 7am.

During the following week Jack became more and more difficult over his daytime milk feeds, and a pattern soon emerged of him taking only 120–150ml (4–5oz) at each daytime feed and only

---

90–120ml (3–4oz) at his 6pm feed, before waking up desperately hungry between 2 and 3am. When his mother contacted me for advice, the daily records she sent me showed that, until things had started to go wrong, the structure and timing of milk feeds and solids were correct. However, I noticed that she had decided to introduce certain fibrous foods earlier than I recommend. Banana, which I advise introducing at six months, was added to his breakfast cereal at five months. Jack loved banana, and this prompted his mother to offer it to him regularly at lunchtime along with mashed avocado, another food that I believe takes longer to digest.

In addition to the large amounts of banana and avocado, when meat was introduced at six months it resulted in Jack cutting back too quickly on his milk intake because he wasn't hungry enough to take it. The quantity of foods that I believe take longer to digest had been introduced and increased too quickly and in excessive amounts. As a result, he had to wake in the night to make up for the milk he still needed and was no longer getting during the day. It was clear from the feeding charts that Jack, who then weighed 6.8kg (15lb), had cut back too dramatically on his milk intake during the day because his solids had been increased too rapidly (especially at breakfast).

Myra, desperate to increase the amount of milk he was taking, decided to mix more formula into his breakfast cereal, which resulted in him having eight teaspoonfuls of breakfast cereal plus mashed banana at breakfast. I advised Myra to cut back the breakfast cereal to four teaspoonfuls, with one or two cubes of pear or peach purée instead of banana. Lunch generally consisted of six tablespoonfuls of a savoury casserole followed by rice and fruit, and was also contributing to Jack's decreasing appetite for milk. I suggested that Myra replace the rice and fruit with fruit and yoghurt. At teatime Jack was given another savoury dish, again usually made up of fish or chicken, mixed with rice and formula milk to help boost his milk intake. I advised her to replace the meat dish with some carbohydrates, such as pasta or a baked potato with vegetables.

Within a week Jack had increased his three daytime milk feeds to 210–240ml (7–8oz) a feed. Although he continued to wake up during the night for a further 10 days, I convinced his mother that it was now being caused by habit rather than a genuine need for milk, and she followed my suggestion of settling him back to sleep with some cool, boiled water. At the end of two weeks Jack was eating three well-balanced meals a day and drinking 690ml (23oz) of formula from the bottle and taking a further 120ml (4oz) of formula in his cereals.

I believe that the types of foods Jack was first weaned on were the cause of his rapid decrease of milk. Being given too much banana and avocado during the early stages of weaning causes babies under six months to cut back too quickly on their daytime milk. In Jack's case the problem was made even worse by the fact that he weighed only 6.8kg (15lb) and that he was being given meat twice a day as well as hard-to-digest foods.

It is a common mistake to introduce too much of the wrong types of food too early or at the wrong time and thus create a problem of milk underfeeding. It is the main reason for babies under six months cutting back too quickly on their daytime milk, which results in a genuine need to feed in the night.

Larger baby sleeping through, then suddenly waking in the night

By the time they reach four months the majority of babies are capable of sleeping right through the night from the last feed, although a totally breastfed baby may still need a feed between 5 and 6am if they are not getting enough to drink at the 10/11pm feed. One thing that many of these babies have in common is that they weigh more than 6.8kg (15lb) and have not been weaned yet or are only taking small amounts of solids.

- As the weaning guidelines recommend six months before the introduction of solids, if your baby is a bigger baby, then the waking up could be genuine hunger and you may need to go back to feeding in the night if you do not wish to introduce solids before six months.

- If you feel your milk supply is quite low at the late feed, it may be worth expressing a little milk earlier in the morning (to add to the milk you express around 9.30pm in the evening) and offering it as a top-up after your baby has had his late breast feed. Some babies can be very sleepy at the late feed and often replacing the breast feed with a bottle of expressed milk so that they take more milk can help the baby sleep right through the night. The other advantage to offering the baby a bottle of expressed milk at this feed is that it can be given by your partner and you can get to bed earlier, which is surely no bad thing!

- If you do not wish to introduce solids before six months then you must keep your baby's milk intake up until he is well established on solids. A fully formula-fed baby weighing this amount could need around 1.1 litres (40oz) of milk a day divided between five feeds if they are to sleep through the night. A fully breastfed baby will need five full breast feeds a day and possibly a sixth in the early hours of the morning, until solids are introduced. Once solids are introduced you can start to reduce the amount of milk your baby is taking to 570ml (20oz) a day, but this has to be done gradually as solids are increased.

- If you are struggling with wakings in the night despite introducing solids, I would suggest that you first try waking your baby fully at 10pm and giving him a split feed at 10 and then 11.15pm. Try this for at least three nights, as the combination of the split feed and being awake longer at the late feed can often help babies sleep longer in the night. You may find that if you do this your baby will then cut down on his first feed of the day. I think it is worth accepting this could happen for a short period if it helps your baby sleep through the night. Obviously, if your baby cuts down on his first morning feed, you would need to feed him earlier than 11am. I would advise that you offer him as much milk as he wants, followed by some solids, but then also offer him a small top-up prior to his lunchtime nap. This will avoid the problem of him waking up early from the lunchtime nap because he had his mid-morning milk and solids earlier.

- If you find that your baby still wakes up in the night or very early despite being fed at 10 and 11.15pm, then I would suggest that you try dropping the late feed for a few nights. He will more than likely wake up in the middle of the night, and when he does it is really important that you give him a full feed, so that he settles back to sleep until nearer 7am. It is pointless to give him a small feed to then have him wake at 5 or 6am again. Feeding him in the night will of course reduce the amount he takes first thing in the morning, so you will have to follow the advice given in the first option and feed him earlier than 11am with half the milk feed, followed by the solids, followed by a top-up milk feed prior to his lunchtime nap.

● When following either of these methods the key is to cut back very quickly on the 10/11am milk feed so that the baby will increase the solids. Likewise you may have to cut back slightly on the 2.30pm milk feed, so that your baby will happily start to take more solids in the evening. As the solids are gradually increased during the day and your baby is feeding and settling well in the night, you can very gradually start to decrease the night feeds. The most important thing is to get your baby sleeping soundly for 12 hours at night. I appreciate that many of you will say that your baby is not needing to be fed in the night, but in my view if feeding them gets them back to sleep, it is a better option than repeatedly being up in the night trying to settle with dummies, water and cuddles. Please be assured that once you have established a good night's sleep with only one feed, you will soon manage to reduce and eliminate that feed as the solids increase.

Waking twice a night

Between four and six months I think that the majority of babies are capable of sleeping through the night from a late feed to nearer 6/7am. However, some exclusively breastfed babies may still need a feed at around 5am until they reach six months and are fully weaned on to solids.

- If your baby has been sleeping a longer stretch at night or right through the night and starts to wake up twice in the night, refusing to settle without a feed, there are several things that could be the cause, but the first one to always consider is hunger. In order for a baby to sleep through from the late feed to nearer 6/7am in the morning, it is important that they receive all their daily milk intake between 6am and 11pm.

- A breastfed baby should be offered both breasts five to six times a day. It is possible that your milk supply is low at the late feed and it is worth offering a top-up feed of expressed milk from a bottle after the breast feed. If you are already doing this and it has not made a difference I would advise that you try replacing the breast feed with a full bottle of expressed milk. Sometimes breastfed babies can get quite sleepy at this feed and do not take enough from the breast to help them sleep a longer spell in the night.

- Bottle-fed babies need approximately 70ml (2½oz) of milk per pound of their body weight. A baby weighing 6.4kg (14lb) would therefore need to drink approximately 995ml (35oz) of milk between 6am and 11pm to help them sleep right through the night. If your baby is taking less than 150ml (5oz) at the late feed, this could be the reason that he has started to wake up in the night again. To ensure that your baby takes a bigger feed at the late feed you need to structure your daytime feeds so that he is hungrier at this time. To ensure that your baby is hungry for a late feed at 11pm, he would need to have his first feed of the day between 6 and 8am in the morning, the second between 10am and 12 noon, the third around 2/3pm and the fourth between 5 and 7pm. I find that by offering a smaller feed at 2/3pm and a split feed at 5/6.15pm it encourages the baby to take a bigger feed at the late feed. Some babies do need slightly more than what is recommended for their age. If you are unsure as to how much you can increase the amount you are giving your baby, please discuss it with your health visitor.

● It may also be worthwhile introducing a split feed at the late feed again for a short while to see if that will get your baby sleeping longer in the night. I would advise that you start to wake your baby up no later than 9.45pm, so that he is wide awake by 10pm. Offer as much of the first breast or bottle that he will take, then allow him a good kick on his play mat for at least 20 minutes, being careful not to stimulate him too much with lots of talking. Then at 10.45pm take him to the bedroom, change his nappy, dim the lights and offer the second breast or the second half of the bottle feed. I would recommend that you make up a fresh formula feed for the second half of this feed. I usually found that by doing the split feed at the late feed, the baby would actually take slightly more, and that, along with being properly awake for over an hour, helped him go back to sleeping longer in the night.

● If all of the above doesn't improve things, it could be that despite increasing all of the day feeds and the late feed your baby may not be satisfied on milk alone. This is particularly true of babies who are weighing 6.8kg (15lb) or more. Some bigger babies who are taking the required daily amount of milk during the day are still waking up genuinely hungry in the night. If this is the case it would be worth discussing with your health visitor if solids need to be introduced earlier than six months. If you decide to wait until six months, you will have to accept that your baby may genuinely need a feed in the middle of the night again until he is weaned.

- I always recommend that the late feed is not dropped until a baby is well established on solids. However, if your baby reaches four months and is having a late feed and then waking up again once or twice more in the night, despite trying all of the above recommendations, then I would suggest that you try dropping the late feed and seeing if your baby will sleep slightly later. It could be that he will sleep to nearer midnight, take a full feed then and then sleep nearer to 6am. While not ideal it is better than having two or three night wakings. See pages 141 and 160 for other reasons a baby may wake in the night.

Should you wean before six months?

This is a decision that I know many parents find difficult and it is not helped by the fact that you will get so many different opinions on the subject. For example, one mother with a baby over four months who had been consistently sleeping through the night, but is starting to wake up in the night looking for a feed is often advised to wean. Another mother with a baby of the same age may be told the complete opposite, and that their baby's increased hunger should be met by extra milk feeds, even if it means going back to feeding in the night. Health officials are told to advise parents that it is best to wait until six months to introduce solids, but many recognise that some babies may need to be weaned slightly earlier if their needs are not being met by milk alone.

I appreciate how hard it must be for parents to make a decision about weaning when the advice given is so conflicting. But the reality is that the final decision must be made by you. If your baby is between four and six months and has started to wake up in the night again, but you are unsure about introducing solids, you must accept that he may need to be fed in the night again until solids are introduced. If you agree that your baby should wait until six months before having solids introduced, it is important that his increased hunger is met by introducing further milk feeds. Babies who have been sleeping through the night with only a small feed, and are waking earlier should have the 10/10.30pm feed increased. Babies who are taking a full feed at 10/10.30pm and waking in the middle of the night may need to have a small milk feed in the middle of the night to get them through until 7am.

It is important to remember that as your baby grows, so will his appetite. It is unreasonable to expect him to manage on only four milk feeds a day when he is showing signs of increased hunger. Therefore, even if you have dropped the fifth feed, you will probably need to reintroduce it until he starts weaning at six months. If you are breastfeeding and your baby goes through a growth spurt between four and six months, and you have not been expressing at regular times to keep your milk supply in excess of what your baby was needing, then you will need to introduce extra feeds for several days in order to satisfy your baby's appetite and increase your milk supply. Often the extra feeds are enough to get things back on track with the night waking, but sometimes with larger babies (over 6.8kg (15lb) in weight), it may not be, and you will have to continue to offer extra feeds until after six months when solids are well established.

Baby taking solids waking in the middle of the night due to hunger

Once solids have been introduced, and once they have been established twice a day, your baby should start to cut back on his late feed, eventually sleeping 11–12 hours a night. As soon as solids are introduced it is very important that any milk feeding after 7pm and before 7am in the morning is greatly reduced, and eliminated altogether before the baby reaches seven months. But even babies who have been going a longer spell in the night can suddenly start to wake up several times a night if milk feeding and solid feeding is not structured properly. Getting the balance of milk and solids right in the first months of weaning can be tricky and if your baby cuts back too much on his daytime milk because of his solid food he may still be waking in the night hungry.

● Where solids are introduced before the recommended stage or too rapidly, babies can cut back too quickly on their daily milk intake. As a result they wake in the night to make up for the milk they are no longer getting during the day.

● It is very important to ensure that solids are introduced at the right times. In *The Contented Little Baby Book of Weaning* I give a guide to what to introduce and when during the first year. If you are unsure as to whether your baby is getting the right balance, please check the guidelines in this book.

● Breakfast is usually offered at some point in the early stages of weaning, once a baby begins to show signs of hunger well before 11am. However, often babies will take too much solid food at breakfast, which in turn affects the amount of milk they can take at lunchtime and this has a knock-on effect for the whole day. To ensure that your baby continues to increase his solids intake but not at the expense of his milk you will need to change things slightly. I would suggest that you only offer solids at breakfast if he drinks 240ml (8oz) of milk or has had a full breast feed at his 7am feed. When he shows signs of being hungry for lunch long before 11am you can then slowly introduce breakfast again.

● Check the amount of carbohydrates (rice or cereal) you are giving your baby at breakfast is in line with what's right for his age. Do not be tempted to offer solids before the milk feed, as a full milk feed is still important first thing in the morning at this age.

● Some fruits, such as banana and avocado, are harder to digest than others. Again, check that you're not feeding your baby any of these before the recommended stage. Although these two foods are very popular first stage weaning foods, I normally do not recommend offering them until the weaning process is well established, simply because they can fill the baby up too much and reduce his milk intake. If you do choose to use these foods early, just keep a very close eye that they do not cause your baby to reduce his milk intake too soon.

● Once your baby is well established on solids, he will eventually reduce and drop his late feed, therefore it is very important that you get the balance of solids and milk right in the evening. If your baby is having too much solid food in the evening, or being fed them too late, then he could reduce the amount of milk he takes after the bath, which would result in him still needing a big feed at the late feed, long after the stage by which he should have dropped it. To avoid this happening, try to make sure that your baby has his evening solids at least one and a half hours before his bedtime milk. For example, if he normally has his milk after the bath at around 6.30pm, then solids should be offered no later than 5pm. It is also important that solids are not increased too rapidly which may also cause him to reduce the amount of milk he takes after the bath.

● If your baby weighs over 6.8kg (15lb) he should be content with a full feed of 240ml (8oz) – at most 270ml (9oz) – at one feed. However, if you find that he still continues to wake up in the night looking for a feed in spite of the above, then simply drop the 10pm feed again and feed him when he wakes in the night. The majority of babies still need one feed in the night between 7pm and 7am until they reach six to seven months and are fully weaned, so your baby is not being unreasonable if he still needs a late feed. However, provided you keep his daily milk intake between 7am and 7pm at the correct level and increase his solids at the right pace, he should within one month of weaning start to naturally decrease the late feed to around 90–120ml (3–4oz) if he is formula-fed. By the time he is fully weaned and on three meals a day, he should naturally have dropped this feed, usually around seven months at the latest. A totally breastfed baby may continue to need a bigger feed at the late feed for a little longer.

CASE STUDY: Poppy, aged five months

Problem: Low milk intake

Cause: Introducing formula milk and solids too quickly

Poppy was a placid, easy baby, who was breastfed exclusively until she was six weeks old. At this stage she suddenly started to wake up around 10pm demanding a feed. She would then wake up again around 2am and 5am and refuse to settle back to sleep without a feed. This pattern continued for a further two weeks. Her mother Susan was becoming so exhausted getting up twice a night that she decided to follow the advice of friends and introduce a bottle of formula at the 10pm feed to see if it would get Polly back to sleeping longer in the night. Within a week Polly had started to sleep through to 3am, and by the time she was 12 weeks she was sleeping through to 7am from her last formula feed at 10pm.

By 16 weeks, Poppy was sleeping through the night from the 10pm feed, but started demanding to be fed much sooner than usual during the day. With a good weight gain each week, she was now weighing well over 6.8kg (15lb). Poppy was such a good weight and was showing all the typical signs of needing to be weaned that Susan introduced her to a small amount of baby rice and fruit at four months.

Poppy loved the solids and within a week she was having solids twice a day and sleeping through to 6.30am with only a 90ml (3oz) formula feed at 10pm. Susan decided to drop this feed, as she was sure that Poppy could get through the night without it. But, as she was planning to return to work when Poppy was six months, Susan decided to introduce a bottle of formula at the 2pm feed, so Poppy continued to take some of her milk from a bottle. Poppy was very reluctant to take this bottle and would never drink more than 90ml (3oz) at this feed. However, her weight gain was still good and she continued to sleep from 7pm to 6.30am, so Susan was not overly concerned.

At six months, when Susan returned to work, she introduced protein at Poppy's 11am feed and replaced the breast feed with a drink of cool, boiled water. Poppy was now having a breast feed at 6.30am and 6.30pm, and a bottle of formula at 2.30pm. Within a week of commencing the new feeding pattern, Poppy began waking up at 5am. Susan attempted to settle her back to sleep by patting her or offering her water, but this rarely worked. Such an early start to the day resulted in Poppy being very grumpy and overtired by the time Susan got home from work at 4pm and wanting to go to sleep at 6pm in the evening.

When I received Poppy's feeding chart it was obvious that the reason for her 5am waking was one of genuine hunger caused by the sudden drop in her daily milk intake. I believed that there were two reasons for the reduction in her milk intake. The first was that, unlike most babies, Poppy did not automatically increase the amount she drank at the 2.30pm feed when the 11.30am feed was dropped. The second reason was that her mother's milk supply had decreased very rapidly when she started work and went down to two breast feeds a day. This meant that in addition to the too-small feed at 2.30pm, Poppy was not getting enough milk at the 6.30pm feed, resulting in a genuine need to feed at 5am.

Although Susan's breasts were very full in the morning and Poppy did take a good feed at this time, she could not take enough in this one feed to compensate for the big drop at her other two feeds. By the time Poppy reached six months, she was having three solid meals a day.

A baby of six months still needs at least three full milk feeds a day, and some may need up to five if they have not been weaned. Milk is still very important at this stage as ounce by ounce the vitamin content is still more valuable than the first tastes of solids and it is vital that it is not replaced too quickly with solids, which is what happened in Poppy's case. The problem was made worse by the fact that she was introduced to formula at the same time as she was quickly put on to two solid meals a day. This also affected the amount of breast milk that Susan was producing. Having replaced the 2.30pm feed with formula and introduced solids twice a day within such a short time meant that Poppy very quickly started to take less and less from the breast, resulting in Susan's milk supply decreasing very rapidly.

I explained to Susan that the first thing we had to do was to boost her milk supply so that Poppy did not continue to increase her intake of solids too quickly. Since Susan was at work from 10am to 4pm, it was not possible to put Poppy to the breast more frequently during the day, and expressing at work was not an option. I suggested that she should express in the evening before bedtime and use that milk for Poppy's 2.30pm feed in the afternoon the following day. She should then offer her both breasts at 5/5.30pm before offering solids: this would ensure that Poppy did not fill up with solids, which were reducing her milk intake too much at bedtime. At 7pm she should then be offered the breast again, before being offered a top-up of formula milk. I advised Susan to keep following this plan until Poppy was taking at least 180ml (6oz) of expressed milk at the 2.30pm feed. Once she was taking this, she could then start to give Poppy her solids first at 5pm, as she should have had two-thirds of her daily requirement of milk by this time.

I also advised Susan to keep a very close watch on the amount of solids she gave Poppy at 5pm as it was important that she did not increase them so quickly that Poppy refused to take a good milk feed from both breasts at bedtime. Susan continued with this feeding pattern for a further two months, at which stage she felt that she could gradually decrease, then cut out the 10pm expressing and reintroduce a formula feed at 2.30pm without it causing a sudden decrease in Poppy's morning and evening breast feed.

This is a very common problem that many mothers who are returning to work find themselves having to deal with. I always advise those who wish to breastfeed for more than four months to include at least one expressing during the day once their baby is weaned on to solids as this helps to maintain a good milk supply, which can otherwise decrease very rapidly once a breastfeeding mother returns to work. I also suggest that when replacing a breast feed with a formula feed it is important not to do so at the same time as introducing solids. Susan would have been better establishing a full formula feed at 2.30pm and waiting until Poppy went through her next growth spurt before introducing solids, as this would have allowed more time for Poppy's digestive system to adjust to the formula, and more time for her to establish full feeds at the remaining two breast feeds.

Replacing breast milk with formula milk

If you are starting to replace breast feeds or expressed milk feeds with formula feeds you may find that your baby may become a little fussier when feeding and a baby who would previously take a full bottle of expressed milk may take 60–90ml (2–3oz) less of formula milk at feeds. This is fairly normal as formula milk is digested differently to breast milk, and it can take two or three weeks for your baby to adjust to being fully formula-fed and increase the amount that they need for their age and weight.

If you are stopping breastfeeding and gradually introducing more formula, it is best that you do not do this at the same time as starting your baby on solids. I think it is best to either continue to breastfeed until solids are established, and then gradually introduce more formula feeds, or establish your baby on at least four formula feeds, before introducing solids. In my experience weaning from the breast on to formula at the same time as weaning on to solids can often lead to babies becoming very fussy about either their milk or their solids, and sometimes both.

Ideally, the introduction of formula should always be done gradually, starting with a first stage formula, the composition of which is much nearer to breast milk than other types of milk, such as that for hungrier babies.

'Hungrier baby' formula milk

Extra-hungry types of formula milk are designed for babies who seem to be particularly hungry and many parents decide to switch to this milk at around four months in the hope it will help their baby sleep longer in the night, but I find that it rarely does. In fact it can have the opposite effect with some babies and in my experience it rarely solves a sleeping problem long term. This type of milk can cause severe wind and constipation problems for some babies, particularly babies who are on solids.

Feeding a young baby this type of milk and giving solids can put a lot of strain on their digestive system so it is essential that you seek expert advice before changing to hungry milk. The best formula milk for babies under one year is that closest to breast milk, which is stage one formula. If your baby is not sleeping well it is important to try and get to the real cause, rather than resort to this type of milk.

Constipation

For weaned babies or babies just starting to wean, be careful not to increase the solids too rapidly. Also look at the types for babies prone to constipation. I would advise avoiding foods like banana, which can be binding for some babies.

Sleep

What to expect

Between four and six months the majority of babies need around three hours' sleep a day, usually divided between one short morning nap and one longer lunchtime nap. However, some babies who are not having one longer nap in the middle of the day may need a third short nap in the late afternoon. All babies are different and there are some that may need slightly more than three hours' daytime sleep, but it is important not to confuse a baby who needs additional daytime sleep with a baby who needs more sleep during the day because they are not sleeping so well at night. A baby who genuinely needs more daytime sleep will be sleeping well at night as well as having longer naps during the day. A baby who is sleeping more than three hours during the day and waking early in the morning, or still waking in the middle of the night, is having to catch up on the loss of night-time sleep and is therefore sleeping more during the day. When this happens it is important to get to the cause of why he is not sleeping so long at night (see below).

What to aim for

Between the ages of four and six months the majority of babies are capable of staying awake a full two hours at a time and, if they are having a good two-hour nap in the middle of the day, should manage to get through the afternoon without a nap. If your baby is not sleeping a full two hours at his lunchtime nap, it is worth looking at his morning nap. Babies who are allowed too long a nap in the morning, often reduce the middle-of-the-day nap too much and yet will fight sleep if they are put down for a late afternoon nap. The result of this can often be that they get overtired at bedtime and either don't settle well, or fall into a deep sleep very quickly, not managing to take a full feed after the bath. Try to ensure that you structure your baby's daytime sleep so that he is not sleeping too much during the day, causing him to have disturbed nights. A baby who is sleeping well at night shouldn't really need to have a long morning nap; try to keep that nap to no longer than 45 minutes so that your baby sleeps longer in the middle of the day.

Sleep Problems

Waking up crying from naps and in the morning

Around this age babies should not really be waking up crying. The main causes of a baby waking up crying in the morning or at nap times, is because they are hungry or they have not had enough sleep.

- If you feed your baby the minute he wakes and then he is happy, the possible cause of the crying is that he simply did not feed well enough at his last feed to get him through to his next. If this is the case you should increase the amount your baby feeds. Breastfed babies should be offered longer on the breast and a bottle-fed baby should be offered an extra 30ml (1oz) at the late feed and first two morning feeds of the day. If you find that your baby will not take more at these feeds, there is no harm in offering a split feed at the late feed and offering a small top-up feed just prior to his nap times to see if this helps resolve the problem. Some babies do take longer to take a full feed in one go and if this is the cause of your baby waking up crying, then it is worth offering the small top-up feeds until he is able to take a full feed all at once.

- If you find that despite top-up feeds your baby is still waking up crying, then it is possible that he is going down overtired at his sleep times. This is particularly true if you find that your baby is still fussing when being put down to sleep. If overtiredness is the cause it is important that you start to settle your baby earlier in his cot at sleep times, so that he drifts off to sleep in a relaxed way instead of crying himself to sleep because he has become slightly overtired. While getting your baby used to going down in this way, it may help to use some gentle soothing music for a short spell to help him drift off to sleep. You could also for a few days stay in the room with him, near the cot shushing him, but not physically assisting him to sleep, until he gets used to drifting off to sleep more naturally.

Not sleeping long enough at the lunchtime nap

Many of the mothers I have worked with over the years have told me how much a lunchtime nap is a lifesaver and in the early months you can use it to have some much-needed rest yourself. However, sometimes a lunchtime nap may go wrong and your baby will wake and then refuse to go back to sleep, even when offered a feed. At between four and six months a lunchtime nap should ideally be two hours. However, when babies come into a light sleep – usually 30–45 minutes after they have gone to sleep – some will wake up fully and so the nap is far too short for the amount of sleep they need.

The best way to deal with this initially is not to get anxious about it and accept that your baby might not want to sleep for the full two hours. Let your baby wake naturally, do something else, like go for a walk, then put him down for another nap later. I usually allow the baby 30 minutes after the 2.30pm feed, then a further 30 minutes at 4.30pm. This should stop him becoming overtired and irritable, and get things back on track so that he goes to sleep well at 7pm.

It is most likely that the baby will start to sleep longer and longer at the lunchtime nap until he is eventually sleeping for the full two hours again.

Not settling in the evening

Most babies of between four and six months need approximately three hours' daytime sleep, divided between two to three naps. If they are having much more, this could be the cause of your baby not settling in the evening. The times of the naps can also play a crucial part in whether a baby settles well in the evening.

- A baby who has a longer nap in the morning and a shorter nap in the afternoon could be getting overtired in the evening and not settling well. If this is the case, it would be worthwhile trying a shorter nap of around 45 minutes in the morning, approximately two hours after the time your baby wakes, then giving the longer nap approximately two and a quarter hours from the time he wakes up from the morning nap. If you find your baby sleeps less than two hours at the second nap, he may need a third short power nap of 10/15 minutes in the afternoon to help him get through to bedtime happily.

- Sleeping too late in the afternoon is another cause of some babies not settling well in the evening. If your baby is sleeping around 45 minutes in the morning and a good two hours after 12 noon, then it is possible that he doesn't need a late afternoon nap. I would reduce this nap by a few minutes every couple of days until he is managing to get through to bedtime without the nap. It may be that you have to bring bedtime forward slightly for a week or so, but once he is settling well in the evening that can gradually be pushed back to his usual bedtime.

- Hunger, particularly in breastfed babies, is another cause of a baby not settling in the evening. If you are breastfeeding it would be worth expressing some milk earlier in the day and offering a top-up feed after the bath to ensure that your baby has had a full feed before you try to settle him. With formula-fed babies it is easier to check if hunger is the possible cause. It may be that your baby needs slightly more than the recommended amount at this feed. Check with your health visitor about increasing the amount you give him at this feed.

● Falling asleep while feeding is another reason some babies do not settle well at bedtime. If you find that your baby is getting very sleepy halfway through his bedtime feed, try bringing his bedtime routine forward by 15/20 minutes and instead of dimming the lights during this feed, keep the lights bright until he has taken most of the feed.

● Allowing your baby to fall asleep on you after his feed can start to present problems at this age. Babies who were previously put in the cot asleep and stayed asleep, will at this age often start to wake up after 10/15 minutes and then take anything up to an hour to settle back to sleep. It is important that your baby goes into the cot sleepy, but awake enough to be aware he is going into the cot.

● Overstimulation is another reason your baby may not be settling at bedtime. Bath time at this age becomes much more fun, but make sure that it is kept to no longer than 10 minutes and, once you take your baby to his room to be dressed and fed, do not allow visitors to be around during the feeding and settling time.

Moving up the cot causing waking in the night

It is around this age that you may find that your baby starts to kick off the covers and move up the cot, which can result in him thrashing his legs up and down and waking himself, or even worse banging his head on the cot spars or getting his arms trapped between them. This is for babies who aren't rolling over. Once they're able to roll then you take all the blankets away and put them in the sleeping bag. During the day you have to help them learn to roll front to back etc. to stop them getting stuck in the corner.

When this happens try tucking the bottom of the sleeping bag under the end of the mattress. If the sleeping bag isn't long enough you can just sew an additional length of fabric on the end so that there is enough to tuck under. I would recommend that you still continue to tuck your baby in securely as described on page 84. Given the importance of not overheating your baby reduce the tog of your sleeping bag accordingly or use a sheet instead of a blanket. Please remember that cot bumpers are not advised for babies under a year old, as they can increase the risk of overheating, a contributing factor in cot death.

Once your baby is over six months, he can be put down in just a sleeping bag without any sheets or blankets.

Early morning waking before solids are introduced

Between three and four months some babies may start to lose interest in their late night feed but will sleep through the night so parents decide to drop the feed altogether. This may initially seem fine and for a couple of weeks their baby may continue to sleep through the night, but in my experience they will then find that he will begin to wake earlier and earlier in the morning and will not settle unless given a feed.

The cause of the early morning waking is hunger and this is a very common problem among parents who allow their baby to drop the 10pm feed too early.

● Even if a baby is taking only 60ml (2oz) at 10pm, I advise parents to continue to wake him and offer him a feed until he is past four months and solids are established, the reason being that all babies will go through a growth spurt between three and four months and four milk feeds a day will rarely meet their hunger needs. If they have been allowed to drop the late feed, they will wake up to satisfy their hunger. When this happens, most parents will try to reintroduce the 10pm feed to get the baby going longer in the night again. Unfortunately, this doesn't always work if the baby has got used to being in a deep sleep at this time.

● If your baby wakes in the night it is important that you feed him immediately and get him back to sleep if you wish to avoid early morning waking or him being awake for any length of time in the night. Please do not see this as a regression of his feeding or sleeping. The majority of babies who are having a late feed will sleep around eight to nine hours from their late feed. Therefore, if your baby has dropped the late feed and then wakes around 4 or 5am, he is still doing very well and is only going the eight to nine hours at a different time of the night. By feeding him quickly in the night when he wakes, he will soon start to sleep longer again and eventually right through to nearer 6 or 7am.

- Obviously if you are feeding him around 4 or 5am, he may not be so hungry for his first feed of the day. When this happens all you can do is allow him to drink what he wants when he wakes and then offer a top-up around 8.30am so he is on track for his next morning feed. If he refuses the top-up he will then need to be given his second feed of the morning slightly earlier. When this happens I would suggest that you then offer a top-up just prior to his lunchtime nap, so that he doesn't wake up early from the nap due to hunger, because the feed was slightly smaller.

- Once solids are introduced, it is important they are introduced at the right speed so that the baby does not reduce the amount of milk he is taking too quickly. Until a baby is well past six months it is important that he has most of his milk before he is offered the solids. This ensures that he will take exactly the amount of solids he needs to satisfy his hunger. Milk is still very important at this stage and he still needs a full milk feed of 210–240ml (7–8oz) or a breast feed from both breasts to get through the night. Giving a baby the solids first often leads to him increasing the amount he takes too rapidly and reducing the amount of milk too quickly.

Early morning waking after solids are introduced

Even once solids are introduced and babies are established on three good solid meals a day and taking the right amount of milk at all feeds, some parents may find that their baby starts to wake earlier and earlier in the morning and will not settle back to sleep unless they are fed.

With parents I speak to in my consultancy I will ask to see a food diary to check what types of solids their baby is eating, and it may be useful for you to write down exactly what your baby is eating and drinking for at least three days. What I often find is that although a baby is taking good quantities of solids for their age and weight, plus the right amount of milk, their diet is very low in carbohydrates and the baby is hungry. In this case I advise parents to gradually increase the amount of baby rice they are giving their baby over a period of several days. If lunch is a combination of three to four cubes of vegetables and tea was three cubes of either apple or pear purée, plus one teaspoon of baby rice mixed with a small amount of formula, I would suggest increasing this to three teaspoons of baby rice mixed with milk, while reducing the fruit purée to one cube. Once this is established, I would suggest that parents try to combine at least one cube of a starch vegetable, such as sweet potato, among their lunchtime vegetables. A variety of fruit and vegetables is essential, but they should be balanced with a carbohydrate such as baby rice or sweet potato, as these types of carbohydrate are what help satisfy the baby's hunger. Within a few days your baby should be back to sleeping soundly through to 7am.

I strongly believe there is a huge link between food and sleep and that between the age of five and nine months it is not just getting the right quantities of food that affects sleep, but also ensuring that the right foods are given at the right times. I discuss how to structure weaning in more detail in my book *The Contented Little Baby Book of Weaning*.

Baby not settling for the morning nap

Between four and six months there can be several reasons why a baby is not settling well for his morning nap.

- The first cause you should look at is hunger, particularly if your baby is not sleeping right through the night and is still waking up between 5 and 6am for a feed. If he then wakes around 7am and he has fed at 5/6am in the morning, he would not manage to take a full feed at this time. Therefore when he is ready to go to sleep a couple of hours later for a nap he could be starting to get genuinely hungry. It is worth trying to delay feeding him at 7am when he wakes and instead feed him nearer to 8am, so that he is not getting hungry nearer his nap time. If he is looking for a feed when he wakes up at 7am, then of course feed him, but then offer him a small top up feed 30 minutes or so prior to his nap, so he settles well for the nap. Obviously, this could mean that he is not so hungry at the usual time for his next feed, so delay this feed slightly until you know he is ready to take a good feed.

- If your baby is sleeping through to 7am then taking a full feed, it may be that he is ready to have his morning feed increased, particularly if he is going through a growth spurt. If you are breastfeeding, I would offer longer on the second breast and if you are bottle-feeding, increase the feed by an extra 30ml (1oz). Remember, that some babies do need to be allowed an hour to feed, with a short break in between. If your baby usually takes his feed in 15 to 20 minutes, then give him a little break of 20 to 30 minutes before offering him the extra milk.

- Unfortunately, until a baby is sleeping to nearer 7am, the morning is often made up of split feeds or full feeds with a top-up prior to the nap. Once your baby is sleeping to nearer 7am he should manage to take a full feed and then go nearer to four hours until his next feed.

- If your baby has started waking earlier in the morning, perhaps around 6.30am instead of 7am, and not going back to sleep, it is possible that he is not settling well at his morning nap because he is getting overtired and needs to be asleep around 8.30am instead of the usual 9am. If you are using my routines you will be conscious of not allowing too much morning sleep if you have established a good two-hour lunchtime nap. Therefore instead of letting your baby sleep from 8.30 to 9.45am, I would suggest that you split the nap so that he is having 15/20 minutes at 8.30am and then a further 15 minutes at around 10am. This will keep both your feeding and sleeping on track for the day and ensure that he continues to sleep two hours at the lunchtime nap. Obviously, if you are not establishing a longer nap in the middle of the day, you can let your baby sleep until nearer 10am or when he wakes.

- A final reason that your baby may not be settling for the morning nap easily is that he is ready to stay awake longer, especially if he is sleeping soundly to nearer 7am in the morning. Look at the time he does eventually fall asleep and then put him down for his nap nearer to that time each day.

General Problems

Dribbling and drooling

Dribbling and drooling are a normal part of your baby's development and should not be a cause of concern; in some cases they are simply a sign that your baby is teething (see below). However, some babies do drool excessively and you may find that the area around their mouth is almost constantly wet and can become sore.

One simple reason for this is that babies of this age have difficulty swallowing all the saliva they produce because their head and neck muscles are not fully developed yet. These muscles develop by seven months and your baby will be able to control their drooling. You can help by wiping the excess saliva off your baby's chin and cheeks as frequently as possible. It's also worth protecting your baby's neck with a comfortable bib or a barrier cream to prevent a rash forming.

Other causes of excessive drooling include nausea, throat pain and infections, so monitor your baby's drooling and if you see any signs of fever, irritability, vomiting or mouth sores, see a doctor immediately.

Teething

Although some babies are born with one or more teeth already visible, on average babies start to cut their first teeth at around six months, and the process continues until about three years of age, when all the teeth have erupted. The first teeth to appear are commonly the incisors, starting with the bottom two front teeth and followed by the top two front teeth. In my experience, babies who enjoy a routine from a very early age and have established healthy sleeping habits are rarely bothered by teething, and only a handful have been bothered by teething in the night, and in these cases it is usually when the molars come through and then only for a few nights.

However, for some babies teething is often accompanied by symptoms that can distress both babies and parents. I have found that babies who wake in the night due to teething are more likely to have suffered from colic and have developed poor sleeping habits. The symptoms listed below can vary in severity and may affect your baby's appetite and intake of milk and solids.

- Baby is more irritable than usual and cries more frequently.

- Rubs his cheek, indicating discomfort in the mouth area.

- Mouth ulcers.

- Drooling is heavier than usual.

- Rash on the chin due to excessive drool.

- Coughs from drool in the back of the throat.

- Constant attempts to chew on anything and everything.

- Gums look red and your baby rubs them.

- Sleep is disrupted, with frequent waking and crying.

- Poor appetite and perhaps refusal to eat.

- Cheeks may appear flushed.

Note that symptoms vary from child to child. Some may experience many of the symptoms listed above, while others will not experience any.

- If your baby is suffering, rubbing his gums with a clean finger or an ice cube can provide some relief. Giving him objects to bite can also help to reduce the pain, so offer teething rings (which can be cooled). Beware of brittle teething items that might break and cause choking. Also, avoid those made from PVC, as research seems to indicate that they could be potentially poisonous to children.

- If your baby has been fully weaned sugar-free teething biscuits or rusks, breadsticks or oven-hardened bread can help soothe his gums. Other suitable foods include peeled cucumber, frozen bagels and frozen fruit, as biting on cold objects can help to numb the pain. Offer cold drinks and cold foods at feeding times.

- If your child is very difficult to settle and has a fever, you can give him a painkilling syrup – either paracetamol or ibuprofen (speak to your pharmacist for advice). There are also various anaesthetic preparations, many of them gels, which can be rubbed on the gums to numb the pain. Some also have antiseptic properties to help prevent infection around the area of the new tooth. Remember that children should never be given aspirin.

- If your baby is teething and waking in the night but quickly settles back to sleep when given a cuddle or a dummy, teething is probably not the real cause of his waking. A baby who is genuinely bothered by teething pain would be difficult to settle back to sleep. He would also show signs of discomfort during the day, not just at night. I would advise you to check the section on excessive night waking and early morning waking to eliminate other reasons for your baby waking.

- If you are convinced that your baby's night-time wakings are caused by severe teething pain, I suggest you seek advice from your doctor regarding the use of paracetamol and ibuprofen. While genuine teething pain may cause a few disruptive nights, it should never last for several weeks. If your baby seems out of sorts, develops a fever and suffers from loss of appetite or diarrhoea, he should be seen by a doctor. Do not assume that these symptoms are just a sign of teething. Very often I have found that what parents thought was teething turned out to be an ear or throat infection.

Eczema

It's hard work caring for a baby or toddler at the best of times, but add to that the stress of a child made miserable by sore, itchy skin caused by eczema and you might be finding it hard to cope.

Eczema is a dry skin condition. It occurs when the skin doesn't produce enough of the fats and oils that help retain water. Usually the skin cells are plumped up with water, but when you have eczema gaps are left between the skin cells because they aren't plump with water. This means the skin doesn't have a very effective protective barrier. Moisture gets out from the inner layers of skin and the skin can dry out. It also means that irritants can get through the cells, and the skin can become red and inflamed.

Eczema affects one in five children in the UK. It usually runs in families – if one parent has it a child has a 25 per cent chance of inheriting it, while with two parents as sufferers the risk doubles to 50 per cent. Most children who have eczema have atopic eczema, which is usually hereditary. It is most often found on the backs of the knees or inside the elbows. This type of eczema does sometimes flare up and then go away again. Common triggers are soap, detergents, contact with animals, pollen or house-dust mites, skin infection or overheating.

Around 90 per cent of children who develop eczema before age one will have grown out of it by their teens (often earlier).

The two most important things you can do to help your child's eczema are to make sure you avoid any triggers that may make it worse, and to prevent your baby's skin drying out by keeping it well moisturised. Here are a number of tips you may want to follow:

● Avoid putting your child in woollen clothing as it may cause itching. Some synthetic fabrics can also irritate the skin, so choose cotton wherever you can. Opting for cotton bed linen will also help reduce the risk of irritation.

● Overheating can trigger eczema which often gets worse in winter when babies are spending more time inside centrally-heated homes, as this dries the skin. Don't overheat your house, and be particularly careful when it comes to your baby's bedroom – the recommended temperature for a baby's room is 16–20ºC.

- Keep your child's nails short so that he can't damage his skin by scratching, and consider using scratch mittens for babies at night.

- As with asthma, dust mites can make eczema worse, so make sure your house is as dust free as you can. Wiping surfaces with a damp cloth and vacuuming regularly will help.

- Many parents find that the type of washing powder they use can affect their children's eczema. Generally the advice is to use non-biological powders and avoid fabric conditioners.

- Pets can sometimes cause problems for children who have eczema. Try to stop your child spending too much time around animals if you suspect this may be the case.

- Moisturising the skin with emollients (special moisturisers) is the most important part of eczema treatment. Emollients will stop your child's skin from drying out and reduce the itchiness too. Dr Michael Cork, Head of Academic Dermatology at the University of Sheffield, runs a successful eczema clinic at Sheffield Children's Hospital. At Dr Cork's clinic, parents were given a demonstration on how to use the creams properly, which led to an 80 per cent increase in their use. They found that 25 per cent of children's eczema could be controlled with emollients alone and that there was an 89 per cent decrease in the severity of a child's eczema when emollients were used correctly.

Here are Dr Cork's top tips on using emollients properly:

- Use plenty – about 500g a week.

- Apply three or four times every day.

- You'll need to use more in extreme weather.

- Always apply after a bath.

- Warm the cream in your hands first.

- Put cream on in the direction of hair growth, using long downward strokes.

- Don't rub the cream in as this will cause itching.

Choosing an emollient

There are dozens available on prescription and to buy over-the-counter, but how do you know which is best for your child? Take advice from your GP on which products to use, and when and how to use them. Some brands your doctor may advise you to try are Oilatum Junior cream and bath formula; Balneum bath treatment; and Eucerin Intensive cream. Aqueous cream is often prescribed by GPs, but it contains a detergent that can cause the skin barrier to break down, so worsening eczema. A study by Dr Michael Cork revealed that 54 per cent of children found their eczema got worse after using aqueous cream. He explains that it was never designed to be used as an emollient, but as a soap-substitute.

- Bath time is another way of getting moisture into your child's skin if you do it properly. Here are Dr Cork's tips for parents:
  - Bath children once a day.
  - Use a special bath emollient liquid designed for eczema.
  - Use a bath mat as the oils make the bath very slippery.
  - Pat, don't rub skin dry afterwards to avoid itching.
  - Use a fresh towel for every bath time and don't let children share towels.

- Your doctor may prescribe a steroid cream or ointment which will be used for a specific period of time to help control eczema. People are often very worried about using steroids for young children but they are safe, although you must always follow your doctor's instructions as to how to use them.

For more help contact The National Eczema Society, tel: 0870–241 3604; www.eczema.org

Sleep regression

Having worked with babies for over 30 years, I found that once they were in a good routine and sleeping through the night, aside from during illness, they would continue to sleep well. Of the 300 babies I cared for and the thousands of babies whose parents I have advised through my consultancy I have never had parents coming back to me saying their baby's sleep had regressed. However, I now find that I am getting an increasing number of emails from parents asking for advice on how to deal with their baby's 'sleep regression'.

It seems that some people believe that at certain ages babies go through a developmental stage that can affect their sleep, resulting in them waking in the night again. My own personal view is that sleep will only backtrack in the night if parents are not one step ahead of their babies' ever-changing feeding and sleeping needs. If there were such a thing as genuine 'sleep regression' due to developmental changes, then I am convinced that from the thousands of parents that I have advised at least some of them would have come back to me and said that their baby's sleep kept backtracking. Indeed it has been the opposite. I regularly hear from parents I advised, often many years ago, about how well their child has continued to sleep. If your baby has experienced what you believe to be sleep regression, I would urge you to check the nine routines in my book *The New Contented Little Baby Book*. The reason that I have nine different routines in the book is because I believe that during the first year a baby's needs keep changing. Parents who are one step ahead of their baby ensure that these feeding and sleeping needs are met and gradually changed before things go wrong. Being one step ahead of a baby's needs, will in my opinion avoid 'sleep regression'.

6

Six to Nine Months

You may be surprised by the rapid changes you see in your baby's development during this period. One of the biggest changes – at the start of this phase – will be in his feeding as weaning is recommended from six months.

If you have been recommended to wean before six months, you will have slowly worked your way through most of the first stage foods, of puréed vegetables and fruits and baby cereal. It is around six months that a baby's natural store of iron, which he is born with, is getting very low. Therefore it is important that you then start to introduce your baby to the second stage foods, such as lentils, poultry, fish and meat between six and seven months. If you have started weaning at six months it is important that you progress through the first stage weaning foods more quickly than what is recommended with early weaning. Instead of introducing the first stage foods of vegetables and fruits every three to four days, you can introduce a new food every couple of days, along with increasing the amounts he is having.

When weaning at six months I recommend you should immediately go to the tier system of weaning at lunchtime, as this will encourage your baby to increase his solids more rapidly. At this age if you continue to offer a full milk feed before the solids, you may find that your baby will become very fussy about weaning, and rejects many of the foods you are introducing. Start off by offering half of your baby's milk feed, then solids, then the remainder of the milk feed. Gradually over several days reduce the amount of milk he is having before his solids, until he is having his solids first, followed by a small amount of milk. A few days after you have introduced solids at lunchtime you can start and introduce solids in at teatime. I usually find that around 5pm is the best time, as it allows enough time for digestion between the solids and the baby's bedtime milk feed. It is important that he still takes a full milk feed after the bath, and allowing enough time between the solids and the milk feed will ensure this.

Once solids are established at lunch and teatime, you will then start to introduce a small amount of solids for breakfast, after he has had his morning milk feed. When this happens you will find that you can gradually push lunch slightly later.

Regardless of whether you started weaning before six months or at six months, between six and seven months it is important to start including chicken, meat, fish, pulses and dairy products. When introducing these foods, I would recommend that you introduce a new food every three days to ensure your baby doesn't have a bad reaction. Some babies also balk at the stronger tastes of these foods therefore I would recommend that you introduce these foods slowly.

Although all babies are different, in my experience the majority of babies are taking around six to eight cubes (a cube is usually around one tablespoon) of solid food at lunch and tea at this age. If you start by replacing two of the vegetable cubes with two cubes of the more simple chicken, fish, meat or pulse recipes, then increase the amount by one or two cubes a day until your baby's meal consists totally of one of the protein meals.

Once your baby is happily taking his protein lunches, you can then start to replace the cereal, vegetables and fruit he is having in the evening with proper savoury meals such as pasta bake, sweetcorn chowder, vegetable risotto or other such carbohydrate-heavy meals.

It is also really important to begin to clean your baby's teeth as soon as the first one appears. At this stage you will probably find it easiest to use a small piece of clean gauze wrapped around your finger, along with a small amount of special baby toothpaste, which can be massaged all around the baby's gums and teeth. Later, when more teeth have appeared, you can move on to a soft baby toothbrush for cleaning.

Your baby's sleep patterns will change during this phase too. At the start, he will sleep for two and a half to three hours in a 12-hour day. This will usually be divided between two to three naps. By nine months most babies will have reduced their sleep to around two and a half hours a day divided into two separate naps, one in the morning and one after lunch. By this stage it's a good idea to see if you can occasionally let him have his lunchtime nap somewhere other than at home – perhaps at a friend's house or in his buggy – just to ensure he gets used to being able to sleep away from home. If he gets used to only sleeping in his cot, life can become difficult as he gets older and only needs a short catnap when out and about or on holiday, but getting him used to sleeping in his buggy or baby chair should prevent this.

Between six and nine months your baby will start to roll on to his front and may prefer to sleep on his tummy. When this happens, it would be advisable to remove the sheet and blanket to avoid him getting into a tangle with them. In the winter months, the lightweight sleeping bag will need to be replaced with a warmer one to make up for the loss of blankets.

Babies often start to move around more during this period, and your baby may be crawling or bottom shuffling. As your baby gets more mobile, you will want to make sure that you have child-proofed your home as best you can with stair gates and safety catches to help prevent accidents, and you will need to move anything breakable or potentially dangerous out of your baby's reach.

If you are planning to return to work, do think carefully about the type of childcare that would best fit in with your family, and ensure that you leave plenty of time to sort this out as getting a place in a good nursery, or finding a nanny or childminder you really like, can take a while.

Many babies start to have a comforter during this period, and may become attached to a blanket, muslin, particular toy or a dummy. It's a perfectly normal stage of development that can help give a child a sense of security if he feels vulnerable, but you don't want your child to become too dependent on a comforter. I have known small children to get so attached to their comforter that they refuse to leave the house without it and are unable to take a short nap in the buggy or car unless they are holding it. It may therefore be a good idea to restrict the use of the comforter to sleep and rest times to prevent this from happening.

Most babies have a development check at around eight months, at which your child's height, weight, hearing and eyesight will usually be tested, along with his general development. This is a useful check-up for parents to reassure them that their baby is on track. Parents do sometimes worry when they start comparing their baby with other people's children, but it's really important to appreciate how much variation there can be in size and development at this age. If you do have any concerns, however, this can be a good time to raise them.

You will find that your baby is able to concentrate more now and that he is making more sounds, and trying to communicate. More and more of his personality will emerge as he continues to develop.

Feeding

What to expect

From six months, although he will cut down on the 11am breast or bottle feed of milk as his intake of solids increases, your baby still needs a minimum of 600ml (20oz) of breast or formula milk a day, inclusive of milk used for mixing food. Once your baby is established on three solid meals a day, he should manage to sleep for around 11–12 hours at night without a milk feed, provided he is taking all of his daily milk quota between 6/7am and 7/8pm in the evening. Sometimes, if a baby is not taking a full feed after the bath, he may need to be offered a late feed for a bit longer. If the late feed has been dropped, then some babies, in particular breastfed babies, may continue to wake around 5/6am and genuinely need a milk feed if they have not had a fun feed after the bath.

What to aim for

Once your baby is between six and seven months, as solids are increased and protein is introduced he should be ready to reduce and eventually drop his second milk feed of the morning. When he is only taking an ounce of milk at lunchtime, after his solids replace it with a drink of water or well-diluted juice from a beaker. But if you find that his lunchtime nap is affected by cutting out the small milk feed, then it would be wise to continue with offering it for a little longer. When this feed is dropped, he may need to increase the mid-afternoon feed. However, if you notice that he is cutting back too much on his bedtime feed, continue to keep the mid-afternoon feed smaller. Between six and seven months your baby should be eating a proper tea at around 5pm, with only a small drink of water from a beaker. He would then have a full milk feed at around 6.30pm.

By nine months, if your baby is formula-fed, he should be drinking all of his water, diluted juice and most of his milk feeds from a beaker. I would recommend that you start off using a soft spout on your baby's bottle, and then progress on to a hard spouted beaker. If you continue to offer milk from a bottle, your baby is likely to drink more milk and fluids than he needs, which can decrease his appetite for solids.

If your baby is not cutting down on his late feed or he is waking in the middle of the night once solids are established, it may be that he is not getting the right quantities of solids for his age or weight, or needs a bigger feed at 6.30pm. Keep a diary of all food and milk consumed over a period of four days to help pinpoint why he is not cutting out that last feed. As mentioned previously in my experience most babies are taking around 6 to 8 tablespoons of solids at this age, although some bigger babies can need more than that. If you are confident that he is getting the correct amounts and is taking the late feed or waking in the night from habit rather than genuine hunger, I would suggest that you gradually start to reduce it. If you reduce it by 30ml (1oz) every three to four nights, provided he does not start to wake up early, you should continue to do this until he is taking only 60ml (2oz). You can then drop it altogether and he should then sleep through from 7pm to 7am. If your baby is breastfed you can try reducing the milk feed by a couple of minutes every three to four nights. Provided he does not start to wake up early, you should continue to do this until he is only taking a few minutes on the breast and, provided that he continues to sleep to nearer 7am, you can then drop this feed altogether. Between six and nine months a typical day would look similar to the following:

7am	milk followed by breakfast
9.15/9.30/10am	short nap (no longer than 45 minutes, less if he has reduced his lunchtime nap)
11.30/12 noon	solids with a small drink of water from a beaker
12.15pm	some babies may still need a small drink of milk before their nap

12.30/1pm	nap (around two hours)
2.30pm	milk feed
4pm	may need a short nap around now if midday nap was too short
5pm	solids with a small drink of water from a beaker
6/6.30pm	bath
6/7.30pm	milk feed, story and bed

Feeding Problems

Six-month-old baby refusing milk

At six months, although he will have cut down on the 11am feed as his intake of solids increases, your baby still needs a minimum of 600ml (20oz) of milk a day, inclusive of milk used for mixing food. Babies who started weaning at six months could still be having four to six milk feeds a day, though you are aiming to reduce this rapidly if solids are not to be refused. If your baby is getting under the recommended quantity and refusing to accept milk (most likely in bottle-fed babies) then it is important you address the issue. Each ounce of milk contains a perfect balance of vitamins and minerals, therefore while it is important that a wide variety of solids are introduced from six months, it is equally important that the amount of milk your baby drinks does not drop below the recommended daily minimum.

- If at this stage your baby is drinking follow-on formula milk, and you have noticed a change in his appetite I would advise changing this back to the first infant milk as I have noticed that with some babies follow-on milk affects their appetite. First stage formula milk is the closest to breast milk and is the only milk that is needed during the first year.

- In order to concentrate on establishing your baby's milk feeds and two good solid meals a day, I would recommend that for a few days that you do not give him any solids at breakfast. Instead try to ensure that he takes a full milk feed, even if it means that you have to allow him a break in between taking the feed.

- Once your baby is back to taking two 210–240ml (7–8oz) bottles of formula, one in the morning and one in the evening – and a 120–150ml (4–5oz) bottle at 2.30pm, his milk intake will be back on track. You can then introduce a small amount of breakfast solids again but only after he has taken at least 180ml (6oz) of his milk feed. The milk that is used in his breakfast cereal should ensure that his total daily milk intake is now at the right level.

- Do also make sure that the amounts of solids that you are giving your baby are correct for their weight. Some parents find that they are in fact overfeeding their baby, particularly carbohydrates, which will also mean they are not hungry at mealtimes and will fuss. Getting the right balance of all the different foods from the different food groups is very important at this age.

Refusing solids

Babies aged six months or older often refuse solids because they drink too much milk, especially if they are still feeding in the night.

- If your baby is still having a late feed I would advise that you gradually cut it back by 30ml (1oz) every three nights. With babies who are having a breast feed, you should reduce the time on the breast by a few minutes every three nights. As you cut the milk feed back at the late feed, you should start to see an increase in the amount of solids that your baby is taking during the day. Obviously, you do not want to decrease the late feed too quickly and so much that your baby wakens earlier in the morning. However, if you do not see an improvement in your baby's appetite for solids, then I would recommend that you drop the late feed anyway and instead offer a milk feed when he wakes early. This has the advantage that your baby is learning to sleep a much longer spell without milk.

- If you drop the late feed and your baby is waking up between 5am and 6am it is important that you feed him straight away, but settle him back to sleep until 7am, so that he does not get used to being awake at this time of the morning. When he does get up at 7am, he should not be offered further milk, as the milk he had earlier should be counted as his breakfast milk. He should instead be offered his breakfast solids, followed by a small top-up milk feed after the solids.

● By the end of six months, a baby's milk intake should be a minimum of 600ml (20oz) a day, divided between three drinks a day and small amounts used in food. If your baby still refuses solids at this age, despite cutting down on his milk intake, it is important that you discuss the problem with your doctor or health visitor.

Refusing protein

While your baby may have sailed through first stage weaning, second stage weaning can be more problematic, with babies not accepting the introduction of new foods, particularly protein such as meat. If a baby starts to refuse certain solids at this age, I advise going back a few steps – sometimes even just to milk – and then reintroducing vegetables and finally the protein.

● Some babies will find the first tastes of chicken and fish and meat too strong. To ensure that your baby does not take an instant dislike to a protein recipe, I would advise introducing it slowly. For example, when you have cooked your first chicken casserole recipe, do not be tempted to suddenly replace six cubes of vegetable purée with six cubes of chicken casserole. Instead replace one of his lunchtime vegetable cubes with one of the chicken casserole cubes, gradually replacing another each day. This way your baby will slowly get used to the different tastes and textures and by the end of a week will be eating a complete serving of chicken casserole.

- The other reason your baby might be refusing protein is because he is eating too big a breakfast. Too much cereal and fruit at breakfast is a significant reason for babies refusing foods later in the day as the quantity of carbohydrate is filling them up and they are simply not hungry enough later. To ensure you get the balance right, gradually reduce the amount you are offering at breakfast until your baby is happily taking a decent amount of solids at lunch. For example, if once the cereal is mixed with milk it is making up around six tablespoons and you are adding two tablespoons of fruit purée, it may be that you need to reduce breakfast to around three tablespoons of cereal with three of fruit, then gradually increase the amounts again.

Refusing lumpy food and finger foods

By the second stage of weaning your baby should start learning to eat more solid pieces of food and you should be continuing to introduce a wider range of tastes and textures, progressing from purées to pulsed food and then to meals with soft lumps to encourage chewing. It is also important to introduce finger foods, which your baby can hold comfortably and bring to his mouth to suck or nibble on. However, problems often occur at this stage as some babies find it more difficult to move from puréed food to more solid food and refuse the unfamiliar – they may not accept these new textures, or will gag when offered them.

I think that the term 'introducing lumpy food' is what can be confusing to parents. Many parents I've worked with will often purée their baby's meals as usual but leave a few lumps in the meal. This can be a shock to some babies who find themselves being given their favourite meal – which has always had a smooth texture – and suddenly finding it has lumps. I always advise changing the texture of purées very gradually, slowly progressing from puréed to pulsed, so that your baby does not notice a sudden change in the consistency of the food.

If you find that your baby is refusing more solid types of foods, I would recommend that you go back to puréeing his food for a week or so, then using the guidelines below start to offer more solid food again. In my experience moving your baby very gradually from purées to more solid food will ensure that he does not refuse or become upset when offered them.

- Around the age of seven months, instead of puréeing all of your baby's meals, you should start to pulse all meat and fish casseroles and mash vegetables and fruit. Once he is used to eating his food in a pulsed form, you should start to offer small amounts of finger foods at each meal, such as softly cooked pieces of vegetables and fruit.

- When he is happily eating most of his food in a pulsed form and managing small pieces of softly cooked pieces of fruits and vegetables, you can then move him on to the next stage of preparing his casseroles in a more adult style.

- For casserole- type dishes cut the meat or fish into the size required to cook them, but cut all the vegetables into pieces the size you know that he can happily manage at the moment. Cook the meal as usual, but once cooked transfer the protein to a separate bowl along with some of the cooking stock and a small amount of the vegetables, and pulse this. Divide the pulsed mixture equally between freezerproof baby storage containers in portions, then equally divide the remaining stock and vegetables between them. When serving the meal, it should look similar to the way you would serve an adult casserole, so that the vegetables are distinguishable and not all mixed together.

- Once your baby is happily eating his casseroles this way, you can start to offer him very thin slithers of chicken, meat or fish taken from food you have cooked yourself (without added salt) alongside his other finger foods. When he shows signs of managing to eat these, when you cook his next casserole you can then stop pulsing the chicken, meat or fish, instead cutting it up into the bite-sized pieces that you know he can manage.

- If your baby gags, do not make a fuss or panic – this will simply alarm him even further. Allow him to cough and clear his throat of the food, and then continue eating. Always supervise your baby when he is eating and ensure that he is sitting upright and fully supported. I recommend that all parents attend a first aid course, so that in the event of food getting stuck in their baby's throat that they know how to act quickly to avoid the baby choking.

- At this stage of weaning it is important not to pressure a baby into eating. Once babies start to eat their food chopped, sliced and diced, and more finger food is included, they will usually eat less than when their meals were all puréed. This is very normal and trying to force your baby to eat more than he wants could result in poor food associations. In my experience the majority of babies will take 6–7 tablespoons of puréed food at any given time in the weaning process; however, once they reach nearer nine months and their meals are served in a chopped and diced form, a lot of them will be happy with just 3–4 tablespoons, plus a selection of finger foods. Although it will appear that he is eating less than previously, this is normal – the pulsed food is thicker and slower to eat and you've just got to let your baby get to a stage where he can judge his own appetite. Don't expect him to eat 6 or 7 tablespoons of casserole plus lots of finger food. At this stage, meals should be a combination of casserole-type foods, prepared as above, only served as smaller amounts, then a selection of finger foods after the spoon-fed food. If your baby refuses to eat the casserole, simply end the meal without a big fuss, but don't offer the familiar food, such as the purée or yoghurt.

- While it is important not to fill babies up with too much fluid during their meals, at this stage I would recommend that you do offer your baby a small amount of water once they have eaten a reasonable amount. It takes a lot more effort on your baby's part chewing and swallowing food served this way, than it did swallowing smooth and runny purées, therefore allowing him small sips of water every few mouthfuls will help him become more accepting of foods that are diced, sliced, chopped or served as finger foods.

● Finally, at this stage whenever possible try to eat at least one meal a day with your baby. Babies love to mimic adults and eating together will most certainly encourage your baby to eat more solid food and finger foods. You will find many recipes in *The Gina Ford Baby and Toddler Cook Book* and my *Feeding Made Easy* that can be made as family meals.

CASE STUDY: Hugo, aged six months

Problem: Refusing vegetables

By the time Hugo was five months old he was a very healthy weight and was drinking up to 300ml (11oz) of formula at each feed. After discussion with their health visitor Hugo's parents decided that Hugo was ready to be weaned.

At first Hugo was somewhat reluctant to take solids but his parents slowly persisted, not introducing puréed fruit until he was happily eating baby rice for a week. The fruit was a roaring success but then it came to vegetables. When she contacted me in desperation, Hugo's mum described these to me as a disaster as far as Hugo was concerned. She had tried carrot, sweet potato, butternut squash, but he refused everything apart from fruit purées.

I told her that Hugo probably had a sweet tooth which had to be addressed but that this would require a great deal of patience and resilience on her part. I advised taking Hugo back to stage one weaning, offering him small amounts of vegetable purées with his baby rice, and for the time being eliminating the fruit purées completely. The next couple of weeks proceeded with varying degrees of success: now and again Hugo was prepared to eat vegetable purées but most days the tears rolled down his cheeks.

It took great strength from Hugo's mum to remain persistent but after a couple of weeks Hugo finally accepted a spoonful of carrot and green bean purée on its own. Once his lunchtime meal was going smoothly I suggested she offer him a cube of fruit purée to end the meal – this always made Hugo smile.

His teatime meal was successful – he opened his mouth for every spoonful of fruit and rice – it was easy to see which was his favourite meal.

When Hugo was six and a half months old Hugo's mum decided it was time to introduce protein. This change ran smoothly and once he was happily eating eight cubes of protein and vegetables she thought it would be nice to replace a couple of those cubes with fruit purée as dessert at lunch and tea. She also started to feed Hugo a small amount of cereal at breakfast time.

This went well for a week then lunchtime became difficult again. The tears flowed constantly, Hugo's back arched and his mouth clamped shut every time his mum offered him a spoonful of savoury food, though by reverting to baby rice she managed to persuade him to eat some. She wondered whether his appetite had decreased so she decided to halve the number of cubes she offered, though the cube of fruit she offered at the end of the meal always cheered him up. They would see a slight improvement for a couple of days but then Hugo would become really cross.

In despair Hugo's mum contacted me again. It was clear to me that Hugo was refusing solids so I advised that for the next week we concentrate on establishing two good meals a day. To do this, we needed to temporarily cut out breakfast and bring forward lunch. I suggested Hugo's mum give him 185ml (6½oz) of formula to drink at breakfast, bring his lunch forward to 10.30am and just serve protein and vegetables. If he still looked hungry after six cubes of savoury foods then I suggested she give him a couple of teaspoons of rice mixed with formula. He then had 200ml (7oz) of formula after his lunchtime nap. I also suggested cutting out protein at teatime – since I believe this can have an effect on a baby's sleep – and replace it with a tea high in carbohydrates.

After three and a half weeks, during which Hugo's mum avoided giving him any fruit, Hugo was happily eating protein and vegetables at lunchtime and vegetables at teatime combined with rice and formula – his tricky eating habits were a thing of the past.

Early morning poo

During the early stages of weaning it can be quite common for babies to start to wake up early because they have done a poo. This can be very frustrating, particularly if your baby had been sleeping through to nearer 7am. Fortunately, I can assure you that this does not last for long and does sort itself out as your baby's digestive system gets used to a more varied diet of solids.

I have found that for a short period avoiding giving fruit (apart from banana) and green vegetables in the evening can sometimes help, along with ensuring that tea is more carbohydrate-based with root vegetables. If a baby is not doing a poo after his breakfast milk and solids, it is also worth increasing the fruit at breakfast so that his body gets used to passing a poo after breakfast and not before.

Refusing water

During the first year milk is still the most important fluid for your baby. However, once protein is introduced at six months at lunch, and the milk feed is dropped, you can start offering your baby a drink of water with his lunch. Do not worry if your baby takes only a few sips, it can often take many months before a baby will drink a couple of ounces. The main thing is that you keep offering water every day with his lunch. If you are worried about his fluid intake you can always give him a small drink of milk just prior to his lunchtime nap.

Refusing to drink from a beaker

It is advised that by one year of age babies are taking all their milk feeds from a cup or beaker. By that stage, the amount of milk a baby requires has reduced from 500ml to 350ml each day and if a baby is drinking in excess of this it affects his appetite for solids. However, many parents encounter difficulties switching their baby from a bottle to a beaker, with many babies refusing to take the beaker. In some cases, babies may never even have taken a bottle of any kind so they may be switching directly from breast to beaker, which is even harder, so it is best to start making the transition between seven and eight months. Initially I would suggest a gentle transition, and I found that a parent I advised recently had great success with this approach. However, if your baby is still refusing to make the switch you may wish to follow the alternative solution outlined below.

- By around seven or eight months, encourage your baby to have his breakfast milk in a soft-spouted bottle-to-cup trainer bottle. Even if he is not keen at first, try for a few days, giving him as much milk as he will take in the trainer bottle and then give him the rest in his baby bottle so that he won't be missing out on much-needed nutrition.

- By the end of the first week, you should find that he is taking all his breakfast milk from the trainer bottle. Continue with this approach until your baby is taking all his milk feeds in trainer bottles.

- By nine months, your baby will have been using the soft spouts for several weeks and should be ready to progress towards getting rid of his bottle altogether. The next step is to offer your baby his morning milk in a hard-spouted beaker (without a valve). As before, give him what he will take, even if it's just a couple of ounces of milk, then switch back to his usual trainer bottle to finish his feed. Allow him to make the transition slowly and proceed as above until he is taking all his milk feeds from the beaker.

- If your baby is still finding the transition difficult try one of the hard spouts for the bottle-to-cup trainer bottles he was used to.

- If at nine months, your baby is still refusing to drink his milk from a beaker, you may need to be a bit firmer in your approach. Offer him the beaker when he is at his hungriest, which would be at 7am in the morning. Keep offering it to him every 20 minutes until nearer 8.30/9am, trying not to offer solids until he has taken at least 60ml (2oz) of milk from the beaker.

- Do the same just prior to his lunchtime solids and directly after. You can then offer him a breast or bottle feed at 2.30pm and as usual after his bath.

- It could take several days or even longer for him to increase the amount he is taking from the beaker in the morning, but once he is happily taking around 150–180ml (5/6oz) of milk in the morning, you can then start to offer him a drink of milk from the beaker at 2.30pm.

- By nine months your baby needs a minimum of 500ml (18oz) of milk a day. If he takes 150–180ml (5–6oz) in the morning, 150–180ml mid afternoon and 180ml in the evening that would be a total of 480–540ml (16–19oz) a day, so try to make up any remainder he needs by mixing it with cereal or into sauces.

Excessive night feeding

Parents are often told that once their baby is eating three solid meals a day he should not need a milk feed in the night. However, I often find that if a baby's daytime feeding routine changes or becomes disrupted for some reason, he may not be getting the nutrition he needs during the day and will start to wake during the night genuinely needing to be fed. Parents often resort to giving their baby milk to get them back to sleep and a vicious cycle emerges where they drink too much during the night and aren't hungry enough for their required solids during the day.

When this happens it is really important to count any middle-of-the-night milk feeding as part of the baby's breakfast milk, otherwise a vicious circle of feeding in the night and not taking enough solids during the day will evolve. For example, if your baby is waking around 4am and drinking a 150ml (5oz) or 180ml (6oz) bottle of milk, when he then gets up at 7am it is important that the amount of milk he has had in the night is deducted from his morning breakfast milk so that his appetite for solids is not reduced. Instead of offering a further 150ml or 180ml bottle, offer just 60–90ml (2–3oz) and then the solids. If your baby has taken a full 240ml (8oz) bottle of milk in the night, it would be better to go straight into solids, then offer just around 60ml (2oz) after these, to ensure that his solids are not reduced by having too much milk between the middle-of-the-night feed and the breakfast feed. At around this age a baby needs 500–600ml milk a day and if he is given a lot more than this because of night feeding he will more than likely not eat enough solids during the day and then keep waking up in the night through genuine hunger.

● As the baby's solids increase during the day, the amount that he needs to drink during the night will normally naturally decrease. Once this happens you would then bring back the full milk feed when he wakes and give it to him before his breakfast solids.

● With breastfed babies it is difficult to know how much they are taking in the night. Therefore to eliminate feeding in the night I would recommend that you express and offer your baby a bottle of expressed milk when he wakes, so that you can follow the same plan as for a formula-fed baby. If you have a baby who refuses the bottle, I would advise that you offer your baby as much milk as he will take in the night from the breast so that he sleeps through to 7am. As his solids increase during the day, you can gradually reduce the length of time he is on the breast by a couple of minutes each night every two or three days.

● With bottle-fed babies I have found that the majority will actually start to sleep later and later in the night and sleep through naturally to nearer 7am, once they are on three full solid meals a day. If you find that your baby continues to wake up and look for a small bottle or breast feed despite eating three full meals a day and reducing the amount that they drink in the night, you should then spend a few nights settling them back to sleep with a cuddle instead of feeding them.

● Finally, it is important at this age that your baby still takes a full formula feed of close to 240ml or be offered both breasts at bedtime. Try to ensure that teatime solids are given at least one and a half hours before his bedtime milk, so that he ready to take a full feed.

CASE STUDY: David, seven months

Problem: Excessive night feeding

Cause: Given too much convenience food

With a difficult toddler to deal with alongside baby David, David's mother had started to change David's routine. She started to cut out his bath and massage in the evening to attend to the screaming toddler, and he was given jars of baby food rather than the fresh food that had previously been an essential part of his dietary requirements. Soon David started to wake up every night at around 10pm and would not settle back without a feed, even though he had dropped this feed a good six weeks previously. Worse still, he started to wake up when his sister was crying in the night. His mother ended up giving him a formula feed in the night so that he would settle back quickly and allow her to return to a hysterical toddler. This excessive night-time feeding resulted in David eating even fewer solids than usual. Although she was exhausted trying to deal with two sleepless children, David's mother followed my advice and made two batches of chicken and vegetable casserole and two batches of lentil and vegetable casserole. Within two days of introducing the correct amounts of this food for his age and weight at lunchtime and mixing his teatime rice with a home-made fruit or vegetable purée, David began to drink less in the night. Although he continued to wake for a further four nights at 10pm, his mother was able to settle him back to sleep with a small drink of cool boiled water. Within a further three nights, David was back to sleeping from 7pm to 7am. I believe that the main cause of his sudden night-time waking was genuine hunger caused by not receiving the correct amounts of the right sort of food for his age and weight. In my experience, the occasional use of convenience food is fine, but babies who are being fed constantly from jars and packets are much more likely to develop sleep problems related to feeding.

Constipation

By this age you're likely to be familiar with what looks normal in your baby's nappy and you'll have an idea of how regularly they pass stools, so if you notice a change in their stools or a change in their behaviour, it may be that your baby is constipated. Signs to watch out for are your baby crying or straining and showing discomfort when he poos, being irritable during his awake time, only doing a poo every two to three days or passing dry, hard, pellet-like poos.

Due to the composition of breast milk, breastfed babies are less likely to become constipated. However, when a breastfed baby is weaned on to formula sometimes constipation can become a problem, especially if the baby is weaned around the same time as they are being weaned on to solids.

During the transition period of weaning your breastfed baby on to formula, if you find that constipation is becoming a problem, it is important to offer your baby a small amount of cool boiled water in between feeds, until his body is used to digesting formula easily and he is passing a bowel movement every day. I do not believe that it is normal for babies to go several days without a bowel movement. In my experience this usually leads to them becoming very uncomfortable and distressed.

Regardless of whether they are breastfed or formula-fed, once a baby is being weaned on to solid foods it is important to get the balance of fluids and solids, along with including the right types of solids, so that constipation does not become a problem.

If your baby is showing signs of constipation it is important to make sure that you have not increased solids so much that he has reduced his milk feeds. By seven months most babies will be taking between 6–8 tablespoons of puréed or pulsed food three times a day. If your baby is taking a lot more than this amount and has reduced his milk intake, it would be advisable to cut back on the amount of solids he is having, to ensure that he is drinking enough milk. You can also offer small amounts of cool boiled water in between feeds to help alleviate constipation. However, do not offer so much water that your baby reduces his milk or solid intake. Around 30ml (1oz) or so between feeds is usually enough to help with constipation, along with ensuring that your baby is eating the right types of foods.

Including enough fibre in your baby's diet is also important if you wish to avoid your baby becoming constipated. In *The Contented Child's Food Bible*, my co-author, Paul Sacher, a paediatric consultant, explains the importance of fibre: 'More often than not, constipation is caused by poor diet, particularly a lack of fibre. Diets full of processed foods are usually low in fibre and high in fat, which can slow down the rate at which foods move from the stomach through the digestive system. Fibre is not absorbed like the rest of the food we eat: it passes through the digestive system unchanged, acting like a broom and helping to sweep everything through the gut and keep it running smoothly.

'Fibre is found in cereals, fruits, vegetables and nuts. Unfortunately, many children do not eat fruit and vegetables or anything unrefined, such as wholegrain bread. The modern habit of grazing rather than eating proper meals probably also plays a part in the development of constipation because there is nothing bulky enough to encourage movement through the intestine. In addition, some children drink excessive amounts of milk, which does not contain any fibre and therefore exacerbates the problem.'

Paul recommends that one of the following high-fibre foods is included at each meal:

- lightly cooked vegetables such as broccoli and green beans; leave the skin on potatoes to maximise their fibre content; serve raw vegetables, e.g. carrots, baby sweet corn, mange tout, with dips, e.g. hummus, tzatziki or guacamole.

- pulses, e.g. baked beans, peas and lentils.

- wholegrain cereal, e.g. Weetabix, Shredded Wheat, porridge, muesli

- wholemeal, granary or rye bread, or white bread with added fibre

- oatcakes

- wholemeal pasta

- brown rice

- fruit (but make sure you leave the skin on (if edible) and wash it thoroughly)

Please note that unprocessed bran should not be given to children because it can cause blockage of the intestinal tract and also prevent absorption of minerals from food.

Sleep

What to expect

By the time a baby reaches six months he needs around two and a half to three hours' sleep a day, divided between two to three naps. Provided they are sleeping well at night, by the time they reach nine months babies will usually have reduced their sleep to around two and a half hours a day divided between two naps, usually one short one in the morning and a longer nap in the middle of the day. However, if a baby is not having a long nap in the middle of the day, they may need a short nap in the late afternoon if overtiredness is to be avoided at bedtime.

One of the biggest changes at this age is moving your baby into his own room. Because he will have been used to always having people around him during nap times and in the evening, it is best to do this gradually. Start off with settling him at either the morning or lunchtime nap in his own room. Once he is sleeping well at either of these times, you can then move on to settling him in his own room from 7pm. If your baby is not used to sleeping in the dark for his daytime naps, I would suggest that you allow him a small night light for naps and at bedtime, until he is used to sleeping in his own room. Gradually phase this out once he is settling and sleeping well at these times.

What to aim for

Babies who are sleeping well to 7am will still need a short morning nap of around 20–30 minutes if you want them to sleep longer at their nap in the middle of the day. The morning nap should be pushed to nearer 9.30/10am, with the lunchtime nap starting somewhere between 12.30pm and 1pm. I have observed that parents who do not push this first nap on during the second part of the first year often end up with their baby starting to wake earlier in the morning. If your baby is sleeping well and has to be woken at 7am, you can leave him to sleep later if this routine would fit in better with your own. He would not then need a morning nap, but may not manage to get through to 12.30pm for his lunchtime nap. If this happens, try bringing his lunch forward to 11.30am and put him down at 12.15pm for his lunchtime nap.

If your baby is still waking in the night, it is possible that he is having too much daytime sleep. Check that he is not sleeping more than three hours between 7am and 7pm and remember that allowing your baby to sleep past 7am may be part of the problem. A baby who is sleeping until 8am plus having a further two naps in the day may be getting too much sleep. A typical day in the life of a six- to nine-month-old baby who is sleeping well at night would look something like that outlined on page 182. If your baby is sleeping more during the day than this suggests, try gradually cutting back on his daytime sleep. He may be irritable for a week or so until he gets used to having less sleep, but if too much is the cause of his night-time waking, cutting back should result in him sleeping better at night.

Sleep Problems

Rolling from back to tummy

Between the ages of six and nine months the majority of babies start to roll from their back to their front and, until they learn to roll back on to their back, they can get quite upset. You may find that for a few weeks you have to help them resettle by rolling them back on to their back.

- To avoid this becoming a long-term habit, help your baby practise rolling backwards and forwards during his playtime. Lie down on the floor next to your baby and with the use of toys encourage him to roll back and forth to grab the toys. Some babies do not like going on to their tummy, but it really is important that they are put on their tummy several times a day, so that they have a chance to strengthen their muscles, learn to push themselves up and roll from their tummies to their backs.

● Once your baby has become confident about rolling back and forth from his tummy to his back at playtime and has become mobile in his cot it is a good idea to get him used to going down for some of his daytime naps on his tummy. Try not to rush to him the minute he cries out during his sleep times. Allow him a short spell to settle himself, otherwise he will become dependent on you to help him get back to sleep.

● Once he is used to rolling from his back to his tummy and tummy to back he will then progress to being able to push himself up fully with his hands to a crawling position. At this stage it is important that you do not rush to him immediately if he gets into a difficult position, allow him a short spell to see if he can get himself out of it. Also at this stage if he rolls on to his tummy and wants to sleep in that position, as long as he can manoeuvre himself around the cot there is no need to keep putting him on his back, and this can sometimes unsettle him further.

● Once he is happy to sleep in any position, I would advise putting him in a sleeping bag if you have not already done so, and removing the top sheet and any blankets. This will avoid the problem of him kicking the blankets off and getting cold in the night or getting into a tangle with the bedding.

Sitting up in the cot and not able to get back down

Another problem that you may face at this age is that your baby is able to get himself up to a sitting position from lying down, but can't manage to get himself back down again. When this happens you should start putting him into the cot sitting up instead of laying him down. Kneel down at the side of the cot so you are face-to-face with him, and encourage him to lay himself down. Almost make a game of it. Start by practising at his daytime naps, then once he's learned how to do it for himself, you can try it at bedtime. You will have to help him at first, but by being persistent in teaching him, he will soon learn to get himself from the sitting position to the lying position.

Early morning waking

By this stage, your baby should be sleeping through the night and, depending on your routine and the time you start your day, sleeping well until 7 or 8am. However, there are various reasons your baby might suddenly start waking earlier – even as early as 5.30 or 6am. Not only is this distressing for parents – who wants to start their day that early? – your baby may also become discontented.

- The most likely cause of sudden early morning waking is too much daytime sleep. However, you first need to rule out other causes, particularly hunger. Make sure that your baby is having enough milk for his age (see pages 180 and 195 for a guide), and if weaned that he is having a protein lunch and a carbohydrate-based tea.

- Check his room to make sure his sleeping conditions haven't changed, i.e. that there is no early morning light creeping in, and that the room is warm or cool enough, so you can rule out a temperature issue.

- If neither of the above is the case, it is most likely that your baby is sleeping too much during the day. The maximum amount of daytime sleep for a baby of this age is three hours, although all babies are different and some simply need less sleep than others. Any sleep that your baby has between 7am and 7pm (or equivalent if you're on a later schedule) needs to be included in this quota, so if you are letting your baby go back to sleep after he wakes then this time needs to be included, e.g. even if he sleeps 10 or 15 minutes past 7am you will need to reduce his morning nap by the same amount.

- For a few days the best thing to do is try to resettle your baby with a milk feed. Offer him as much of a feed as it takes to get him sleeping soundly until 7am, then you can start to look at his daytime naps and the total amount of time he is sleeping between 7am and 7pm. After a few days of giving him a feed so that he is sleeping soundly until 7am, you can very gradually reduce the amount of milk he has in the early morning, eventually eliminating it altogether. Remember, when offering him his first feed you should reduce the amount he normally would have at 7am by the amount he has had in the early morning, so he is not put off his breakfast solids.

- Now you can start to push the morning nap on and keep it to 30 minutes.

- Next, look at the time of his lunchtime nap. This should not be any earlier than 12.30pm to ensure that your baby will not be overtired by bedtime. Once you have shortened the morning nap you should find that the lunchtime nap will lengthen, until he is sleeping nearer to two hours.

- Less sleep during the day should mean that your baby is naturally less wakeful in the morning and more likely to drift back off to sleep himself if he does wake.

Dropping the third nap of the day

The third nap of the day is usually the first nap that babies will drop, usually somewhere between the age of three and four months. However, if a baby is not sleeping almost two hours at their second nap of the day, they will probably need a short nap late afternoon if they are to get through to bedtime without becoming overtired. Depending on how long they slept at lunchtime, this nap should be around 15–30 minutes. If they slept for around one and a half hours at lunchtime, then a 15-minute nap should get them through to bedtime; if they slept for less than an hour, then they would probably need nearer 30 minutes.

Night waking

I frequently read that between six and seven months babies are capable of sleeping an 11–12-hour night without a feed. In theory this is possibly true, but the reality is that unless a baby's feeding needs are being met properly during the day, it is very possible that any night wakings could be due to hunger. This is particularly so of breastfed babies if they are not getting a big enough milk feed after their bath. I believe that some babies may still need a late feed at 10/11pm until they are well established on three solids meals a day.

● If you have dropped the late feed and your baby suddenly starts waking up in the middle of the night or early morning, you should not discount hunger as the cause. Please refer to the feeding guide on pages 180–2 to check that your baby is receiving the right amount of solids and milk to sleep through the night. If your baby is not eating enough solids, you may find that either you have to reintroduce a late feed, or give him a feed when he wakes to ensure that his nights do not become very unsettled.

● However, with both breastfed and bottle-fed babies that are still feeding at the late feed and then waking up and looking for another feed around 5/6am, it could be that feeding twice in the night is the actual cause of them not taking enough solids during the day, and then genuinely needing to wake up and feed twice in the night. If this is the case it would be best to drop the late feed. While they may wake earlier in the night, if they take a big enough feed they will not need to wake up a second time, which means that the one feed in the night should reduce the total quantity of milk they take in the night, while also getting them to sleep through to the morning and increasing their appetite for solids the next day.

- As they increase their solids during the day, provided they are taking a full milk feed at bedtime, they should start to sleep later in the night, gradually reducing their need to feed in the night at all.

- The other cause of night waking at this age is too much daytime sleep. Please refer to pages 202–3 for a guide to how much daytime sleep your baby should be having. If he is having a lot more than the guidelines, gradually reduce the amount of sleep he is having until he is having near enough the recommended daily amount.

Not settling in the evening

Between six and nine months most babies need on average two and a half to three hours' sleep a day divided between two naps, possibly three depending on how long they sleep at lunchtime. At this age feeding should be well established so it is rare that a baby of this age doesn't settle due to hunger. The main causes are either too much daytime sleep or too little.

- If a baby is having too much sleep after 3pm they may not settle so quickly in the evening. It is therefore important to look at your baby's middle-of-the-day nap as at this age it really shouldn't be much more than two hours. If he is having over this, gradually cut back the amount your baby is sleeping by five minutes every day until he is settling well in the evening.

- If your baby is having a shorter lunchtime nap and you are giving him a late afternoon nap, you should gradually cut back the late afternoon nap until he is settling well in the evening.

- Sometimes a baby will have a short lunchtime nap and refuse to have a short late afternoon nap, therefore becoming overtired. If your baby is having less than one and a half hours at the lunchtime nap, it is important that you gradually reduce the morning nap until your baby is sleeping longer at lunchtime.

- If you are unable to reduce the morning nap because your baby is waking early in the morning, it is important that you resolve the early morning waking problem, so that his need for a longer morning nap is eliminated (see page 207 for how to deal with early morning waking).

Dummy addiction

A dummy can be a great comfort to some babies in the early days, particularly a sucky or sensitive baby. I have used dummies with the majority of the babies I have cared for and it never created a problem because I never allowed the baby to fall asleep with the dummy in his cot. However, an older baby who has become used to falling asleep with the dummy in the evening, will more than likely begin to wake up at least two or three times in the night because the dummy falls out and he then can't get back to sleep without it. This is not a problem that resolves itself and some babies can end up waking up every hour looking for the dummy. If not dealt with, dummy dependency can continue for two and sometimes three years. Unfortunately, it is not a problem that can be resolved without some degree of crying, but, fortunately, unlike some other problems, it is usually resolved within a few nights.

- Providing you follow the guidelines carefully, a period of sleep training, using the controlled crying method on page 365, should resolve the problem within three nights. However, it is very important that both parents are in agreement about going down this route, as if it is not carried out consistently it will simply make the problem worse. There is no point embarking on sleep training and then after a period a parent who cannot cope with the crying gives the baby back his dummy – it can make matters worse. To ensure that crying is kept to a minimum I would recommend that for a couple of days prior to eliminating the dummy you take the dummy away during your baby's daytime sleeps. On these days I would advise that you take your baby out in his buggy for naps, so that you're gradually decreasing his dependency on the dummy before you begin the sleep training. This is a much gentler way of reducing his dependency.

- On the first night of eliminating the dummy I would recommend that you stay in the room with your baby, reassuring him until he falls asleep, without actually holding him to sleep. Stand by the cot and if need be shush and pat him until he is asleep. If he wakes in the night repeat the same process as above.

- The second night I would stay in the room until he falls asleep, but allow 10-minute intervals between shushing and patting him. When you are not standing by the cot reassuring him, you can sit on a chair in the room and verbally reassure him. If he wakes in the night, repeat the same process as above.

- On the third night, settle your baby in his cot sleepy but awake and without the dummy, then leave the room. This is very difficult as your baby may start to scream but both you and your partner need to wait 10 minutes before just one of you enters the room. Gently stroke your baby's tummy for a couple of minutes, then quickly leave the room. It is important not to talk to him or take him out of his cot. Repeat this process for the next 45 minutes, ensuring the same person goes into the room, by which time your baby will fall asleep.

- If your baby wakes in the night you need to repeat the process.

- You also need to be sure not to confuse your baby so it is essential that you don't give him his dummy at daytime naps either. However, you also don't want him to get fretful at his naps and overtired, so take your baby for a long walk in his buggy at each of his daytime naps as the motion of the buggy should calm him and make him less likely to scream for the dummy.

- The next night follow the same procedure for settling your baby, only this time wait 15 minutes before going in. The following day take him out in his buggy again at nap times to ensure that he sleeps without the dummy and doesn't get overtired.

- On the third night allow him 20 minutes to settle without going in. At this point your baby should be sleeping through the night without the need for the dummy at all. The next day try to put your baby in his cot for daytime naps. If your baby does still need some kind of sucking or comfort, he will quickly find his thumb and within a week should be happy to settle himself in his cot without any crying at all.

General Problems

Boredom

Babies over six months can get particularly frustrated and bored. Unlike younger babies, they will not be content to lie for 20 minutes or so under the cot mobile or on the activity mat. The toys listed below are some that are popular with older babies. (Always check that they conform to British Standard BS5665.)

- Colourful balls are a great hit with older babies. Some have several buttons that, when pressed, make different sounds. Others are clear, with an object inside that wobbles when the ball is rolled.

- Activity centres that fix to the side of the cot or playpen are designed to help develop a baby's manual skills. They have a selection of dials, buttons and bells that make different sounds, and some incorporate a musical device. The one that is designed to look like a teddy bear is very popular.

- Baby bouncers that are suspended from a door or special frame are excellent for older babies who have enough neck control to support their heads.

- Soft toys, such as snakes, crocodiles and birds that are designed to squeak, crinkle, rattle and make different noises are great for a multi-sensory experience.

- Stacker toys, composed of different stackable shapes, will help develop your baby's hand and wrist control. Choose brightly coloured ones, where each shape has a different texture and makes a different sound.

Be careful to avoid overstimulation. I find it helps to have quiet toys and soft books for the wind down period before a nap or bedtime, and to keep noisy games, toys and high-level stimulation for the baby's wakeful, social time.

Separation anxiety

By the age of six months babies begin to realise they are separate from their mothers and may show signs of separation anxiety or stranger anxiety. The happy contented baby who was so easy-going and relaxed and who would happily go to anyone suddenly becomes clingy, anxious and demanding. He screams if his mother leaves the room for even a few minutes and often gets hysterical if approached by a stranger. Some babies will even get upset when relations they know well attempt to talk to them or pick them up. This behaviour is a totally normal part of the baby's development. All babies go through this stage to some degree between the age of six and 12 months, and it is usually around nine months that it becomes most obvious. In my experience, babies who are used to being with someone else on a regular basis usually suffer less from separation anxiety. If your baby suddenly becomes more clingy around this age, it is important to understand that he is not being naughty or demanding. Forcing him to go to strangers or leaving him alone in a room to play by himself will not solve the problem and may lead to him becoming more fretful and insecure. Because this stage often coincides with the time a mother returns to work, a baby who has always slept well at night can start to wake up in the night fretful and anxious. Responding quickly and positively to his anxiety rather than ignoring it will, in the long run, help him to become more confident and independent. However, it is important that you do not give your baby so much attention that he begins to feel that he is being rewarded for his night-time waking.

Although this stage can be very exhausting for a mother, it rarely lasts long. The following guidelines can help make this difficult period less stressful and hopefully keep any sudden night-time waking to a minimum.

● If you are planning to return to work when your baby is between six and 12 months, it is important that he gets accustomed to being left with someone else for short spells before he reaches six months of age. He should be gradually left for longer and longer periods until he is happy to be left for the length of time you will be separated once you go back to work. Ideally, he should have had a settling-in period with the childminder or nursery of a month – and a minimum of two weeks – before you go back to work.

● It is also important to get him used to large groups and new experiences long before you start back at work. Try to arrange regular play dates with a small group of the same mothers and babies. Once he appears to be happy and responding to the regular faces, increase the number of people and vary the venues.

● Provided you are confident that your baby is happy with his carer, do not prolong your goodbye. A hug and a reminder that you will be back soon, using the same approach and words each time you say goodbye will, in the long term, be more reassuring than going back to try to calm him.

● During this period advise your baby's carer that your baby must not be subjected to too many new things at once or to handling by strangers. The calmer and more predictable his routine, the more quickly he will get over his feelings of anxiety.

Fear of strangers

At around six months you might find that your sociable baby becomes much more wary of strangers. Don't let this worry you; it is a natural part of his development. It is thought that this fear is a biological response relating to our origins: for a baby to survive in a primitive environment, a fear of strangers was a protective response. We have an expectation that babies are happy to be handed to loving relatives and friends for cuddles when they are small, but even young babies can find being passed from one loving relative to the next, tiring and at times distressing.

- If your baby begins to cry when approached by strangers, or to look away when someone is trying to engage him, don't try to push him to communicate. It is much better to explain that your baby is becoming self-conscious and having a shy period, than to expect him to smile on cue!

- You can help your baby's response to friends and family members you see regularly by talking to him about them. If you have a photo montage on the wall, you can show your baby photographs and name the people in them.

- Role play can help too. Try giving your baby's toys the names of friends and family with whom you want him to become familiar.

- For close relatives or friends who spend time with your baby frequently it can be upsetting if he is distressed or tearful when he sees them, but this usually passes once the person has been there for a while.

- Discourage people from making too much fuss of your baby when they first arrive. Sometimes a baby can find physical proximity threatening. It is better if he is allowed to respond to a new person being around him in his own time, once he feels comfortable with the person, than when someone is attempting to make eye contact, communicate with and hold him.

● Although your baby will learn how to deal with greetings and attention as he grows up, some children remain shy. It is much better for you to adapt to this, and try to understand how it feels to be a shy child, than to push your child into situations where he feels distressed.

Going to nursery: the first day and beyond

If you have chosen a nursery, I imagine you have done so having researched and visited all the day nurseries in your local area. Personal recommendations are worthwhile, but remember that what suits one baby may not suit the different personality of another. Look for a nursery with a friendly, caring environment and one that does not have a high turnover of staff – your baby should not have to keep getting to know new faces. Many nurseries have a 'key worker' scheme in which one or two selected carers will take special responsibility for your child. This makes it easier for him as he can begin to relate to the familiar faces he will see every day.

Leaving your baby and going off to work for the first time is not easy and you will no doubt worry that your baby will feel abandoned. If you've been through a settling-in period at the nursery, this will make it much easier for you both. Do remember that many babies will cry at first when they are left at nursery and this is very normal. It is really hard to leave a crying baby, but if your baby is upset when you leave, that doesn't mean he is going to stay upset for the rest of the day. Nursery staff are usually adept at dealing with babies who react this way, and babies often stop crying fairly quickly once their parent has left. Most nurseries will be more than happy for you to call to check that your baby has settled down once you get to work.

Another aspect of returning to work that can come as a shock is the sense of guilt that many women feel. It isn't easy to leave your baby with someone else all day, particularly if you are working full-time and fairly long hours. It is inevitable that you will feel some guilt, but once your baby is used to being at nursery and you are used to being back at work, you may find that this is the best solution for your family. If you are fulfilled at work, this can have a positive effect on your relationship with your baby and the precious time spent together will be relished and enjoyed.

Your child's first day at nursery is a milestone, but it can be a daunting experience, overshadowed by worries and concerns. You're bound to feel some anxiety. There are quite likely to be some teething problems and it can take a while to get used to this major change in your lives, but feeling confident that you've made the right choices along the way, and knowing that you're as prepared as you can be, will make all the difference to you both. Below are some tips on how best to navigate this period and the potential hurdles that can arise.

- Expect your baby to take a little while to adapt to a nursery environment, and where possible, take steps to enable yourself to introduce him to his nursery gently. Leaving him for short trial sessions on a regular basis before you return to work will get him used to the new environment and will enable him to understand that you will always return to him at the end of the session. It will also help you to get used to leaving him.

● Don't be surprised if your baby finds the separation difficult at first. If you always use the same words when leaving him he will come to know the routine and realise that you will reappear again. In the beginning he may be a little tearful at being left each time. If you can build a friendly rapport with the staff, especially those directly involved with him, then he will learn to trust them as he sees you smiling and talking with them. Your body language and facial expressions will help him feel at ease. However you are feeling inside at the prospect of leaving him, by remaining cheerful, positive and smiling – particularly when saying goodbye – you will really help him get used to his new experience.

● Many parents are initially concerned about how their baby will cope with eating and sleeping alongside other babies when they have been used to the quiet of home. Most babies adapt amazingly well. You may find your baby does not sleep at nursery quite as long at lunchtime as he does at home, but this may lengthen once he grows used to the different noises and sights.

● Be aware that during the first few weeks, however well he sleeps at nursery, he may well be tired when he returns. The adjustments he needs to make, the new surroundings and people are a lot for him to take in. Although you are eager for him to keep his usual bedtime, in the first weeks after starting nursery you may need to make this earlier until he is more settled. As he may not be at nursery every day you can adjust bedtime depending on what has happened during the day. On the days he is at home and at weekends, you can remain on your present routine if it suits you. Once he has got used to being at nursery, he will probably manage to go back to his usual schedule, albeit most likely with a slightly shorter lunchtime nap.

- Once they start nursery some babies simply never manage to have a long lunchtime nap again and only manage an hour or even less. This can be a problem in the very early days until they adapt to getting through the day on a shorter lunchtime nap. If this is the case with your baby it may be that you have to tell nursery to let him have a slightly longer morning nap, if he will do so. His lunchtime nap, although shorter will then come later, but it will help him get through to bedtime without becoming so overtired. It may be that at nursery they have to follow this sleep pattern of the daytime sleep being split into two equal naps – in the morning and afternoon, as opposed to one shorter morning nap and a longer lunchtime nap. On the days he is at home, there is no reason why you can't switch this back to giving him the shorter nap in the morning and longer nap at lunchtime. I find that in time most babies will eventually adapt to a different routine at nursery to the one they have at home.

- If your baby will not take a longer morning nap and ends up having two shorter naps, then the other option is that when you pick him up from nursery you drive him around an extra 10 minutes, to see if he will take a short catnap in the car. Although this can seem like a real inconvenience at a time when you just want to get your baby home, in my opinion it is worth it if it helps your baby get through to bedtime without becoming overtired.

- Remember that if he has a good lunch and an early tea at nursery, you can't expect your baby to eat another full meal when he gets home. However, neither can you expect him to get through from 3.30/4pm to the morning without further solids. All that is needed is a small snack to get him through to bedtime happily; just be careful of offering him so much food that he reduces his bedtime milk feed. Some nurseries are prepared to offer babies a snack instead of a full tea at 3pm, so it is worth checking with your nursery if they are happy to do this, for the first few weeks at least. If not then you will need to balance out the solids your baby has at nursery with the solids he has when you get him home. As you still want him to take a good milk feed I would recommend that you offer solids no later than 5.45pm and ensure that you do not give him too big a meal, which might put him off his bedtime milk which is still important at this age. Because he will more than likely be quite tired and time is limited at this point in the day, I would recommend quick and easy meals, such as a small bowl of pasta with sauce, a thick vegetable soup with bread or mini sandwiches. For babies who are very tired and fussy at this time I used to find that a bowl of cereal would sometimes do the trick.

- As your child grows older, you should get regular updates from the nursery on his progress. He will at some point move on from the baby room into the next age group, and the activities on offer will become wider and more varied. Many children will stay at the same day nursery right through until they start school, while others will move on to different types of pre-school or nursery before this. As your child gets older, you are likely to see some positive benefits from time spent at nursery. It can help with social skills and development, and children who have been to nursery usually find the transition to school far easier.

If it goes wrong

Occasionally, problems can arise. A baby may not seem to have settled despite weeks of reassurance that things will get better, you may start to question the way things are done or feel unhappy with some aspects of the care your child is receiving.

This doesn't necessarily mean that you have chosen the wrong nursery as teething problems are not uncommon, but it is important that you address any worries you have right away rather than letting things build up.

- Talk to your child's key worker or to the nursery manager, and you may be able to resolve the situation fairly quickly.

- If you aren't happy after following the complaints procedure, don't feel that you can't look at other nurseries. It would be better to live through the disruption of moving nursery than to constantly worry that your child isn't being looked after in the way you would like while you are at work.

7

Nine to 12 Months

Between nine and 12 months your baby should be eating and enjoying all types of food, with the exception of food with a high fat, salt or sugar content. Peanuts and honey should also still be avoided. It is very important that your baby learns to chew properly at this stage. Food should be chopped or diced, although meat may still need to be pulsed or very finely chopped. By the end of his first year, your baby should be able to manage chopped meat.

Try to include some finger foods at every meal, and if he shows an interest in holding his own spoon, do not discourage these attempts – have two baby spoons when you are feeding an older baby and give him one to try to feed himself. When he repeatedly puts it in his mouth, load up the second spoon and let him try to get it into his mouth, quickly popping in any food that falls out. It is important that he enjoys his meals even if a certain amount of it lands on the floor. With a little help and guidance, from 12 months most babies are capable of feeding themselves part of their meal. I recommend trying to have breakfast or lunch with your baby so that he can copy you eating. By the end of this stage, he will be eating three full meals a day and when your baby reaches a year, you can replace the night-time bottle with a beaker too.

Some babies will start to show signs of separation anxiety by this stage, being suspicious of people they don't know. You may notice that your baby seems more clingy when strangers are around or wary of them. He may even try to hide his face from new people, or turn his head away from them. This is a perfectly normal stage of his development, but it can be difficult if it coincides with you going back to work and employing a nanny or childminder, or taking him to a nursery. I have found that babies who spend time with more than one adult are less prone to separation anxiety than those who are exclusively looked after by a sole carer. Separation anxiety can be upsetting if your child is visibly distressed by your friends or family, but try to remember that this is a normal phase of development. At the same time, babies at this age often start to find other children fascinating and may seem to enjoy the company of their peers.

Babies often start to move around more during this period, and your baby may be crawling or bottom shuffling. By the time he reaches a year, he may be able to walk if you are holding on to him, and he may even be capable of taking his first few steps unaided. As your baby gets more mobile, you will want to make sure that you have child-proofed your home as best you can with stair gates and safety catches to help prevent accidents, and you will need to move anything breakable or potentially dangerous out of your baby's reach. By the end of this phase, your baby is fast becoming a toddler.

Feeding

What to expect

Between nine and 12 months babies need a minimum of 500ml (18oz) of milk a day, inclusive of milk used in solids. This amount is usually divided between three milk feeds of 180–240ml (6–8oz) in the morning, 120–150ml (4–5oz) mid afternoon and a 210–240ml (7–8oz) bottle at bedtime. By the time they reach one year this should be down to a minimum of 350ml (12oz) a day, usually divided between two feeds and any used in solids. Babies who are allowed to drink excessive amounts of milk, which is more likely to happen when being fed from a bottle, are more likely to become fussy about solids as they fill up on milk and are not hungry for their solid food.

If you have not already done so it is important to get your baby drinking milk from a beaker. I would recommend that you start by offering the mid-afternoon milk feed from a beaker. Do not worry if your baby reduces the amount he usually takes at this feed as many babies drop it by the age of one year anyway. Once a beaker is introduced in the afternoon, and then the morning, the daily amount of milk the baby takes usually drops slightly, because most babies drink less first thing in the morning and mid afternoon when the milk is given in a beaker. Once you have established your baby on a beaker mid afternoon and first thing in the morning, provided he has shown that he can take 150ml (5oz) from the beaker, you can then look to replacing the 210–240ml (7–8oz) bottle at bedtime with a drink of milk from a beaker. Between nine months and one year most babies become more efficient at drinking from a beaker, so your baby should manage to drink between 180ml (6oz) and 240ml (8oz) at bedtime.

Babies who are still being exclusively breastfed should have all their water and any well-diluted juice offered to them from a beaker by the time they reach one year of age.

What to aim for

The majority of meals at this stage should consist of food that has been chopped, sliced or diced and each meal should include some finger foods. This is also a good time to introduce raw vegetables and salad foods. Your baby should be given a spoon and encouraged to feed himself with some of his food at mealtimes.

Between nine months and one year a typical day for a baby waking at 7am could look something like the following. If you are starting your day earlier or later the routine below can be adapted accordingly.

7am	milk from a beaker followed by breakfast
9.30/45am–10am	short nap (15–30 minutes)
10am	some babies may need a small drink of water and a small snack
11.45am/12 noon	solids with a drink of water from a beaker

12.30pm–2.30pm	nap (2 hours)
2.30pm	milk feed or drink of water from a beaker
5pm	solids with a small drink of water or milk from a beaker
6/6.30pm	bath
6.30/7.30pm	milk feed, story, teeth cleaning and bed

Feeding Problems

Refusing the bedtime bottle/low bedtime milk intake

As they reach their first year some babies start to cut back or get very fussy with their bedtime milk and can drink as little as 90–120ml (3–4oz). This reduction can often result in early morning waking, so to avoid this happening I would recommend that you check the list below.

● The first thing to look at is the mid-afternoon milk feed. If your baby is still having this milk feed from a bottle and drinking more than 120–180ml (4–6oz), this could be the possible cause of him reducing his bedtime milk. I would recommend that this milk feed is reduced to no more than 120ml (4oz) to see if that will increase the amount of milk your baby takes at bedtime.

- If you have already reduced your baby's mid-afternoon milk feed I would recommend that you replace that milk feed with water and move the feed earlier, just prior to his lunchtime nap. Because it is not long since he has eaten his lunch, he will be less likely to take such a big feed, and giving it to him prior to his nap will allow a longer time between the milk feed and his solids at 5pm. You may find that he gets hungry a little earlier than usual and that is fine as you can bring his tea forward by 15 minutes, which in turn will mean he is more hungry for his evening milk.

- Another cause of a baby being fussy with his bedtime milk is being fed excessive solids at teatime. This is more likely to happen if a baby is still being served his food in a puréed or pulsed form and is eating in excess of 8 tablespoons of food. Try cutting his solids back slightly to see if that helps increase his bedtime feed.

- Having too short a gap between teatime solids and bedtime milk is another reason your baby may cut back his milk. Try to allow at least one and a half hours between solids and his bedtime milk. Bringing his tea forward by 15 minutes will also sometimes help increase the bedtime milk feed. (For example, if tea is usually around 5pm and milk around 6.30pm but your baby is not taking enough milk, then solids could come forward to around 4.45pm.)

- When structuring milk feeds you should aim to get your baby drinking nearer to 180–210ml (6–7oz) at bedtime. If you have to cut out the mid-afternoon feed to achieve this and your baby is less than a year and only taking 150–180ml (5–6oz) in the morning, it would mean that his daily milk intake will be 330–370ml (11–13oz), which is about 150ml (5oz) short of the recommended amount for a baby between the ages of nine and 12 months. This shortage can be added to your baby's food in his breakfast cereal and by offering him plenty of milk sauces in his meals. Once he reaches a year he needs a minimum of 350ml (12oz) of milk a day, which he can easily get from two milk feeds a day – one first thing in the morning and the second in the evening.

● Between nine and 12 months most babies become much more active as they begin to crawl and pull themselves up and 'cruise' around the furniture. The extra physical activity can cause them to become overtired around teatime. If this is the case with your baby I would recommend that you try giving him an extra 15 minutes' sleep at lunchtime. If he refuses to sleep longer, it would be advisable to bring forward his tea so that he does not get overtired and refuse to eat.

Fussy feeding with solids

Between nine and 12 months it is important that most of your baby's food is served sliced or diced. As your baby's growth and weight gain start to slow down at this age, continuing to serve puréed or pulsed food means that you could be overfeeding your baby, which is often a cause of fussiness at mealtimes. Understandably, if your baby is used to eating 6–8 tablespoons or more of puréed or pulsed food at mealtimes and is suddenly getting fussy after 3 or 4 tablespoons, you may worry that he is not getting enough to eat.

- Excessive milk intake is the other main cause of babies of this age being fussy with food. As I explain on page 230, it is still important that your baby has a good milk feed at bedtime, but look closely at the rest of his daytime milk and see if he is either drinking too much milk or having too much milk too close to his mealtimes.

- It's also worth taking a look at what his intake of other fluids is and whether he is perhaps having too much to drink during his meals or too close to his mealtimes. Try to offer other fluids around one and a half hours before his meals. And at mealtimes encourage him to eat most of his meal before drinking large amounts of fluids. Some babies will get fussy with solids and will not eat until they have had a drink. If this is the case put just 30ml (1oz) or so of water in his beaker initially, then once he has eaten a fair amount of solids you can top the beaker up with more water.

- Just as it is important to time when you give fluids between meals, the same should be said of snacks. Offering snacks too close to mealtimes or offering the wrong types of snack can be the cause of babies being fussy with their solids.

- At this age babies are much more aware of colour and texture, so how you present your baby's meals is important if he is not to get bored. Continuing to purée or pulse all the food can also lead to a baby becoming more fussy through boredom.

- Try to stick to regular mealtimes and, if your baby is fussy the minute you put him in the high chair, it is better to take him out immediately and try a few minutes later rather than cajole or force him to eat. If he is still fussy 20 minutes later it is better to skip the meal and wait until his next scheduled meal or snack than start offering him alternatives.

- It is often around this age that more processed foods are introduced to a baby's diet. While it is fine to use commercial food occasionally, be careful that you are not offering them too much or too often as processed foods can be high in sugar. Tinned soups and tinned fruit contain sugar, as do baked beans. Some yoghurts can also contain a lot of sugar. If you give your baby commercial foods too often, it is likely he will become addicted to them because of the sugar content then start to become fussy and refuse home-cooked foods. If you are using ready-made food always check the list of ingredients on the label and avoid those foods which have a high amount of sugar, starch and filler in them.

Although I advise offering a selection of finger foods to babies of this age the choice should not be endless. At this age the amount a baby eats at individual meals can become very erratic and it is best never to force the baby to feed. Allow a certain length of time, but if it becomes obvious that he is not interested, clear the food away. He should not be coaxed or cajoled into eating – all babies will eat well if they are hungry enough and not overtired. It is best to judge a baby's food intake over several days at this age, not by what he eats at individual meals.

Refusing vegetables in a diced or sliced form

Some babies who have happily eaten vegetables puréed in a casserole will often become quite fussy when offered them in diced or sliced form.

- If you find that your baby is regularly refusing vegetables I would recommend that you try offering them to him at the beginning of the meal, before offering the protein and carbohydrates. You will be more likely to have success if you do not put a huge amount of food on the plate. Start off with 2 tablespoons of sliced or diced vegetables and put them on a plate for your baby to share with you. A little role play, including a couple of his favourite toys, can often work as you can pretend to feed the teddies and eat some yourself. Even if he only takes a minuscule amount that will be a start. I often start by giving a baby of this age just a teaspoon of vegetables and it can take several weeks before they will take a decent amount, but I find that offering very small amounts and increasing them slowly over a longer period of time works well with a lot of the babies who have become fussy about eating vegetables prepared in this way. To ensure that your baby is receiving the important nutritional content of vegetables you can continue to offer vegetables disguised in soups and pasta sauces.

- This is also a good time to introduce your baby to raw vegetables and salad vegetables. Some babies actually prefer raw vegetables to cooked ones. Serving crunchy vegetables such as carrot, cucumber and peppers with a hummus or salsa dip can really work well with some babies.

● You can also try spreading vegetable purées on toast or rice cakes, so that your baby gets used to eating them more textured.

CASE STUDY: Theo, aged 11 months

Problem: Refusing to eat at mealtimes

Cause: Timing of drinks and continuing to offer mashed foods

Theo had always been a good feeder, enjoying a wide range of freshly cooked foods. At around eight months, his mother noticed he was starting to reject more and more of his favourite meals. By the time she contacted me, Theo had reached 10 months and mealtimes had become a battleground with him clamping his mouth shut the minute a spoon was put anywhere near his mouth. His mother would try lots of different tactics to try and get him back to his old eating habits. She would spend ages singing, clapping and playing all sorts of games at mealtimes to get Theo to smile so he would take just one extra mouthful. If this approach failed she would then try offering him endless choices of meals, with him often taking no more than a mouthful from each choice.

When I received Theo's food diary I could see that there were several very obvious things not helping his feeding problems. One was the timing of his drinks, which were too close to mealtimes and taking the edge off his appetite; another was the fact that Theo was

---

still drinking his morning and evening milk from a bottle. He was consuming over 240ml (8oz) at both of these feeds, which was also taking the edge off his appetite.

I advised Theo's mother to offer him no more than 180ml (6oz) from a beaker first thing in the morning and no more than 210ml (7oz) from his bottle in the evening. These amounts, along with milk used in cereals, would still exceed 350ml (12oz), the minimum recommended at one year of age. Any other fluid should be offered midway between meals, not an hour before. At mealtimes I advised that Theo should not be given his juice until he had eaten at least half of his solids.

It was also obvious from the food diary that most of Theo's food was still being mashed and mixed up and that very little finger food was being offered. I explained that babies of Theo's age become interested in the colour, texture and shape of their food and I suspected he had become very bored with all his food still being mashed and mixed up into one bowl. It was very important that he should be offered a selection of finger foods at most meals and that he should be allowed to feed himself, regardless of how messy he got.

Theo's feeding did improve considerably, although he still had days when he was fussy. As he had just started learning to walk, I suspected that tiredness might also be a cause of his fussiness and I advised his mother to start his meals slightly earlier on days when he had been extremely energetic.

Gagging or coughing when offered foods with lumps

A bad experience with a lump of food stuck in the throat can be quite scary for a baby and may be enough to make him refuse to swallow any foods containing lumps. On the other hand, being overly cautious and not offering your baby foods with lumps can lead to problems later on, as learning to chew is a step on the way to learning to talk. I have encountered families where the baby has coughed and spluttered after eating a particular food, causing such distress to the parents that they have reverted to puréed foods and stayed there. Not offering foods of different consistencies and failing to challenge your child's feeding abilities will stunt his development.

● In many cases, gagging is behavioural and a baby's way of controlling what foods he will and won't eat. If your baby gags and you immediately offer him puréed food, he will quickly learn that gagging leads to a 'soft option'. If he gags, remain calm, do not make a big fuss, reassure him, then offer the food again.

● If your baby continually gags or coughs when being fed, he may have a medical problem and should be assessed by a speech and language therapist who is trained in swallowing and feeding problems. Speak to your GP about this.

● It is important never to leave babies alone when they are eating in case they choke. Make sure you are familiar with the procedure for dealing with a choking baby. Having said that, choking on foods is very rare, and as long as you are present when your child eats, you should not be scared to offer foods that contain lumps. Obviously, foods such as whole nuts and grapes should be avoided.

Refusing food from the spoon

Between nine and 12 months it is very common for babies suddenly to start refusing foods from the spoon you offer him. When this happens it is really important that you do not force the issue. It is part of a baby's natural development to want to take control of his own feeding and forcing him to take food from a spoon could lead to long-term feeding issues.

● Allowing your baby to take control of his own feeding is really important, even if it gets very messy. The key thing is not to force him to eat. Also remember that at this age the amount of food a baby eats does normally reduce. You may find that some days your baby will eat loads and other days he will seem to eat hardly anything. Try to analyse his food intake over three or four days as opposed to day by day.

● By this stage most babies will have been taking on average 6–8 tablespoons of food at mealtimes. You may find that after 2 or 3 tablespoons your baby starts to clamp his mouth shut and refuse any further food. When this happens it is better to split the meal into a small amount of solids from the spoon and then make the remainder of his meal up with a selection of finger foods. If you keep forcing him to take the amount he used to eat happily you could end up with him refusing to take food from the spoon altogether.

- If your baby goes through a stage of refusing food altogether from a spoon, try puréeing his casseroles or meat and vegetables together and spreading it on toast or small pieces of bread roll.

Screaming when put in the high chair

At this age the two main reasons most babies get upset when they are put in the high chair is either overtiredness or they are simply not ready to eat. This often coincides with the morning nap being reduced or eliminated.

- If you have just reduced your baby's morning nap, or have eliminated it altogether, see if overtiredness is the cause by bringing his lunch forward slightly until his body clock is totally used to his new nap times.

- If that doesn't solve the problem you should then look at how much your baby is eating at breakfast and what snacks he is having and at what time. Around this stage the majority of babies do reduce the amount they eat and it could be that your baby is simply not ready for lunch. If he is having it much before 12pm you could try delaying it by 15 minutes to see if that resolves the problem. If not then I would try reducing his breakfast and mid-morning snack for a few days, to see if that helps things.

- If he continues to scream when put in his high chair it would be worth trying to put the high chair in a different room for a short spell to see if a change of scenery helps.

- And finally, if none of the above have any effect, I would abandon the high chair for a week and try giving him his meal in a booster seat that attaches to an adult dining chair so that you both can sit at the table together. You will probably find that after a short spell away from the high chair he will be happy to go into it again.

Throwing food on the floor

This is a problem that often occurs at this stage – babies will start to play up, refusing to eat and throwing food around. If this happens, quietly and firmly say 'no' and remove his plate. Do not make a fuss or try to cajole him, wait 10 minutes or so and then offer the food again. If he still doesn't want to eat, end the meal and do not offer substitutes. Do not offer him a biscuit or yoghurt half an hour later, as a pattern will soon emerge where he will refuse lunch knowing he will get something sweet if he plays up enough. He should be left until the next meal or scheduled snack time.

CASE STUDY: Tim and Ollie, twins aged 11 months

Problem: Refusing finger foods

Cause: Too-small appetites

At almost a year old, twins Tim and Ollie were underweight and only interested in eating puréed food for their main meals. They had both suffered from reflux since they were three months and getting them to take even the minimum daily requirement of milk had been a challenge until they were about 11 months. They had finally started to drink 'enough' milk, but their weight gain was still very poor and their parents had problems progressing from puréed food to more textured, grown-up food.

When their parents contacted me for help, the first thing we had to focus on was making sure the twins gained weight, which meant increasing the amounts of solids they ate and decreasing their milk intake. Only once their weight gain had started improving could we focus on textured food.

Although the twins had finally started to drink 'enough' milk I told their parents that at a year this should be cut back in order to ensure they started taking solids as their main food source. The boys were having around 630–720ml (22–25oz) a day divided between three feeds and I wanted them to reduce this to around 510ml (18oz) a day as by 12 months they should only be drinking a minimum of 350ml (12oz). I advised the parents to give them 150ml (5oz) first thing in the morning and mid afternoon, followed by 210ml (7oz) in the evening. I also suggested that they switch their 'hungrier baby' formula milk back to first stage milk, as the composition of the 'hungry' milk is such that it would be filling the boys up and reducing their appetite for solids. This advice worked almost immediately.

With less milk over the course of a day, the twins' parents were able to give them larger portions of the puréed foods they loved without too much problem. They gave them a full range of foods and I advised adding fat and calories where possible – butter, cheese, full-fat milk, olive oil, etc. They did this for a month and were thrilled to see that both boys put on weight. During this time, I also advised the twins' parents always to offer finger foods. Although they were happy to take toast, rice cakes, soft biscuits, etc. most other finger foods were rejected. However, their parents made sure that they always had something new to try.

Once the twins had starting putting on weight, I advised giving them their favourite foods but alongside this to start to give them some different, slightly more textured foods, such as soft cubes of vegetables or pasta in a smooth sauce. While Tim seemed to enjoy them, Ollie didn't! He would more often than not spit the bits out or reject the food altogether. His mother kept on trying but also ensured Ollie was given meals he would eat happily to ensure he ate something.

At this point I also advised that the twins started to have their afternoon milk cut down, but not out. They didn't seem as hungry for it anymore and often only took 15–30ml (½–1oz), so their mother didn't press them to take any more and just ensured they had water when they needed it.

At around this time, the twins' feeding problems had been going on for what seemed to their mother a very long time and she was starting to feel desperate. I had a long talk with her to reassure her that adapting to new things was going to take the boys time, and any anxiety they sensed in her wasn't going to help the situation and would affect them. We talked through the facts: that they are slim boys; however as both she and her husband were lean toddlers, this was probably genetic. Also they were incredibly active, so they were burning up their calories quickly. The main thing I made their mother realise was that they would not starve; all babies/toddlers will eat when they are hungry. This last point gave their mother confidence to be more relaxed when feeding them and stopped her resorting to puréed food if the twins wouldn't eat the textured food she offered.

With this new confidence we continued to move the twins on to textured food. Again we revisited their feeding routine and made four key amendments: having their morning milk and breakfast earlier; only giving them yoghurt and fruit for breakfast instead of porridge; adding more textures to the puréed foods they enjoyed at lunchtime (i.e. peas, bits of chicken, couscous); and dropping their afternoon milk completely. This strategy worked quite quickly with Tim and he seemed to enjoy his food, but Ollie wasn't convinced. I advised their mother to give Ollie porridge if he didn't eat his lunch in order to give him some carbohydrates to sustain him.

Within a few days, the twins were definitely eating a bit better but they started waking earlier and earlier in a very grumpy mood. Normally their mother would be able to leave them chatting in their cots until just before 7am, even if they woke at 6am, but not anymore. They woke any time from 5.15am on and by 6am would be screaming.

They would then guzzle their milk and cry for more when they'd finished their bottles. I concluded that they weren't getting enough food to sustain them through the night and advised giving them baby rice with a small amount of food after their tea in order to boost their carbohydrates. I also advised their mother to cut their morning nap from 45 minutes to 20 minutes but increase their lunchtime nap from 1 hour 20/30 minutes to 1 hour 40 minutes. I again advised that their mother wouldn't necessarily see a change overnight as their systems needed to adapt to it. After three days of not much difference they suddenly seemed to click back into their normal sleeping habits; in fact they started sleeping even later until around 7am.

Three months on, and although it had been slow, progress was made, particularly with Tim. He is now happy with more textured food and will try most finger foods. Ollie, who has always been the trickier one food-wise, is also definitely better at taking his textures than he was three months ago. It was never going to be a speedy process but sometimes slow and steady is the best way forward.

Sleep

What to expect

Between nine and 12 months most babies will be having around two to two and a half hours' sleep a day, divided between two naps, provided that they are eating well and consistently sleeping

11–12 hours at night. Around this age some babies who have slept really well to nearer 6/7am in the morning may suddenly start to wake up earlier or reduce the amount of time they sleep at their middle-of-the-day nap. This is usually a sign that the baby is ready to cut back further on daytime sleep. Some babies who start waking up around 5am and managing to get happily through to nearer 9/9.30am before needing a nap, may need their daytime sleep cut to a strict two hours. I have had experience of babies who have started waking regularly at 5am and the only way to resolve the problem was to cut their daytime sleep to a 15-minute morning nap and a one-and-three-quarter-hour middle-of-the-day nap.

Another cause of early morning waking is when a baby starts to reduce the amount of sleep he has at his middle-of-the-day nap. When this happens the baby tends to get tired more quickly in the late afternoon. This results in parents putting him down either too early or too late, at which point he goes off to sleep overtired. Both of these can contribute to early morning waking. Therefore if your baby is cutting down on his middle-of-the-day sleep, it would be advisable to reduce the amount he sleeps in the morning, until he is back to napping longer at the middle-of-the-day nap.

What to aim for

If you want to avoid the problem of your baby waking up earlier in the morning or reducing his lunchtime nap I would advise that you keep a close eye on the morning nap. A baby who is sleeping well at night should not need a long nap in the morning, therefore I would recommend that if he is not already doing so that you gradually push the morning nap later and later until it is coming somewhere between 9.45am and 10am and limit it to around 15–20 minutes so that he still settles and sleeps well for his longest nap in the middle of the day.

If your baby has got into the habit of waking at 5/6am and not going back to sleep, it can initially be difficult to reduce the morning nap. When this happens I would recommend that for a few days you allow a 45-minute nap in the morning. Allowing a longer nap for this short period will enable you to push his lunchtime nap much later and only allow him one and a quarter hours. Once your baby is sleeping a bit later, it is important that you then push the morning nap on as late as possible and reduce it to around 15–20 minutes. Then go back to giving your baby somewhere between one hour and 40 or 45 minutes for the middle-of-the-day nap.

If your baby is showing signs of wanting to sleep to nearer 8am, then I would recommend that you eliminate the morning nap altogether to ensure that he sleeps well at the middle-of-the-day nap.

Sleep Problems

Not settling well at the lunchtime nap

While most babies are still having two naps a day at this age, there are some who need less daytime sleep and one of the indications of this is that they take longer to settle to sleep at their afternoon nap. If your baby is taking longer to settle for his afternoon nap

I would recommend that you start to push his morning nap later and gradually reduce it until he is settling to sleep quickly again for his lunchtime nap. Once you reach the stage where he is having only 10/15 minutes in the morning and is still taking a while to fall asleep, then it would be sensible to cut out the morning nap altogether. If you allow him to reduce his lunchtime nap, you could end up with him being overtired at bedtime, which can have a knock-on effect and cause early morning waking. Once you drop the morning nap, you may find that for a short spell you need to bring his lunchtime nap slightly earlier – see the next problem for more detailed guidelines on dealing with nap times.

Early morning waking and cutting out the morning nap

When early morning waking suddenly appears at this stage, it is often a sign that a baby is ready to reduce his overall daily sleep and perhaps even drop the morning nap.

It can be tricky going from two naps down to one, and getting rid of the morning nap often results in a baby's midday nap being brought forward too early. An earlier lunchtime nap means an earlier wake-up time, which can have a knock-on effect the next day where the baby can become so overtired when he is put to bed at night that he goes into a deep sleep very quickly. This can then lead to early morning waking. In order to avoid overtiredness, some parents resort to putting their baby to bed earlier, but this also can have a knock-on effect with the baby waking up earlier in the morning.

With either scenario, a vicious circle can quickly evolve where the baby gets into the habit of waking up early. He can then become so tired that, rather than the parents being able to reduce and eliminate the morning nap, they find themselves having to increase it so their baby gets through happily to the lunchtime nap.

If your baby is over nine months and showing signs of waking earlier, not being ready for his morning nap or reducing his lunchtime nap (all signs that a change in sleeping needs is imminent), I would suggest the following tips to help to prevent early morning waking becoming a problem.

- Gradually push the first nap of the day later in the morning and reduce it to 15 minutes. This will allow you to push the afternoon nap on and the reduction of the morning nap should encourage your baby to sleep better at lunchtime, which will also help avoid him going down overtired in the evening. What many parents do not realise is that during the transition period of dropping the morning nap, they may need to slightly reduce the lunchtime nap, until the morning one is totally eliminated so that their baby's overall daytime sleep is reduced. Once the morning nap has successfully been dropped, the lunchtime nap can then be slightly increased again.

- If your baby is showing signs of not being ready to sleep at 9.45–10am, do not be tempted to drop the morning nap as doing it too early will mean that his lunchtime nap could come too soon, resulting in him going to bed either overtired or too early. Keep pushing your baby's morning nap on until he is managing to stay awake until close to 11am, then allow a nap of no more than

10 minutes. Once he is managing to get through to 12.45–1pm for his lunchtime nap, you should be able to cut out the 10-minute nap and get him through to around 12.15–12.30pm for his nap, which would then be increased back to two hours. If you find that your baby is becoming too tired to eat a proper lunch, you can always bring his lunch forward slightly for a short period until his body clock adjusts to the new nap times. I usually find that once they have had lunch babies perk up enough to get through to 12.15–12.30pm.

Resisting bedtime

At this age a lot of babies who have settled well at bedtime will suddenly start to resist sleep when they are put in their cot, with many screaming the minute they go near it. In my experience the most common cause is too much daytime sleep. Usually, because a baby has been sleeping really well for months parents have continued to give them a long morning nap of around 45 minutes, followed by a two-hour nap in the afternoon.

- The first thing to look at is the timing of the morning nap. If your baby is going down at around 9am or 9.30am, I would advise that you gradually push the nap on a little – to 9.45/10am – while also reducing it until your baby is having only 20 minutes. Once you have pushed on the morning nap, you would then need to push the lunchtime nap to around 12.30/1pm so that your baby doesn't end up getting overtired at bedtime. By reducing the morning nap time to 20 minutes you should fairly quickly see an improvement and your baby should go back to settling well in the evening. However, it is important to keep a close eye on his daytime sleep as some babies do actually need to drop the morning nap between nine months and one year if they are to settle well in the evening and sleep to nearer 6/7am in the morning. See page 248 for more about how to reduce and eliminate the morning nap.

- Occasionally I do find the cause of the baby resisting bedtime is overtiredness. Again this is usually linked to the morning nap. Some babies who are ready to cut their daytime sleep, will often cut back on their afternoon nap first. This is more likely to happen with babies who are being allowed a longer morning nap. When the baby cuts back on the lunchtime nap, it means he has to be awake longer in the afternoon from the time he wakes from his nap until he goes to bed, which in turn can result in him being overtired and resisting bedtime. The solution to this problem again involves reducing and moving on the morning nap, so that your baby has less sleep in the morning, which will encourage him to sleep slightly longer at his lunchtime nap, ensuring that he does not go down in the evening overtired.

CASE STUDY: Megan, aged 12 months

Problem: Waking several times a night

Cause: Standing up in the cot

Megan had always slept well but at the age of 10 months suddenly started to wake up two or three times a night. Her parents would find

---

her standing up at the end of the cot crying. They realised that although she was able to pull herself up to a standing position using the spars of the cot, she had not learned how to get herself down again. They would lay her down and quickly leave the room, and within minutes she would settle herself back to sleep. The same pattern would happen at least one more time in the night and, more often than not, twice more.

I explained that many parents went through a period when they had to go in and help their baby lie back down but I had rarely heard of this happening two or three times a night; it was more likely to happen near morning when the baby came into a light sleep. When I asked about Megan's daytime naps, her parents told me that she had always slept well, and was still having 45 minutes in the morning and up to two and a half hours at lunchtime. I was sure that the reason Megan was waking and standing up so often in the night was partly due to her parents not cutting back her daytime sleep.

Between nine and 12 months the majority of babies cut down on the amount of sleep they need, and parents should always look at the amount of daytime sleep their baby is having if there is a change in the night-time pattern. I advised Megan's parents to continue to help her to settle in the night when they found her standing up, but at nap times and in the evening they should put her in the cot and by holding her hands on the spars help her to get down to her sleeping position. It was important that they helped her but as she became more capable, assisted her less and less.

I also suggested that they cut her morning nap back to 30 minutes for the next three days, and then cut her lunchtime nap back to a strict two hours. Within days of cutting down her daytime sleep, Megan was only waking up and pulling herself up twice in the night. By the end of the first week Megan was also lowering herself down to her sleeping position without any help from her parents. I then advised her parents that they should now adopt the same procedure in the night as they had at nap times and in the evening. For several nights they should assist Megan to get down, then gradually help less and less. At the end of the second week they would go in and stand by the cot and tell Megan to lie down but not help her. It took a further week before Megan stopped calling out for her parents in the night. Whether she was standing up and getting herself back down or just not getting up at all they weren't sure, but everyone was getting a good night's sleep and Megan went back to being a very happy little girl during the day.

When this problem first arises, parents should immediately start to teach their baby to lower himself when put in the cot, so that a long-term dependency does not develop. It is also important to look at how much sleep a baby is having during the day, as too much will result in him having much more energy in the night when he comes into his light sleep.

Getting stuck in the corner of the cot

Once a baby starts to crawl and move around his cot, he will often crawl right into the corner and get stuck. When this happens you may find that for a few weeks you will have to go in and move your baby further down the cot until he learns how to manoeuvre himself out of the corner. I have heard some parents say that the baby should just be left as he is as that is the only way he will learn to get himself out of a difficult position. While this may work for some babies, more often than not it just results in a baby working himself up into a state and by the time the parents do relent and go in to help him, he is wide awake and can often take an hour or so to settle back to sleep.

When you find yourself in this situation I would suggest that you immediately go to your baby and help him out of the corner. Then ensure that during his awake times during the day you put him in his cot for short spells to play so that when he is awake he can practise how to get out of a difficult position. Although it might feel as though your baby's sleeping is backtracking, you shouldn't worry and should simply view it as part of your baby's normal development. This stage rarely lasts longer than two or three weeks and the more practice your baby has during the day of manoeuvring around his cot, the sooner he will learn to get out of the difficult position and go back to sleep quickly at night.

PART 3
The Toddler Years

8

One to Two Years

As he passes his first birthday, your baby will move towards being a toddler and over the next year you will see some big developmental changes. Your child will start to learn to walk and talk, and although each child develops at his own individual pace, this is a time at which he starts to have a degree of independence as he begins to be able to do some things for himself, such as undressing – you will have to learn to adapt to this too.

Physical independence is one of the most marked changes during the 12–18-month phase. Most children take their first steps soon after their first birthday, but this does vary hugely from one child to another and it can take a while for confident walking to become established. Learning to walk can lead to some frustrations if a child is wobbly for a while and is falling over a lot, but he will gradually become more stable with time.

Once your toddler has been walking independently for about six weeks or so, you can take him to a shoe shop for his first proper shoes where you should make sure he is properly measured and fitted. Getting your child's first shoes can feel like a real milestone in his life for you as parents.

The other big change during this period is in your child's ability to communicate as he will start to learn to talk. It is important to remember that the more you talk to your child, the easier it will be for him to learn to communicate with you as toddlers learn to speak by listening. Do remember that it is perfectly normal to find it hard to make out much of what he is trying to say as he starts to try to speak. By the time your toddler gets to 18 months, he will on average have a vocabulary of somewhere between 20 and 40 words.

From 18 months, your child's speech will likely go through a rapid phase of development and by the age of two he will start to make the foundations of sentences. By two he may be able to put two words together to explain concepts or to tell you what he wants: a two-year-old may say 'Daddy gone' or 'more milk', but he won't yet be able to manage more complex sentences. Continue to ensure that you talk to him as much as you can, always explaining what you are doing as you go about your daily activities. Finding quiet periods to read to your child and sing nursery rhymes together will really help too.

Try not to constantly compare your child's speech with that of his peers as children do develop at very different speeds. One toddler may be chatting away happily when another can barely manage a few words and yet both can be within normal ranges of development for their age. If you do have any real concerns about your child's speech, you should talk to your health visitor or your family doctor about this.

Toddlers will gradually become more independent in other ways at this age, and you may find that your child is starting to pull off hats and socks as he learns to dress himself. By the age of two, most toddlers are able to take off some of their own clothes and may be able to put some on too – although undressing is often easier than dressing! Do try to allow your toddler to have a go himself as he will be able to do more if you offer positive encouragement.

He will need more of your attention once he is mobile and can interact with things and with other children too, and toddlers can be quite demanding. As a parent, it is essential that you start to set clear boundaries for your toddler so that he is always aware of what is and is not acceptable behaviour. This is not about being strict with your child, but about helping him to learn how to behave. Toddlers can go through challenging behavioural phases, but they need to understand that kicking, hitting, biting or scratching is unacceptable. Aggressive behaviour can quickly make your child unpopular with other children and parents and setting boundaries which encourage your child to behave well will help him socially too. The best way to help your child to understand what is and isn't acceptable is to focus on reinforcing and encouraging good behaviour. If he learns that when he is behaving well he will get more of your attention – cuddles, praise etc. – it follows that when he is naughty he isn't going to get your attention so he will soon tire of playing up and misbehaving.

For some families, a big change during this phase can be the arrival of a new baby brother or sister. If your toddler has been moved out of his cot and into a big bed to make room for a new baby, this can set up feelings of anxiety and resentment. Your toddler's routine can be disrupted by the arrival of a new baby and he may need lots of reassurance at this stage. If your toddler feels that he isn't getting as much attention as usual during the daytime, he may start to wake up more during the night so it is a good idea to try to ensure you spend some time focused on him whenever possible.

During this phase, it is quite common for toddlers to have some tantrums which is why people often refer to this stage as the 'terrible twos'. This is most likely to begin around the time that they learn to walk, partly because they often get very frustrated at not being able to do all that they would like to, and having tantrums is a normal part of development. If your previously calm toddler suddenly begins to have tantrums where he shouts, screams and hurls himself about or kicks out at something it can be quite worrying at first, but try to remember that this is often his way of showing his frustration. During this stage he is learning to do so many things from scratch, and he will find it difficult to understand his own limitations. He may understand exactly what you are saying to him, and yet he can't really express his own feelings clearly or tell you what he wants, and he may want to do things that are still physically beyond him.

Tantrums can intensify right through the 18–24-month period, but often start to decline after a child's second birthday. You can help by setting clear boundaries for your child, as it is important that he understands what is and isn't acceptable behaviour and has a clear idea of this in his head. Having a structured day, with regular sleep patterns, can also make it easier as overtiredness can lead to tantrums. By this age, any issues with your toddler around sleeping, feeding or behaviour are often intertwined, and you may find that getting one part of this right leads to improvements in other areas too. I believe it is very important during the toddler years that your child continues to follow a regular feeding and sleeping pattern. When this routine is combined with love, encouragement and support, your child will be in the best position to embrace the many challenges he will encounter during his first toddler years.

Feeding

What to expect

With a little help and guidance, from 12 months most toddlers are capable of feeding themselves part of their meal. It is important that your child enjoys his meals even if a certain amount of it lands on the floor. You can also encourage him to feed himself by making sure that you always give him a spoon of his own. Initially, he will need help to load the spoon with food and to get it into his mouth, but the more practice he has at doing this for himself, the sooner he will be able to do it without help. If he has lots of encouragement, he may be able to manage to feed himself with a spoon by the age of 18 months. Do keep offering lots of finger foods which will also help encourage your child to feed himself.

It is worth bearing in mind that your child's growth slows down during his second year, and that many children have a decrease in their appetite at this stage. If you aren't careful, mealtimes can turn into a battleground, so don't ever force a child to eat if he really doesn't want to, but equally do make it clear that there will not be snacks available as an alternative to meals.

What to aim for

This is a time of rapid change, and your toddler will need three regular meals a day to help keep their energy levels up, along with a mid-morning and a mid-afternoon snack, such as a piece of fruit or a rice cake, and a drink. You do need to be careful with snacks for children of this age though, as they can feel full up quickly, so you should try to make sure that you have a two-hour gap between snacks and meals if you can. I have often seen parents who are concerned that their children aren't eating enough at mealtimes, only to discover that they are being fed lots of snacks in between meals and are feeling too full up to eat a proper main meal later on.

Between 12 and 24 months a typical day would look similar to the following, although adaptations will have to sometimes be made with sleep, depending on social activities. From one year old it is recommended that a baby needs a minimum of 350ml (12oz) of milk. However, some babies will start to cut right back or even refuse milk altogether during the second year. If this is the case with your child it is important to supplement his diet with plenty of yoghurt, cheese and/or other calcium-rich foods to ensure that he still receives the right amount of calcium each day. You will also need to ensure that he is offered regular drinks of water to ensure he is getting enough fluid during the day and in the evening.

7/7.30am	awake, 180–240ml (5–7oz) of milk or other fluids followed by breakfast
9.30/9.45am	short nap of 15/30 minutes (gradually reduced and eliminated)

10am	drink of water and small snack
11.45/12 noon	lunch
12.30/1pm	nap (no more than two hours)
3pm	drink of water and small snack
5pm	tea with a small drink of water from a beaker
5.45pm	bath and bedtime routine
6.30/7pm	150–210ml (5–7oz) of milk or other fluids
7/7.30pm	asleep

Feeding Problems

Fussy eating

Few things upset parents as much as fussy children who turn up their noses at perfectly good food. I know mothers can be driven to the point of tears when, at the end of a long day, their carefully prepared meal ends up in the bin or the dog's bowl. But there is nothing more likely to stop a child from eating than tension and anxiety. As much as it can be difficult, I advise parents never to argue with a child about eating what is on their plates – it simply results in everyone getting upset. Instead, make it clear there is no alternative and remove the food immediately. I have watched parents cajole children into eating, bribe them with puddings and threaten them with punishments if they don't eat. None of these is the ideal way to approach fussy eating, and the threat of a punishment is more likely to physically prevent a child from eating as he becomes tense and upset. Could you eat a plate of food after someone had threatened you? With eating disorders and problems of obesity among children on the increase, it is important to be very careful about what messages we attach to food and eating.

It is also true that during the second year, growth slows down and there is often a very noticeable decrease in a toddler's appetite. Elizabeth Morse says in her book *My Child Won't Eat*: 'If a child grew at the same rate as in the first year, he would be 29 metres long and weigh 200 tons by the age of 10.' Unfortunately, many parents are not aware that the decrease in their toddler's appetite is normal and become anxious that he is not eating enough and often end up coaxing, cajoling and force-feeding him with a spoon, making him eat more than he really wants or needs. It is vital during the second year that mealtimes do not become a battle of wills. How you deal with any fussiness or food refusal at this stage will affect your toddler's attitude to food for years to come. Try to bear in mind that most children will eat what they need, and are unlikely to be starving themselves. That said, fussy eating is a difficult thing for parents to endure and there are things you can do to help prevent and solve the problem.

● Try to stick to set mealtimes whenever you possibly can. Young children know where they are with a regular routine, and it will help avoid some of the problems that can arise at mealtimes, such as fussy eating or worse, tantrums.

● Be realistic about how long you expect your child to sit quietly at the table during mealtimes. Of course, you should expect him to sit and eat his own meal properly, but it is unfair to expect a toddler to stay at the table during a long adult lunch. Let him get down from the table once he has finished eating.

● Children who fuss at mealtimes are often not really hungry. If your child is eating too much between meals, or drinks a lot just before a meal, he is less likely to eat well at mealtimes and this can lead to battles. I always advise parents to keep a food diary for a few days monitoring everything that their child eats and drinks, as this often reveals that the overall food intake is actually much higher than parents might have thought. Sometimes, it's their liquid intake which affects the amount a child eats and you should keep an eye on the quantities your child drinks as this will make a difference to his appetite.

● Never try to force-feed a toddler who is refusing to eat as this will almost inevitably lead to tears and will make mealtimes a source of anxiety for parents and their child. If a child is not hungry, there is no point in forcing food on him, but it is important not to start offering biscuits or puddings as an alternative or as a reward or punishment if a child won't touch his meal. Saying, 'If you don't eat your greens, you can't have any pudding' will immediately teach a child that greens are a punishment and pudding is a reward. Similarly, do not give sweets, crisps, biscuits or chocolates as treats. If a child is used to being offered bribes if he eats, he will learn to expect this.

- If your toddler is getting fussy and refusing food, try serving smaller portions on a bigger plate. Give him lots of praise when he eats it all. Gradually increase the portion by a tiny amount every three or four days until he is eating normally. Similarly, try to have realistic expectations of how much your child can eat – sometimes parents expect toddlers to eat overly large quantities of food. Offering small quantities and then giving your child more if he is still hungry is better than piling a plate high with food, which can be daunting.

- Sometimes a toddler will go through a stage where they will scream the minute they are put in their high chair. When this happens I would remove them from the high chair immediately and take them to another room to calm them down. After a period of 10 to 15 minutes of calm I would then return them to the high chair and try again. If the same thing happens I would simply take them out of the high chair and wait until the next allocated snack or meal time before offering food. If the problem is behavioural I find that taking this approach the problem is quickly resolved. If the screaming is not behavioural it could be your toddler is overtired, in which case simply bringing the meal forward by 15 minutes or so should help. If bringing the meal forward does not resolve the problem then the next thing to look at is whether your toddler's meals are being offered too close together and he needs a longer space between them. As above, offering snacks or too much fluid before a meal can also reduce his appetite. Finally, sometimes avoiding the high chair and having a picnic on the floor for a few days can be enough to break the problem if it has simply become a habit.

- Remember that children learn by observation. The best way to encourage good behaviour and table manners is to set a good example. If you don't sit down at the table and eat a meal but instead resort to snacking while dashing about, you can't expect your child to sit at a table and eat peacefully.

- As your child learns to feed himself, some spills and mess are inevitable, so don't constantly reprimand him for less than immaculate table manners as this can lead to anxiety. However, by the time your child is three he should be able to eat without making too much mess. If your expectations are realistic, you are less likely to encounter bad behaviour.

- In order to encourage your child to eat properly at mealtimes, it is also important to avoid making mealtimes into an opportunity for playing games or to allow him to watch television while he eats. This will distract your toddler and it will be harder for him to eat properly if he is focused elsewhere.

- It can help to make sure that your child has his main protein meal at lunchtime. Toddlers do sometimes get tired when they are busy all day, and by the time they get to their tea they can be a little fractious and will be more fussy. If you have made sure that your child has had the necessary protein at lunchtime, you can then offer a quick and easy tea of something simple such as pasta, soup or a baked potato.

● Allow your child to taste things from your plate. Someone else's food will often look more tempting than the food in front of him.

● If your child refuses to eat a particular food, try not to lecture him or get upset. Simply remove his plate and try again another day. Chances are your child will get bored of his own behaviour, especially if it doesn't incite a response from you.

Breastfeeding and returning to work

If you are planning to return to work and would like to continue to breastfeed, it is important that you try to make sure that you have established a good milk supply, especially if you want your baby to have expressed breast milk during the day. As your baby will most likely be emptying both breasts at the 7am and 6pm feeds, you will need to express most of the milk for the feeds to be given in your absence during the working day or between 9pm and 10pm in the evening.

I would recommend that you express approximately 90ml (3oz) first thing in the morning and then fully express both breasts in the evening.

The following guidelines give suggestions on how to incorporate working and breastfeeding:

- The longer you can spend at home establishing a milk supply, the easier it will be to maintain it once you return to work. Most breast-feeding experts advise a period of 16 weeks.

- Expressing from the beginning of the second week at the times suggested will enable you to build up a good stock of breast milk in the freezer.

- Introducing a bottle of expressed milk at the late feed by the second week will ensure that there will not be a problem of your baby not taking the bottle when you return to work.

- Check with your employer well in advance of returning to work that there will be a quiet place available where you will be able to express. Also check that they are happy for you to store the expressed milk in the refrigerator.

- Once you have established a good expressing routine using the heavy-duty expressing pump, you should begin practising with a battery-operated one. With a single expressing pump you may find that switching from side to side throughout the expressing will help the milk to flow more easily. It may also be worthwhile considering a mini electric pump that will enable you to express both breasts at once.

- Make sure that the nursery, or your nanny or childminder, is familiar with the storage and handling of breast milk, and how to defrost it.

- Establish the combined feeding routine that you will be using for your baby at least two weeks in advance of your return to work. This will allow you plenty of time to sort out any difficulties that may occur.

- Once you return to work, it is essential that you pay particular attention to your diet and that you rest well in the evening. It would be advisable to continue expressing at 9.30pm to ensure that you maintain a good milk supply. Also, make sure that you keep a good supply of breast pads at work, and a spare shirt or top!

CASE STUDY: Benjamin, aged 28 months

Problem: Food refusal

Causes: Demand feeding and excessive fluid intake from dependence on a bottle

Benjamin was breastfed on demand until he was nearly one. He had always been a poor feeder, looking for a breast feed every two hours, even after he was weaned on to solids. There was very little food that he enjoyed as a baby, apart from baby rice or rusks mixed with fruit purée or baby fromage frais. Occasionally, Benjamin would take a liking to a new recipe for a few days, but the interest never lasted longer than this and his mother would always resort to giving him a breast feed or fromage frais when he started to get upset about a certain food.

When Benjamin reached one year his mother Catherine decided to take a more structured approach and limit the breastfeeding on demand, so over a period of two weeks, she gradually increased the length of time between breast feeds and replaced them with a bottle of formula. While he still continued to be fussy about solids, Benjamin's eating during the day did improve slightly, and Catherine managed to get him off the two middle-of-the-night feeds following advice given in Dr Richard Ferber's book *Solve Your Child's Sleep Problems*. He would still wake up once or twice in the night and would be given a drink from a bottle of well-diluted fruit juice. At his various wakings during the night Benjamin was drinking at least 240ml (8oz) of juice.

When Benjamin was 14 months old Catherine discovered she was pregnant. On the recommendation of a friend she bought *The New Contented Little Baby Book* and, following its advice, decided not to breastfeed her second baby during the night. Isabella was a very easy baby, and by five months was sleeping a good 11–12-hour stretch at night. When solids were introduced she took to them really well, and by seven months was eating three good meals a day from a wide variety of the different food groups. While she continued to have two breast feeds a day, she was happy to take the rest of her milk and fluids from a cup. This became embarrassing for Catherine as Benjamin, who was now nearly 28 months old, was still having all his milk and fluids from a bottle. His diet was also still very limited. Apart from sausages and ham, he refused all other forms of protein. He would hardly touch breakfast, apart from a small yoghurt, because he was still full from the fluid he had been drinking during the night. He would eat vegetables but only in soup, and his lunch and tea were nearly always the same thing. Lunch was generally a tin of soup with a Marmite or jam sandwich, accompanied by a packet of crisps. Tea would consist of sausages or processed ham and cheese spread or baked beans with sausages on white toast. The soup, crisps and processed meals he ate were of the high-salt convenience variety which were making him thirsty. After all of his meals Benjamin always ate two pots of fromage frais, and during his meals and in between times the only thing that he would drink from a cup was diluted blackcurrant cordial. He also continued to have a full 240ml (8oz) bottle of milk when he first woke in the morning and another at bedtime.

Catherine was very concerned that as Isabella got older, she might start to refuse the healthy food that she was so happy to take and start demanding the type of food that Benjamin was eating. This concern led her to ring me for advice.

When I received details of what both children had consumed over a three-day period, it was obvious that Isabella was eating a very healthy and varied diet for her age. But Benjamin's diary showed that the type of food he ate was indeed very limited and was eaten in very small amounts. His diary also showed that his two milk feeds morning and night, plus the juice he consumed during the night, came to a daily total of around 840ml (28oz). This amount did not include drinks that he had at mealtimes and in between.

I explained to Catherine that while it was very important for babies and young children to receive enough fluids, children of

Benjamin's age cannot comprehend the difference between thirst and hunger, and will often satisfy their hunger needs by drinking fluid. I was fairly sure that part of the reason for Benjamin's fussy feeding was excessive fluid intake. To establish whether this could be the case, I advised Catherine to monitor and record his fluid intake during the day. Two days later Catherine sent me the details and it was much worse than I had envisaged. Between 9am and 5pm, excluding milk feeds and middle-of-the-night diluted juice, Catherine calculated that Benjamin was drinking a whopping 1050ml (35oz) of fluid on top of 840ml (28oz) of milk and his diluted fruit juice in the middle of the night. This was a total of 1900ml (63oz) of fluid a day. It was certainly one of the worst cases of fluid excess that I had heard of, and even Catherine was shocked by the huge amount.

I advised her that in order to improve Benjamin's appetite we should get his total daily intake to a maximum of 1200ml (40oz) a day consumed between 6/7am and 7/8pm. She agreed to this, but with Christmas just 10 days away, she was very hesitant about abandoning his middle-of-the-night drinks, as she was concerned about him screaming in the night for a drink and waking up the family visitors. I suggested that we concentrate on reducing Benjamin's daytime fluids over the Christmas period, and hoped that we would see an improvement in his eating so that we could get tough about eliminating night-time fluids after Christmas.

I advised Catherine to continue to allow Benjamin to have his milk and middle-of-the-night fluids from his bottle so that neither she nor he got overly stressed, but that she had to be tough with him about all other fluids. He could still have a drink when he wanted but it must be from a cup, not the bottle. Over the next three days Catherine recorded a slight decrease in the amount that Benjamin was drinking, but he was still consuming nearly 900ml (30oz) a day (instead of the recommended 350ml (13.5oz) a day), in addition to his two milk feeds and middle-of-the-night diluted juice. However, after a lot of fussing and protesting about not being allowed his bottle during the day, he was reluctantly accepting this fluid amount from a cup.

By this time one set of grandparents had arrived for their Christmas visit, so I suggested to Catherine that she enlist their help in occupying Benjamin during the day so that he did not always have access to a cup full of fluids. She should set certain times of the day when he was offered a drink, and if he had not had a drink within 30 minutes of being offered it, the cup should be removed. If an hour later he asked for a drink, he should be offered a piece of fruit instead.

Within five days, Benjamin's excessive daytime fluid had been dramatically reduced. He was having 180ml (6oz) of milk in the morning when he woke. At lunch and teatime he would drink 90–150ml (3–5oz), and in between meals he would drink 90–120ml (3–4oz). This huge reduction in his daily fluid intake had an excellent effect on his eating, and although he still continued to be fussy about the types of foods he ate, the amounts he consumed increased dramatically. His daily intake of fluids between 7am and 7.30pm was now 720–810ml (24–27oz), and because his eating had improved so much during the day, he was drinking less in the night.

Once Christmas was over, we agreed to resolve the problem of Benjamin still drinking his milk from a bottle both night and morning, and still needing a drink of diluted juice to settle himself back to sleep in the middle of the night. I suggested that we begin by reducing the amount of night-time juice. Over the next four nights, Catherine should reduce the amount in each bottle by 30ml (1oz), and gradually dilute it more and more until she was putting only water in the bottle. I explained that she must be prepared for several unsettled nights once he was being offered only water during the night. She could go in and reassure him every 10 minutes should he get very upset, but she was not to lift him out of the cot or resort to settling him with juice. The first two nights were very difficult for Catherine, as she was in and out of his room several times between 2 and 6am, but she did not relent, and on the third night she managed to settle him back to sleep without offering him a drink.

On the fourth night I suggested that we offer Benjamin only one drink, but in a cup instead of a bottle. That night was a particularly bad one, and Catherine decided that she was ready to abandon the cup of water altogether and use controlled crying in order to get him back to sleep. She then had a further three very difficult nights of sleep training but on the fourth night Benjamin slept through until nearly 6am. On my advice, she abandoned the morning bottle of milk and replaced it with a cup of milk. The first few mornings Benjamin fussed and protested but Catherine persevered and by the end of the week, he happily drank 180ml (6oz) of milk from a cup. We then replaced his bedtime milk feed from the bottle with a cup, so he was now taking all his fluids from a cup. He continued to enjoy a cup of warm milk at bedtime, and this together with the dairy products he ate during the day, ensured he was getting plenty of calcium for strong teeth and bones. The warm milk soothed him, and also enabled him to sleep well at night. Because he was no longer drinking during the night, he did increase the amount of fluid he had during the day, but we ensured that he was offered only water midway between meals so that it did not interfere with his appetite. I advised Catherine that she should fill two bottles each morning – one with water and one with well-diluted juice – with the exact amount he was allowed to drink that day. This would make it easier for her to monitor his fluid intake.

Benjamin's daily fluid intake was now 960–1020ml (32–34oz), and he was eating very substantial amounts at all his meals. Catherine was a bit worried that he was now below the daily fluid recommendations, and for several days increased the amount of fluid he was having. However, she noticed that he immediately became very fussy about his meals, particularly his tea. I advised her that 960–1020ml of fluid a day, along with a good intake of fruit and vegetables daily, was more than sufficient. Benjamin did continue to be very limited in his range of foods, but I reassured Catherine that as long as he was getting a selection from all the food groups, she should not pressure him to try lots of different things. It would be better to establish several weeks of him getting used to happily eating good amounts, then gradually try to expand on the range of foods.

Now that he was happy to eat some of the same types of food as Isabella, Catherine and I devised a meal plan that enabled her to cook food that was suitable for both children and at the same meal. Eating with his sister then encouraged Benjamin to become more adventurous with his food and to expand on the different meals that he would eat.

Benjamin's situation really stemmed from being breastfed on demand long after solids were introduced, and being allowed to drink fluids from a bottle after the age of one year. Toddlers of this age can drink fluid much more quickly from a bottle than a cup and when their fluid intake is not structured to fit in with mealtimes it can result in them confusing hunger with thirst. Allowing them to drink excessive amounts of milk on top of being given the wrong type of snacks, as was Benjamin's case, can take the edge off their appetite and doesn't help them become more accepting of other foods.

Refusing lumpy food

I think that the guidance for introducing more lumpy food can be very misleading. If a baby is used to very smooth, puréed food and then suddenly, at around nine to 12 months, they find that after taking a few spoons of their favourite meal they are having to deal with a solid lump, it is hardly surprising that so many children gag and even refuse more lumpy food. To avoid this happening babies should first go from puréed food to pulsed food, while also being introduced to finger foods such as sliced and diced vegetables and fruit. Moving from puréed food to more textured food can be a difficult transition for some babies and making it a very gradual change will make the process much easier.

CASE STUDY: Thomas, aged 18 months

Problem: Refusing lumps

Cause: Excessive amounts of carbohydrates at breakfast and in the morning

Thomas was weaned on to solids at six months old. At that point he was having five 270ml (9oz) bottles of milk each day, so Thomas's mother thought he would be a hungry baby. However, for the first month of weaning he refused to open his mouth. Thomas's mother tried both feeding him on an empty stomach and after his milk feed, but by eight months he was still only eating baby rice and puréed apple and pear. Each stage of weaning became increasingly difficult.

By 14 months Thomas had moved on to a more varied diet (although food was still puréed) and was drinking 150–180ml (5–6oz) of milk when he woke in the morning, followed by one or two Weetabix or some cereal. By mid morning he would have a couple of rice cakes, oatcakes or breadsticks, and the same in the afternoon. On toddler group days, his morning snack was most likely biscuits. His lunch and tea were nearly always the same – blended casseroles and soups. His mother Emma tried to leave in some lumps, but Thomas usually spat them out. At 18 months she was still struggling to get him to eat lumps and a more varied diet. He started to refuse any type of savoury food, turning his head away when she tried to feed him his usual soup or casserole. As an alternative, she would end up giving him toast, which he fed to himself. He'd also eat a few cheese triangles.

When Emma called me, I immediately thought that Thomas was eating an excessive amount of carbohydrates. His breakfast and mid-morning snacks were affecting his appetite, and were responsible for his fussy eating habits at lunch and tea. I suggested temporarily changing breakfast to puréed fruit and half a tub of yoghurt, which Thomas liked, and to reduce the milk at breakfast to 120ml (4oz). For lunch I advised giving him a protein meal, but not to resort to feeding him foods he did like if he refused his savoury meal. I also suggested that instead of biscuit-type snacks, Emma should offer Thomas a little chopped fruit between meals. For dinner she should try soup or some other carbohydrate meal, followed by bread if he ate the soup. As a last resort, if Thomas did not eat well in the evening, I advised that Emma could give him cereal so that he was not going to bed on an empty tummy. I also stressed the importance of not making a fuss or cajoling Thomas at mealtimes should he refuse to eat. I assured Emma that he would not starve if he missed a meal, and that at his age it was important to allow him the control to decide how much he wanted to eat. However, it was important to structure his food and drink so that the right types of foods were being served at the right time of day, and that he was not filling up on juice and biscuits in between meals. Following my advice, Emma's day with Thomas progressed like this:

7.45am   Emma gave him 120ml (4oz) of milk in a cup. He drank that quickly and shouted for more but she didn't give in.

7.55am   Emma gave him 75g of natural yoghurt mixed with 4 spoonfuls of puréed apple. He took three mouthfuls then shouted for milk and wanted to get out of his high chair. She let him down, putting the unfinished bowl in the fridge, and he ran to the cupboard where the breakfast cereals are and banged on the door crying. She calmly offered him more yoghurt instead.

8–9am
During this hour he had a bit of a tantrum, running back to the kitchen to bang on the cupboard and shout for milk. Emma kept distracting him by going outside.

9am
Thomas realised that all he was going to get was the yoghurt and he finished the rest of the bowl. He also had some water.

9.30–11.30am
Toddler group. Emma realised how many biscuits he would normally have (up to three). Thomas kept going to where the biscuits were and cried when she carried him away but Emma remained firm. He drank a cup of water during those two hours.

12 noon
Emma gave Thomas puréed mince with vegetables and mashed potato with small chunks of carrot on the side. Over the next 20 minutes he ate nearly the entire bowl. He played with it but put spoonfuls in

his mouth as well. Emma kept praising him and he ate about eight spoonfuls.

5pm   Thomas ate all his lentil soup and a piece of bread.

7pm   He had a full cup of milk.

After two weeks of continuing to feed Thomas in this way, his eating had vastly improved. As a family they were able to enjoy fish fingers and mash together, which Thomas loved. Two weeks previously he wouldn't have touched it unless it was puréed.

Refusing milk

At this stage, your child's nutritional needs will be being met by solids but you do need to be mindful of his calcium intake, so continuing to give your toddler 350ml (12oz) of milk each day ensures that you are meeting these needs. A beaker of warm milk at bedtime is also a soothing part of the bedtime routine and I find that most toddlers continue to enjoy their bedtime milk until they are two to three years of age. However, some toddlers can become fussy about milk or start to refuse it altogether. If that is the case then you do not need to worry, as milk is not as essential to their diet at this age as it is for children under a year. It is important, though, to make sure your baby is eating plenty of yoghurt, cheese and/or other calcium-rich foods to meet his calcium requirements. Obviously you can't force your baby to drink milk at bedtime, but in terms of hydration, children of this age still need at least 180–240ml (5–6oz) of fluids at bedtime as it would be unrealistic to expect a child to sleep nearly 12 hours without a drink.

- If you find that your toddler is taking much less than 180ml (6oz) of fluids at bedtime and starting to wake up earlier, you should first look at the times and amounts of when he drinks both milk and other fluids. When a toddler is taking a lot less than 180ml in the evening, I often find that they are waking up and taking a really big feed of 270ml (9oz) of milk or more in the morning (usually 180ml or 210ml (7oz) before breakfast followed by another 90ml (3oz) or 120ml (4oz) after breakfast or mid morning). Or they may still be having a large drink of milk mid afternoon. Either can be the reason the toddler will not take a big enough drink of milk at bedtime. To remedy this problem and get your toddler drinking 180/210ml (6/7oz) in the evening, I would recommend that you allow him around 210ml milk at breakfast, but only offer him water after breakfast, mid morning or mid afternoon, so that he is really ready to drink his bedtime milk.

- It is also a good idea to look at the portion sizes of his meals and snacks. Remember that babies and toddlers do not know the difference between hunger and thirst and often a toddler will eat more than they really need, therefore reducing their appetite for their bedtime drink.

- Another reason that toddlers sometimes do not drink enough at bedtime, is that they become very tired after the bath and too sleepy to drink the full amount they need. If this seems to be the case for your toddler, I would suggest that 30 minutes prior to the bath, you sit and have some quiet time downstairs and offer your toddler as much of his bedtime milk as he will take. That way, even if he gets sleepy after the bath, he will probably manage another couple of ounces.

Refusing water

As the amount of milk is reduced during the second year it is important that your toddler drinks enough fluids. Milk and water are the two recommended drinks for your children, however, continuing to give excessive amounts of milk during the second year could really affect your toddler's appetite for solid food.

If your toddler completely refuses water, it is worth adding some pure fruit juice to his water. Start by adding a splash of juice to your child's usual drink of water, then as your toddler gets used to drinking the diluted juice, you can then gradually dilute it even further until he is taking just water. Many parents are concerned about the effects that the juice will have on their toddler's teeth, but provided the juice is very well diluted and is only given at a couple of drinks each day with meals, it should not affect his teeth.

Getting rid of the bottle

From one year, it is recommended that bottles are eliminated and all drinks, including milk, be given to a baby from a beaker. He needs a minimum of 350ml (12oz) of milk a day and a maximum of 500ml (18oz). If you continue to give your child his milk from a bottle after one year of age, it could seriously affect his appetite for solid food. At this age he is likely to drink it very quickly so he will consume a lot in a short period of time. In my experience the longer a toddler is allowed to drink milk from a bottle after one year, the more difficult it becomes to get them to drink milk from the beaker.

If you have not already done so, I would advise that you replace the breakfast bottle with milk from a beaker. If he absolutely refuses the beaker I would suggest that you get one of the feeding bottles that have the soft spout and get him used to that, before attempting to introduce the beaker again.

You will probably find that it could take a couple of weeks before your toddler will take a decent amount from the beaker, but it is important to keep persevering with it. If he only takes 60–90ml (2–3oz), then offer him a further 60–90ml mid morning and mid afternoon. Once he is taking around 180ml (5oz) from the soft spout bottle or beaker you should then drop the evening bottle.

Once he is accepting milk from the soft spout bottle it should be easier to move on to the beaker. However, if you find that you are having no success with the soft spout bottle or the beaker it would be worth trying one of the feeding cups with a plastic straw. I have often found that toddlers who refuse to drink milk from a beaker will happily do so from a beaker with a straw.

Night-time feeding

If your toddler is still needing to be fed to sleep and wakes several times a night refusing to settle back to sleep without a feed, it is important that you look very closely at his daytime feeding before embarking on any form of sleep training. All too often parents attempt to sleep-train toddlers with disastrous results. They are told that their toddler does not need to feed in the night and that using controlled crying will quickly resolve the problem. After two or three nights of the toddler screaming for hours, these parents usually abandon controlled crying, claiming that it did not work for them. I believe the advice that toddlers don't need feeding in the night should be replaced with '*shouldn't need feeding in the night*'.

A possible reason that sleep training has not worked for these toddlers is that they are genuinely hungry at some of their night wakings. This is a result of demand feeding in the very early days. Because the milk feeds were never structured properly, the baby was never given the opportunity to increase his daytime feeding. A vicious cycle soon evolves where the baby needs to make up his daily nutritional needs in the night because he did not feed well in the day, along with the wrong association of falling asleep on the breast or bottle, which leads to a very serious problem. Because this is more than just an association problem, it is important that steps are taken to improve the daytime feeding before sleep training is used to eliminate the association problem.

● If your toddler is waking up really hungry in the night, it is probably because he is not eating enough solids during the day. However, it would be very difficult to go cold turkey and eliminate all night feeds immediately, for the simple reason he would cry and cry because he really was hungry.

- In order to increase your toddler's solid food during the day, it is essential to count any milk feeds after his bedtime milk feed as part of his daytime milk. For example, if your toddler is waking at 2am every morning and drinking a 210ml (7oz) bottle it is important that you count that as his breakfast milk and go straight into solids at breakfast time and then after breakfast offer him a small amount of water to drink. Because the minimum daily amount of milk required at this age is 350ml (12oz), you do not need to offer your toddler any further milk until bedtime, at which point he would need between 180ml (6oz) and 240ml (8oz).

- As your toddler's food intake increases during the day you can gradually decrease his middle-of-the-night feed. Do not do this too quickly – try reducing it by 30ml (1oz) every couple of nights, which will ensure that he will not wake a second time through genuine hunger.

- As he decreases the amount of milk drunk in the night, you can start to offer him the amount he has dropped after his breakfast solids. Once you are down to a couple of ounces in the middle of the night, you should then return to offering him his milk first in the morning.

- If you are managing to get him back to sleep with a couple of ounces of milk and cuddles, you can then replace the milk with a couple of ounces of water and cuddles. After he has managed a few nights of settling himself back to sleep quickly after the water and cuddles, you can then drop the water and settle him with just cuddles.

- After a few nights of settling him with cuddles I would recommend that you use the gradual withdrawal method outlined on page 370 to teach him how to self-settle when he wakes.

It can take around two weeks for this method to work, but it is a much gentler way of dealing with the problem than going cold turkey and taking the bottle away and leaving him to cry. The only exception to this would be breastfed babies. In my experience some breastfeeding babies are genuinely waking up in the night hungry, due to the mother having a low milk supply in the evening. If you are breastfeeding, I would recommend that you try offering your toddler both breasts before the bath and then a top-up of expressed milk or some cow's milk after the bath, to see if that helps improve things. If he continues to wake in the night looking for a feed, I would recommend that you follow the same advice as I have given for a bottle-fed toddler, but instead of reducing the milk in the night by 30ml (1oz) every couple of days, reduce the length of time he is on the breast by 3–5 minutes every couple of days.

Sleep

What to expect

During the first part of the second year the amount of sleep that a toddler needs can vary hugely depending on the individual toddler, averaging anywhere between 13 and 15 hours in a 24-hour period, which is usually divided between night-time sleep and one or two naps. It is usually during the first half of the second year that toddlers will be ready to drop their morning nap and go from two naps a day to one, although some may have already done this just prior to their first birthday. Going from two naps a day to just one nap can be difficult for some toddlers to cope with, as the middle-of-the-day nap usually has to be brought forward for a short spell when the morning nap is dropped. This can often result in the toddler becoming overtired in the evening as the time between him waking from his middle-of-the-day nap and the time he goes to bed is longer.

This overtiredness can result in problems in settling in the evening. If this is not dealt with properly, a child who has always slept well can, during the second year, suddenly start waking up much earlier in the morning or even in the night.

The huge changes in children's lives at this time can sometimes affect sleep too, and children who slept very well during their first year can suddenly seem to have disrupted sleep patterns once they become toddlers. This may in part be attributed to the sheer physical exhaustion of becoming more mobile and becoming more engaged which is inevitably tiring. If daytime sleep is disrupted by lots more activities during the day, this can have an impact too. Alternatively, too much daytime sleep can lead to problems.

What to aim for

At the age of one, a baby will usually be having around 14–15 hours of sleep across 24 hours, divided between a long night-time sleep and one or two naps (lasting up to a total of two hours) during the day.

The majority of toddlers who are sleeping well at night will, between nine and 15 months of age, cut back their morning sleep to 10–20 minutes a day, and by 18 months have cut it out altogether, having a two-hour nap in the middle of the day. If a child is sleeping well between 7am and 7pm, he will usually need to start to cut down on the amount of sleep he needs at some point between the ages of 15 and 18 months. Occasionally, though, I do find that some children who are not sleeping so well at night, will start to sleep better if their morning nap is eliminated altogether. You may notice that your toddler takes longer to drop off during his daytime naps, he may wake up again quickly after a very short sleep in the day, he may take longer to settle at night or wake up very early in the morning – all these changes can indicate that your child is ready to cut back on his sleep. There are also some toddlers who actually need to cut down their daily sleep much earlier than 18 months. If you find that your toddler is resisting bedtime or waking up earlier in the morning, then you may have to look at reducing his daytime sleep to less than one and a half hours. I have had some toddlers who need to have their daily nap time reduced to one hour or even less if they are to sleep a good 11–12 hours at night.

Although some toddlers may need more daytime sleep, it is also important to remember that a child who genuinely needs more sleep in the day, will most likely sleep well at night too. All too often I hear parents saying that their toddler needs more daytime sleep than the average, yet their toddler is waking up very early or not going to bed until later – both signs that he is having *too much* daytime sleep.

CASE STUDY: Matilda, aged 18 months

Problem: Night-time and early morning waking

Cause: Too much daytime sleep

Matilda had never slept through the night consistently for more than a couple of weeks at a time. But when she did wake, usually around 11.30pm and 5.30am, she could usually be settled back to sleep fairly quickly with a little bit of patting and her dummy. When Matilda started nursery at around 14 months she quickly stopped waking up at 11.30pm and would sleep straight through from 7pm to 5.30am, when she would quickly resettle back to sleep when given the dummy until 7.30am in the morning. This pattern lasted for about a month when Matilda's 5.30am waking suddenly started to become earlier and earlier, until she was regularly waking around 4.30am, but unlike in the past where she would settle back to sleep quickly when given the dummy, most days it would take two hours or sometimes longer of patting before she would fall back to sleep. On the days she went to nursery she had to be woken at 7.30am in order to be in nursery by 8.30am. She was then put down for a nap around 9.30am for one to one and a half hours, followed by a second nap around 2pm for an hour. On the days she didn't go to nursery Clare would let her sleep until 8am, she was then tired again by 11.30am at which point Clare would let her have a short nap of 40 minutes so she wasn't overtired to eat her lunch. She would then have a second nap of one hour at around 2.30pm.

By the time Matilda reached 18 months she was consistently awake every night from around 4.30am for up to two hours and sometimes longer, but she also had started resisting bedtime and would often take up to an hour to settle in the evening, and it was at that point that Clare got in touch with me.

After reading the seven-day sleeping and feeding diary that Clare had sent me, I was convinced that the middle-of-the-night waking and the resisting sleep at bedtime was being caused by too much daytime sleep and suggested to Clare that we would need to gradually cut it back if we wanted Matilda to sleep consistently through the night.

Clare was not convinced of this and was concerned that Matilda who got tired and grumpy very quickly, and was extremely difficult to deal with during the day, would become even more so. I explained that it was a vicious circle that Matilda was getting so tired during the day because she was awake so much at night and she was sleeping during the day. I calculated that on the days that she went to nursery Matilda was having three hours' sleep between 7am and 7pm and on the days she was at home she was having around two hours and 40 minutes between 7am and 7pm. I believed that to get Matilda sleeping to nearer 7am in the morning we would need to cut her sleep to around one and a half hours a day. I assured Clare that we would do this gradually and that as she started to sleep better at night, she would not be so irritable during the day and it would be easier to reduce the day-time sleep.

The first thing I advised Clare to do was to wake Matilda up no later than 7am every morning, regardless of what time she had done in the night. For the next few days she should allow a total of no more than two hours' sleep a day, dividing it between a morning nap of 30 minutes and a lunchtime nap of one and a half hours. Reducing the daytime sleep by 40 minutes to one hour meant that on the first night Matilda was fast asleep by 7.15pm. She then slept soundly to 5.30am, when she settled back to sleep within 20 minutes once she was given the dummy and a little bit of shushing and patting.

She followed the same pattern for three nights and during the day she would have a morning nap of 30 minutes around 9.30am and then a second nap of one and a half hours at 1.30pm. For the next three days I suggested that the morning nap should be pushed on to nearer 9.45am and reduced to 15 minutes. Reducing the daily sleep by a further 15 minutes resulted in Matilda over a period of a week starting to sleep to sleep nearer to 6/6.15am, but then she was awake for the day. I advised that they bring the morning nap back to 9.30am and increase it to 30 minutes again, and put her down at 1.30pm as usual but reduce the nap to one hour. Clare was concerned that Matilda would get overtired if we reduced the daytime sleep further, but I was confident that reducing the daytime sleep by a further 15 minutes would help Matilda sleep slightly longer in the night, although she may have to put Matilda down slightly earlier around 6.45pm. Matilda would usually fall asleep within five to 10 minutes and within a few days Matilda started to sleep to between 6.45am and 7am. When this happened I advised that they should then go back to giving Matilda a morning nap of 15 minutes, but push it on to 10.15am, and then put her down for the lunchtime nap at 1.30pm and then increase it to one hour and 15 minutes, which would mean she could then start to put her down in the evening at 7pm again. Within a few days Matilda was settling to sleep within five to 10 minutes of being put to bed at 7pm and most mornings she had to be woken at 7am. At this point Matilda was having a daily total of one hour 30 minutes' sleep, but I was fairly sure that because of her age that her sleep would need to be tweaked again fairly soon. I told Clare to keep an eye on how quickly Matilda was falling asleep at her morning nap; if she found it was taking longer and longer, this was a sign that she would be ready to drop the morning nap. When this happened I advised her to use my advice on page 299 for dropping the morning nap. During the second year when a toddler starts to need less sleep as in Matilda's case it is often a case of regularly tweaking and adjusting the daytime sleep so that the daytime sleep comes at the right time of the day, and doesn't exceed the daily total a child needs. Because all children are different the individual needs of a child can vary dramatically, but in my experience when a toddler starts waking up in the night or waking up earlier, the main cause is usually too much daytime sleep.

Usually by the age of 18 months, the amount of sleep your child needs will reduce to 13–14 hours across a 24-hour period,

and this will often be just one daytime nap along with the longer
night sleep. Most toddlers will usually still need around one and
a half hours of daytime sleep. If your toddler continues to need
a morning nap as well as a lunchtime nap, it can be a good idea
to take him out in his buggy for a quick 10–15-minute nap. If
you put him down in his cot, he is likely to go into a deep sleep
and will be hard to wake. The movement of a buggy or a car,
however, will prevent this and help you to keep the nap as short
as possible. It can take a while to adjust to new sleep patterns, and
you may need to be patient for a while as you work out the new
routine for your child.

You should also bear in mind that children of this age have lots
of energy, and so you will want to try to ensure that your toddler
has a good balance of physical and mental activity. Getting lots of
fresh air and physical activity will help ensure that he is ready to
sleep well at night.

By the time they reach two years old, toddlers will have reduced
their daytime sleep and most will be down to one daytime nap.
Initially cutting back on daytime sleep can make a toddler irritable
for a while, but he will adjust to this with time. One common sleep
disrupter for children of this age is when parents move a toddler
into a big bed, which often happens between 18 and 24 months.
It may be worth leaving your toddler in a cot for longer if he is
not quite ready to move into a bed, as I have found that toddlers
who move into a bed too early are more prone to waking up very
early and getting up in the night, and also to wanting to sleep in
their parents' bed if they wake up at night rather than being happy
settled back into their own bed.

The bedtime routine

If you have established a bedtime of 7.30 or 8pm, you may find that once your toddler stops having his early morning nap he gets very overtired and needs to go to bed slightly earlier. Overtiredness can be a real problem during the second year as it is during this stage that the toddler begins to learn many new skills, which can leave him both physically and mentally exhausted. It is very important to start winding things down after tea and to maintain a very calm, quiet bedtime routine. At this age toddlers who have just learned to walk can become very excitable in the early evening, wanting to run around playing chase or hide and seek. What starts out to be a fun game nearly always ends in tears as the toddler gets a second wind and refuses to calm down.

Sleep Problems

Jumping out of the cot

I always advise that parents should keep their toddlers in their cot well into the third year if possible. However, occasionally a toddler during the second year will manage to get out of his cot unaided. When this happens you will have no choice but to either take the sides off his cot, if he is in a cot bed, or transfer him to a toddler bed. In both cases I would install a bed rail to reduce the risk of him falling out of the bed.

If you have not already done so, I would advise you put a stair gate across your toddler's doorway. I find that parents who have the stair gate at the top of the stairs, often end up with their toddler sneaking through to their room and into their bed in the middle of the night. Once he is actually out of his bedroom and into your bed, it can be very difficult to get him to settle back to sleep in his own bed. By fitting the stair gate across his room it at least keeps him there. You may find that you will have some disrupted nights where your toddler will get out of bed and stand at the gate calling for you, but as exhausting as this is, each time he gets out of bed you must just remain firm and take him back to his bed without any discussion. After a few nights, he will soon give up getting out of bed and learn that there is going to be no interaction in the night.

Dummy addiction

In my experience, with babies between six months and one year a 'cold turkey' approach (see page 212 for a detailed explanation) seems to work within a few days and with older children you can reason with them. However, I find that with children during the second year taking the dummy away can sometimes cause even more sleep issues than it resolves. If your toddler reaches one year and is still dependent on his dummy, particularly to get to sleep, my advice is to wait until he is over two and start trying to get rid of the dummy then. Apart from the possible damage that the constant sucking on a dummy can do to his teeth, you should also consider the peer effect of dummy dependency. Toddlers and older children often become targets of ridicule by their peers if they are known still to use a dummy.

It's rare that a child with a dummy dependency will give it up without a strategy and encouragement from his or her parent but the strategies outlined below are easier to implement when he gets older. If you are planning to eliminate the dummy, the following points should first be considered:

- Do not allow relatives or friends to make fun of your child for using a dummy. In my experience, comments such as, 'Only babies have dummies' or 'You look silly with that dreadful thing in your mouth' can make a sensitive child feel very inferior, causing him much stress and increasing his need for the dummy.
- Never attempt to get rid of the dummy just prior to or straight after the arrival of a new baby.
- Your toddler or child should be in good health and fully recovered from any illness when you attempt to wean him off his dummy.
- Eliminating the dummy should be avoided when major changes are about to take place, for example around the time of moving house, starting nursery or a mother returning to work.

- If a baby under the age of one has a dummy dependency which is causing them to wake at night if the dummy comes out of their mouth, I would encourage the parent to wean the baby off the dummy as described on page 213. This technique is less effective once your child is over a year old, so at this stage my advice in the first instance is to put several dummies in his cot and he ought to be able to find at least one without waking fully. From my experience, there will be another window of opportunity to diminish the dummy dependency when your child is over two years old. In the meantime, I would restrict the use of the dummy to sleep times only and only when they are actually sleeping in their cot.

- However, if your toddler is waking several times a night between the ages of one and two, and unable to locate a dummy for himself, then you may have no option but to get rid of it entirely. How you get rid of the dummy requires care and thought. Trying to eliminate a dummy gradually rarely works as the toddler's constant whingeing and crying over several hours upsets the parent and he or she will relent and give it back. If your toddler is used to having a dummy during the day as well as at night, I would advise that you get rid of it over a weekend when you will be able to elicit help in keeping your toddler busy with lots of activities. He will most probably be miserable for the first day that he is denied it, but getting him out of the house doing things that require lots of physical energy will help to minimise the whingeing. Take him swimming or to the park to play with a ball and go on the swings. When at home try to involve him with finger painting, gardening and water play. It is also probably better not to attempt to put him in his cot for his midday nap, as it is unlikely he will settle without his dummy, and you do not want to get him worked up into a state. If you are out and about, he will hopefully have a catnap in the buggy or car.

- That evening when you settle him to sleep you can try introducing a special new toy that he will hopefully use as a replacement comforter, but obviously not one so small that he would end up sucking it or losing it in the cot. This would simply be a transferral of dependency, when your aim is for your child to soothe himself to sleep without something to suck on. Your toddler will more than likely be very difficult to settle and I would recommend that you have a short-term strategy in place for comforting him while he gets used to not having the dummy. If he is getting very upset at bedtime, you may find that for the first few nights you will need to stay in his room until he goes to sleep, to reassure him. After the first couple of nights, if he is settling to sleep more quickly you can then start to use the gradual withdrawal method as described on page 370 until he has learned to settle himself to sleep without the dummy. The same approach should be used in the night if he wakes crying for his dummy. Once he is settling quickly at bedtime without the dummy you may wish to try waiting for a few minutes or so before going to him in the night, particularly if he is not crying hard and the crying is intermittent. I usually find that once toddlers have learned to settle in the evening without the dummy, they very quickly learn to settle in the night when they wake.

● With a child over two years one has to be much more careful how getting rid of the dummy is approached. The mind and imagination of a child this age are developing very rapidly, and taking the dummy away suddenly could cause much more emotional upset than it would with a younger child. If your child is still using the dummy during the day, restrict it to being used in his room. Gradually decreasing his dependency on it will make it easier for you to persuade him to give it up. My cousin persuaded her little girl of three years to give all her dummies to the tiny babies who were in hospital 'and didn't have a dummy'. For being so thoughtful to these little babies she was allowed to choose a special new toy. This was a great hit, and helped her to settle to sleep happily at night without the dummy. Another good idea is to get a friend to come around and explain that all the shops have sold out of dummies and her little baby really needs one. Making a nice gesture of wrapping the dummy up in pretty paper to give to the baby as a present often makes an older child feel important about the kind gesture he is making.

- Sometimes 'forgetting' to pack the dummy when you go on holiday can work. The fact that children are normally so excited about going on holiday, and bedtimes are usually much later with no pressure of work for parents during the day, can help get over the first couple of days of the dummy being eliminated. Trips to the beach and extra treats of an ice cream for being such a good boy or girl managing without their dummy will also help make the first couple of days go more smoothly.

Dropping the morning nap

If at 18 months your toddler is sleeping well at night and lunchtime and still sleeping between 30 and 40 minutes in the morning, I would advise gradually reducing the morning nap over a few weeks until he is only having 10–15 minutes, to avoid a problem arising at his other sleep times as he gets older. Once he is getting through to his lunchtime nap happily on 10–15 minutes the morning nap can be cut out altogether.

- It can be tricky going from two naps down to one, and getting rid of the morning nap often results in a toddler's middle-of-the-day nap being brought forward too early because he'll get tired sooner. This earlier lunchtime nap obviously means an earlier wake-up time. He can then become so tired that rather than being able to reduce and eliminate the morning nap, parents find themselves having to increase it so that their toddler gets through to his lunchtime nap happily. This can have a knock-on effect whereby the toddler can become so overtired that when he is put to bed at night he goes into a deep sleep very quickly, which in turn can lead to early morning waking.

- What many parents do not realise is that during the transition period of dropping the morning nap, they may need to reduce the lunchtime nap slightly until the morning nap is completely eliminated so that their toddler's overall daytime sleep is reduced. Once the morning nap has successfully been dropped, the lunchtime nap can then be slightly increased again.

- Some toddlers do have difficulty making the transition from two naps to one nap and will get slightly more irritable until their body clock has adjusted. In my opinion it is better to put up with a couple of weeks of grumpiness while you establish one good nap of two hours than to end up with two naps of only 45 minutes each and a toddler who is irritable all afternoon because he has become overtired from too short a lunchtime nap.

Refusing to settle at bedtime

Sometimes a toddler who has always self-settled well suddenly becomes very difficult to settle in the evening, taking longer and longer to go off to sleep. In this situation the solution to the problem is nearly always that his daytime sleep needs to be reduced. While the recommended amount of daytime sleep for a toddler during the second year is around two hours, I have come across many toddlers who need less sleep than this if they are to settle well in the evening and sleep to nearer 7am.

I would recommend that you reduce the amount of daytime sleep your toddler is having by 10 minutes every two to three days until he has gone back to settling well in the evening. If he is still having a morning nap and it is longer than 15 minutes that is where I would start reducing the amount he sleeps. I would keep reducing the nap time by a few minutes every day until he is only having 15 minutes, this will probably mean that you have to bring his afternoon nap time forward. This is fine as it will also help him settling in the evening.

If you have already cut out the morning nap then you should start reducing the middle-of-the-day nap by five minutes every two to three days until he is settling well in the evening again.

CASE STUDY: Lucy, aged 21 months

Problem: Early morning waking

Cause: Needing less sleep than average

Lucy had always needed less than the average daytime sleep required for her age. By 18 months she was down to a 15-minute lunchtime nap, and by 19 months was only having 10 minutes. At 21 months, she started waking around 6am (rather than 7am) and so her mother Abigail knew that her lunchtime nap had to go.

Abigail was dreading dropping this nap, as by lunchtime Lucy was always tired and went into a deep sleep from which Abigail would have real trouble waking her. She wasn't sure how Lucy would cope without a sleep in the day, but in fact there was no need to worry.

For the first six nights Lucy was desperately tired by 6.45pm, and Abigail really had to struggle to keep her awake until 7pm. She persisted, in the knowledge that Lucy's body clock would adjust. On the seventh day things just seemed to click and Lucy easily made it through to 7pm. It was only a couple more days before Abigail realised that her bedtime actually needed to be 7.10pm if she was to sleep until 6.45am. Now, at nearly 24 months Lucy has no daytime sleep and has a 7.20pm bedtime.

Night waking

Unlike babies under one year the cause of night waking in the second year is rarely due to hunger, although it can sometimes be caused by not having adequate fluids at bedtime. At one year of age when the bedtime bottle is replaced with a drink of milk from a cup, the amount a toddler will drink is usually reduced to around 150–180ml (5–6oz). Obviously if your toddler wants more, this is fine as long as he is not reducing the amount of solid food he eats because he is filling up too much with milk. Listed below are the three main causes of night waking with a child during the second year.

- Too much daytime sleep is often a cause of night waking, particularly if a toddler is still having a long morning nap and a two-hour nap in the middle of the day. If your baby is having 30 minutes or more in the morning, I would gradually reduce the morning nap over a couple of weeks and push it later in the morning until nearer 11am so he is only having around 10 minutes or so. Once he is having only 10 minutes you should manage to drop this nap altogether, although he may need to go down slightly earlier for his lunchtime nap for a couple of weeks until he is used to only one nap a day. Aiming for a two-hour nap around 12.30/1pm seems to suit the majority of toddlers.

- Overtiredness can also cause night waking. Again, too long a morning nap can cause this, when the toddler is sleeping longer in the morning and then suddenly starts to reduce his middle-of-the-day nap. The shorter lunchtime nap results in the toddler getting very tired late afternoon and going down to sleep overtired, which can cause him to wake in the night. Unlike too much daytime sleep where the toddler will be inclined to wake around 3/4am, with overtiredness the wakings tend to be before midnight. Again the key to resolving this is to gradually reduce and push on the morning nap until nearer 10.30/11am and only give 10 minutes. Unlike the toddler whose night wakings are caused by too much daytime sleep, the overtired toddler may continue to still need a short morning nap for a little longer, along with a two-hour middle-of-the-day nap.

● The third main cause of night waking at this age is usually caused by the toddler having learned the wrong sleep associations. Sometimes toddlers who learned to self-settle when younger, can forget how to do this. Usually this can happen after an illness or perhaps when on holiday if the routine has been too relaxed. Usually the toddler gets used to falling asleep in a parent's arms and then placed in the cot or the parent will often take to laying next to the toddler on their bed to get them to sleep, before transferring them to the cot. If you think that this is the cause of your toddler's night waking I would suggest that in addition to double-checking that your toddler is not having too much daytime sleep, that you use the gradual withdrawal method as described on page 370 to help your toddler learn to self-settle again. The gradual withdrawal method requires a lot of patience and can often take two to three weeks to see the problem totally resolved, but in my experience it is usually the best method to eliminate night waking with children over one year.

Early morning waking

If your toddler starts to wake much earlier than 7am, he will probably still need to go down for his nap around 9–10am. In my experience toddlers who wake early and go down early for their morning nap usually need to go down earlier for the lunchtime nap. As toddlers are much more active physically during the second year they are then more prone to becoming very exhausted in the late afternoon and often need to go to bed earlier than 7pm. This only reinforces the early morning waking.

I would advise that regardless of how early your toddler wakes you gradually push the morning nap on by five minutes every three to four days, so that his lunchtime nap eventually becomes later. This should have the knock-on effect of him not being so tired in the late afternoon, which means you could gradually delay his bedtime by five minutes every three to four nights. This will hopefully result in him waking up later in the morning. If he does start to wake up later in the morning, it is very important that you begin to reduce the amount of time he sleeps at his morning nap to 10–15 minutes, so that his overall daily sleep is no more than one and a half hours, slightly less than the average amount of sleep needed by a toddler.

CASE STUDY: Max, aged 15 months

Problem: Early morning waking

Cause: Too much daytime sleep and an early bedtime

Max suffered from colic and reflux as a small baby, so for his first four months his mother Sophie had very little sleep. At five months Max was still waking up twice in the middle of the night, so Sophie contacted a sleep clinic to get professional help to resolve the problem. Following their advice Sophie and her husband got Max sleeping through to 6am. However, as the weeks went by Max started to wake earlier and earlier and before long he was waking at around 5.30am every day. Sophie contacted the sleep clinic again. They explained that early morning waking was a difficult problem to resolve and suggested persevering, sometimes getting Max up immediately, sometimes leaving him to cry. For the next nine months

Max woke every morning at approximately 5.15am, with Sophie becoming more and more tired and despondent.

On a typical morning Max would cry as soon as he woke. Sophie would leave him for 15–30 minutes, then she would lie on the nursery floor and play with Max through the bars of the cot for 15 minutes before getting him up and dressed for the day. He never wanted his milk until 7am so she knew hunger wasn't the problem.

At around 12.30pm Max had a nap of between one and one and a half hours and would go to bed at 6.30pm. This pattern continued for over eight months. Sophie felt that she had tried everything suggested by the sleep clinic and had read several books on the subject. It was then that she read a case study about a toddler whose early morning waking problem had been solved on my website, and she contacted me to ask if the same advice would work for Max. I told Sophie that because Max's early morning waking had gone on for such a long time, it would not be as easy to resolve as the case on the website and I would monitor her progress with Max for a few weeks.

The first thing we had to try and achieve was to encourage Max to fall into another sleep cycle after he woke at 5.15am. I told her to remove all toys apart from one soft teddy from the cot as these were confusing – the cot was a place for sleep not play. I then advised Sophie and her husband use a settling technique using the baby monitor to verbally comfort Max instead of leaving him to cry on and off as she had previously been doing. I explained that Sophie's approach was only teaching Max to continue crying when he woke, as he knew she would eventually go in to him.

Every two or three minutes Sophie should say the same words – 'Sshh sshh, it's sleepy time' – over the monitor for a period of no longer than 10 minutes, after which she should go into the dark nursery and verbally reassure him for a further 10 minutes, without picking him up. She should then leave the room for no more than 60 seconds before returning, saying, 'Good morning' and switching on the light, ready to start the day. In this way Sophie could extend the night-time a little and give Max a positive association with the start of the day when she appeared and started chatting cheerfully.

In addition, I suggested adapting his sleep times slightly so that when Max had one and a half hour's daytime nap he would go to bed at 6.45pm and if his nap was shorter he would go to bed at 6.30pm.

Initially, Max cried hysterically when Sophie used the baby monitor or sat by the cot in the dark, but after a few days this did improve and he was considerably calmer, crying much less. However, he still showed absolutely no signs of returning to sleep. I therefore suggested quite a dramatic change to Max's sleep time: Sophie was to put him to bed at 7.30pm. This must have completely confused his body clock as Max woke at 7am the following morning. As this meant that Max had had considerably more sleep at night than he was used to, I advised that Sophie cut his daytime nap down to only 30 minutes; Max then went to bed at 7.30pm again.

The following morning Max woke at 5am and chatted off and on until 6.45am. There were some 15-minute quiet patches so he had returned to sleep for some of the time and I advised Sophie to continue with the 30-minute daytime nap and 7.30pm bedtime. Then one morning Max woke at 5am but this time only cried out a few times before waking again at 6am. I explained that this pattern was a very good sign because it meant Max was learning to settle himself back to sleep when he woke up early in the morning. Another very important development was that Max no longer cried when he woke. Instead he would chatter for 20 minutes before Sophie would get him up – a much nicer start to the day for Sophie.

Over a three-week period, Sophie and I worked on increasing Max's lunchtime nap to 55 minutes and Max continued to wake at 6–6.15am. I explained to Sophie that it could take at least two months for Max's body clock to adjust to a different routine, and that she would have to accept that until this happened there would be times of the day when he would be tired and irritable. However, even with the situation as it stands, Sophie is absolutely thrilled with the later wake-up time especially as Max also plays happily for 20 minutes before she has to get him up.

Co-sleeping to sleeping alone

If you've been co-sleeping your child may have been used to cat-napping on your bed and then not going to sleep until you do. Getting a toddler who has been used to co-sleeping accustomed to sleeping alone in his own room requires a great deal of patience and perseverance. If the transfer from the parents' bed to their own bed in a separate room is not handled properly it can end up being very traumatic for the toddler, resulting in several nights and often weeks of night wakings with lots of crying and screaming.

● First, I would recommend that you get your toddler used to the room that is to be his bedroom during the day, by playing with him there for short spells or reading him stories there. It is important that from day one you put a child gate across the doorway, so that he is used to it being there before you actually move him into the room.

● Once he is familiar with the room, you should aim to start to settle him there in the evening. If he is used to going to bed around the same time as you do, you should bring this bedtime forward by at least an hour to allow for a bath and bedtime story routine. During the first week once you have read him the story and when he is showing signs of tiredness you should dim the lights and settle him in his cot or bed. It is important that you stay with him until he falls asleep. It is fine to reassure him, but try to keep talking to a minimum, repeating the same thing – that it is sleepy time now. If he tries to get out of bed or keeps standing up in the cot, you need to keep laying him down. This can take up to an hour, sometimes even longer. You will probably find that he will wake again at least once more in the night, perhaps even twice. You should go to him as soon as he wakes, reassure him that you are there and stay with him until he settles back to sleep.

- By the end of the first week you should then start to use the gradual withdrawal method to settle him in the evening. When you start to use this method, you can bring his bedtime back to nearer the time that you eventually want to make his regular bedtime (between 7 and 8pm), as it will probably take longer for him to get himself off to sleep than when you sat with him the whole time. But it will be helping him learn to get himself off to sleep without you being in the room. If he wakes in the night it will probably be easier if, for a few more nights, you stay with him until he goes back to sleep.

- When a toddler has been used to going to bed late and sleeping in his parents' bed, it can be difficult to determine how much daytime sleep he actually needs, but once your toddler starts to settle earlier in the evening, it is really important that you start to reduce the amount of sleep that he is having during the day to ensure he will sleep well at night. If he is still having a morning nap, you should gradually push it later in the morning at the same time as reducing it to around 10 minutes. Once he is sleeping only 10 minutes in the morning, you should manage to drop the morning nap so that your toddler is only having one middle-of-the-day nap. The majority of toddlers between one and two years of age can still need a nap of around two hours a day. However, there are always exceptions to the rule and I have worked with many toddlers who by the time they are 15 months may only be having one to one and a half hours a day. Be guided by your toddler and gradually keep reducing his daytime sleep by 10 minutes or so every few days until he is settling well in the evening and sleeping through the night.

● Once he is self-settling quickly in the evening you can then use the gradual withdrawal method in the middle of the night when he wakes. As the night wakings become less and less frequent you should try using a two-way monitor to reassure him when he wakes, so that when he calls out for you, you can reassure him with your voice over the monitor.

● In my experience it can often take two to four weeks to get a toddler who has been used to sleeping in his parents' bed to sleeping happily in their own bed, and there is no benefit in trying to rush this procedure as the last thing that you want is for the toddler to feel insecure by being left to cry alone for any length of time in what should become a happy sleeping environment.

9

Two to Three Years

Your toddler will be becoming his own person by this age, with his own thoughts and ideas. It's important to encourage this and to allow him to develop at his own pace so that he can become confident and self-assured. He will be able to communicate more effectively with you by this age, and this will hopefully lead to less frustration.

By the time he is two, your toddler will be walking steadily and he will become more daring physically as he learns to run, jump and climb. Encourage him to explore and try new things rather than being overprotective. Obviously you don't want him to do things which are risky or dangerous, but at the same time you shouldn't spend all your time telling him to be careful as this can make him over-cautious.

Many children move into a big bed at this time, and may also become more difficult to settle at night. They may also start waking early in the morning, and I often remind parents that a properly darkened bedroom is just as important for a child of this age as it is for a baby.

Another major concern for parents of children this age is when to start potty training. There is no right or wrong time to do this as it depends entirely on you and your child. He needs to be ready for it, but equally so do you as you may need some patience. Your child must be able to understand instructions and to concentrate, but if he is ready I believe potty training can be carried out successfully in as little as a week.

By this age, your child will be able to dress and undress himself, although he will probably still need some help, particularly with zips and buttons. Do try not to do everything for him though as he needs to learn how to do things for himself. One of the most important assets you can give your child at this age is help building his confidence and self-esteem. Try not to constantly correct his mistakes, to compare his abilities with those of his peers or to always expect him to be brilliant at everything. If you are not careful, your own desire for your child to be perfect can start to make it difficult for him to do anything at all and it is important to encourage him to believe in his own abilities.

At the same time, you do need to strike a balance. Sometimes if parents don't set boundaries, children can start to become overconfident at this age. Although initially parents may not think this is a problem it can lead to problems later as an overconfident child is often very unpopular with his peers.

Your child will face new social challenges at this age, as he will be learning how to make friends, how to behave with others and how to take turns and to share. He should be aware of some basic social skills by this age and you will want to make sure that he knows how to say please and thank you. It is also the right time to start instilling good table manners and to teach your child not to interrupt all the time when others are talking.

Children of this age sometimes develop fears and anxieties, and it is worth being careful about what your child watches on television as fears can easily be exacerbated. Children may be afraid of monsters, or of the dark, and separation anxiety can again be a big issue for children between the ages of two and three.

Many children will start at a nursery or pre-school at this age, and choosing the right place for your child can be a daunting prospect if there are a range of choices. When you are choosing a nursery, think carefully about what would best suit your child and your family, and visit as many places as you can before making a final decision. There are many advantages to attending nursery, not just educational benefits but also the wider social benefits of being with other children of the same age and learning to socialise, and this is why parents are often keen to start some nursery or playgroup sessions even if the child is being cared for mainly by one parent at home.

By the time your child reaches the age of three, he will be an individual with his own character, likes and needs. He will also be establishing a degree of independence and starting to make his own friends. He will be more physically active and able to communicate effectively, but parental support to help build confidence and self-esteem is still key at this stage.

Feeding

What to expect

During the third year as a child becomes more independent it is important to let him decide when he has had enough to eat. As in the second year you may find that he will go for two or three days and seem to eat enormous amounts, and then for a few days appear to hardly eat anything. He should not be forced or cajoled to finish a meal, if he genuinely doesn't want to eat. However, he also has to learn that he cannot look for food an hour or so later and should be made to wait until the next snack or mealtime. By the time they reach two years of age a toddler should be totally capable of self-feeding using a spoon and well on the way to mastering the art of using a fork.

During the third year some food refusal and fussiness can become a real problem if your child is constantly offered food substitutes at mealtimes or allowed to eat an hour or so after his usual time. This is also a time when a child becomes more aware of different commercial foods such as cereals and snacks. If your child starts refusing breakfast it can be very tempting to cave in to pressure from him asking for some sugar-laden cereal that he has perhaps seen on television. If he refuses his usual breakfast cereal, then for a week or so offer him a small selection of toast and spreads and yoghurts or cheese and fruit instead, before trying him again with the cereal he used to eat.

What to aim for

Children aged between one and three years need around 350mg of calcium a day. If your toddler is still drinking around 350ml (12oz) of milk a day, he will be getting his daily calcium from milk alone. However, some children can become disinterested in milk at this age. If this is the case, ensuring that your child has a serving of yoghurt or cheese each day, along with calcium-rich cereals and leafy green vegetables, will ensure that he is getting more than his daily requirements.

Similarly, if your child is no longer drinking milk it is important that you ensure that his daily milk intake is replaced with the same amount of water. Children of this age don't often know how to differentiate between thirst and hunger, so keep a close eye on his fluid intake to ensure that he does not become dehydrated. If he no longer wants his bedtime milk, he should still be encouraged to have a good drink of water around the same time he used to drink his milk.

Continue to aim for three healthy meals a day with healthy snacks in between meals. Try to stick to regular meal- and snack-times so that your child does not get overtired, which can lead to fussiness at mealtimes. Once your toddler reaches two years of age you can gradually introduce semi-skimmed rather than full-fat milk as a drink if that is what you and your family prefer to buy, provided he is eating a varied and healthy diet.

At this age it is also important to encourage good table manners, as by now there is no excuse for messy eating. Encourage your child to use his cutlery properly and to rest his fork on the side of his plate while chewing his food. He can also be encouraged to drink from an open-top beaker; again encourage him to rest his beaker next to his plate in between sips.

Encourage your toddler to wash his own hands before and after meals now, as opposed to you wiping them for him.

Between two and three years of age a typical day would look something like the following:

7/7.30am   awake, drink and breakfast

9/10am   playschool or social activity

12/12.30pm   lunch

1pm   short nap/rest time

2pm   playschool or social activity

5pm   tea

6pm   bath/bed routine (may need to start earlier if you have a new baby)

7/7.30pm   settled in bed

Feeding Problems

Fussy eating

How you deal with any feeding problems at this stage may affect your toddler's attitude to food for the rest of his life, so it is vital that mealtimes do not become a battle of wills. In my experience, toddlers who are going through a fussy stage and who are constantly coaxed, bribed or force-fed by spoon, can sometimes end up with a long-term problem of fussiness where they won't sit down and enjoy their meal. If you are concerned that your toddler may not be eating enough, it is a good idea to keep a food diary for one week. Each day list all the food and drink he has taken, as well as the times of consumption. Because a toddler's appetite can vary considerably from day to day, it is important that you calculate his overall food intake over one week. Most parents find that over several days the amount of food their toddler has eaten averages out to meet all his nutritional requirements. However, if your toddler's food diary shows that he is actually eating less than the recommended amounts, it would be advisable to discuss things with your doctor or health visitor. Here are the most common causes of food refusal and faddiness, together with suggestions for resolving each one.

● Fruit juice given immediately before food or within an hour prior to eating can take the edge off a toddler's appetite. Encourage your toddler to eat half of his food before giving him a drink. If possible, try to get your toddler used to drinking water in between meals. If juice is given, make sure it is very well diluted, and offer it no later than two hours before his mealtime.

● Many leading brands of fromage frais are high in sugar, containing sometimes as much as 14.5g (½oz) in a 100g (4oz) pot. Sugar is often the second largest ingredient in the pot. Toddlers can become addicted to these and, if given them often enough, will soon lose their appetite for other foods.

- Try to offer a variety of different foods in small amounts, rather than one or two in large amounts. For example, serving fish with a small amount of carrots, cauliflower, peas and potatoes is more likely to stimulate your toddler's taste buds than serving fish with carrots and potatoes. By offering him a selection of the foods you know he likes, you will be encouraging him at least to try some of the new foods.

- It is best to serve your toddler's main protein meal at lunchtime, and then if he becomes fussy and tired later in the day, you know he has had one good meal and you can be more relaxed about tea, which is likely to be the busier part of the day. He can then be offered something which you know he likes and is easy for you to prepare, such as pasta or a baked potato with a filling, or a thick soup and sandwiches.

- Schedule meals and snacks at regular times and stick to these times. If after 30 minutes your toddler is not showing any interest in eating, remove the food without making any comment on his lack of appetite. However, he should not be allowed anything to eat or drink until the next scheduled meal or snack. Ideally, there should be a two-hour gap between meals and snacks.

- Eating even the smallest of snacks less than two hours before a meal can be enough to affect some toddlers' appetites. The type of snack given is significant. I would not offer foods that take longer to digest, such as bananas and cheese, as a snack to a child who is being fussy about meals as they are more likely to take the edge off his appetite. Carbohydrates such as rice cakes, crisps and biscuits are other snacks that can have a knock-on effect at mealtimes as they can fill a toddler with a small appetite up.

● Avoid giving your toddler puddings or sweets as an incentive for finishing his meal. This only leads to him thinking that the food can't be that good if you are offering him a bribe to eat it. Instead, offer a selection of fresh fruit, cheese and crackers, or plain yoghurt mixed with fresh mashed fruit.

● Try to avoid distractions at mealtimes, such as reading or playing games. Also remember that every time you speak to your toddler he will need to answer. Therefore be careful about getting into long-winded conversations before he has managed to eat most of his meal.

● It is also important to sit down and eat with your child whenever possible. I believe that many eating problems evolve because children reach a stage where they feel very threatened when left sitting alone to eat a plate of food. They cannot understand why they should be expected to eat all the different foods on their plate when Mummy and Daddy are rushing about and only having to eat a sandwich.

Food refusal

I usually find with young children who eat a very limited diet, and particularly those who refuse to eat vegetables, that they are eating either excessive carbohydrates or protein, which can often contribute to the problem of refusal to eat vegetables and can limit their interest in a wider variety of foods.

- Between one and three, guidelines recommend that your toddler needs two portions of protein per day, depending on his age and weight – this can be meat, fish, egg or pulses – and three to four portions of carbohydrate, which can include bread, rice, pasta and cereal, and he should be eating five portions of fruit and vegetables.

- Don't be tempted to overload your toddler's plate. It is better to start off with only two slices of carrot and one broccoli floret and gradually build up the amounts you give him rather than risking him rejecting it from the outset. You can increase the quantity by such a tiny amount that he barely notices, and after a couple of weeks he will be happily eating proper portions.

- Bring colours and shapes into meal preparation, for example, mixing some tiny green peas with some big orange slices of carrot.

- While it is important that a child is never forced to eat foods that he genuinely dislikes, I believe that with the huge variety of foods available, particularly vegetables and salads, it is not acceptable that a child dislikes every single one. Refusal of vegetables is a very common problem among young children and can be avoided if parents give their children a choice and refuse to substitute them repeatedly with the same favoured foods.

CASE STUDY: Alice, aged 2 years and 10 months

Problem: Fantastic feeder to fussy feeder

Cause: Over-compensating for likes and dislikes

Mother Emily went back to work when her baby Alice was six months old and a nanny took over. Alice ate well and with great enthusiasm; in fact Emily remembers that she used to look very surprised when friends' babies wouldn't eat anything that didn't come out of a jar. Alice, in fact, was the opposite: the one thing she wouldn't eat was food from a jar. As Alice got older she continued to prefer 'mushy' foods, such as shepherd's pie, but generally she remained a good eater, and Emily did not see this as a problem. Then Emily decided to give up work when Alice was around 20 months. The nanny left and Alice's eating habits seemed to change overnight.

To Emily's surprise, in the first couple of weeks when she had sole care of her daughter, Alice began to refuse some of her meals. Initially, she would eat a little before pushing the spoon away, but the problem became more pronounced and Alice began to refuse her meals constantly. Emily responded by becoming increasingly anxious. The nanny had been hugely competent and Emily felt that on some level her daughter must be reacting to the change in routine, as she persisted in refusing the wide range of foods she had previously enjoyed.

Emily tried to entice Alice to eat by pretending the spoon was an aeroplane and would offer her alternatives if one of the favourite foods was rejected. Within a fortnight of the nanny leaving, Emily had resorted to giving Alice the few foods she was now prepared to eat – yoghurt and grated cheese. Mealtimes became increasingly upsetting, with Alice pushing the foods on to the floor and Emily almost crying with frustration.

Within two months it had reached a stage where Alice was eating only Weetabix with banana, jam sandwiches, biscuits, chocolate and ice cream. Emily did occasionally try to withdraw biscuits between meals, but Alice would cry and scream until Emily gave in. It would be the same at other people's houses, which in the end made it very stressful for Emily to go anywhere with Alice. The less good food Alice ate, the more she demanded biscuits and cried until she got them. Emily would give in and Alice would not be hungry at mealtimes. She would be hungry again later and demand more sweet things. Emily couldn't get herself out of the habit of giving in to Alice's demands for biscuits and chocolates, and at this point she rang me for advice.

When I spoke to Emily I said that the most important thing was to remove all biscuits, sweets and ice cream from the house and to decide firmly that there must be no eating between meals. We prepared a menu plan for the next seven days and I told Emily that if Alice cried and screamed for biscuits and sweets when she was given her meals, she was to walk away from her. She must not get into a conversation about food.

Emily started the plan at the weekend so that her husband could support her. I suggested that they offer Alice a selection of fruits and yoghurt at breakfast instead of the usual Weetabix and banana. I explained that we should save the foods that we knew Alice would eat until teatime. We did not want her final meal of the day before bedtime to become a battle. By offering only fruit and yoghurt at breakfast, Alice would, we hoped, be hungrier for her lunch. Lunch had always been her worst meal, where she played up the most, refusing all forms of protein since the nanny had left. I suggested that Emily shouldn't overburden Alice with huge platefuls of food, but put small amounts, including some new vegetables, on the plate.

With hindsight Emily recognised that her concern about her daughter missing the nanny had meant she had reacted too quickly to Alice's altered feeding habits. We both agreed that Alice, a bright little girl, had rapidly established that fussy eating was rewarded by her mother's undivided attention. At 21 months of age she began to manipulate her mother with great success. The more Emily responded, the more the pattern was set. Sugary snacks between meals ruined Alice's appetite and made it even less likely that she would eat wholesome food. Reversing these patterns was going to be challenging for Alice's parents. Having been used to getting her own way, Alice had awful tantrums during the first three days. She demanded biscuits, hurled herself on to the floor and vehemently refused her meals. It was very upsetting for everybody. Alice's sleep was starting to be affected – she was waking earlier and, as a consequence, was whingy and prone to tears during most of the first few days. However, Emily and her husband persevered and, to their delight, by the fourth morning, Alice ate her fruit and yoghurt within eight minutes. At lunchtime, within 20 minutes she happily ate fish fingers and peas with baby new potatoes. The pattern was broken.

Gradually, over the next few days, Alice's parents reintroduced cereal and toast at breakfast. Once they became confident that her lunchtime appetite had returned, they were able to increase her breakfast.

I encouraged her parents to give her nutritious finger foods at lunchtime, including cooked carrot batons and pieces of chicken breast and honey-roast ham. By doing this, Alice was able to feed herself, and while she was no longer in a position to choose her meals, she did have a level of control that pacified her. In addition, I told Emily to praise her when she ate, but to ignore her if the food was either rejected or thrown from the high chair. Within the first week, Alice was eating a good breakfast, including porridge, toast fingers and cut-up fruit. Her lunch had the appropriate balance of nutritious food. By the second week she was happily attempting to feed herself most of the meal using her fingers, and she was also allowing her mother to help. On the increasingly rare occasions when food was refused, Emily responded by making no fuss, but offering no alternatives. Her daughter's stamina was improved, she no longer needed or expected sugary snacks between meals, and on the occasions when they were out the only snacks she was allowed were healthy ones in moderation – fruit, raisins and raw vegetables.

Toddlers are very sensitive to the response their behaviour generates. While Alice's response was extreme, it was clearly motivated by her discovery that she could get her mother's attention by not eating. Her mother's lack of confidence in herself meant that she over-compensated for her daughter's fussy eating. Fortunately, they both re-established good feeding patterns, which they have been able to maintain to this day.

Refusing protein

Some toddlers who have happily eaten chicken, fish, lamb and beef during their first year, will suddenly start to refuse some, if not all, of these protein-rich foods during their second year. As a parent this can be quite worrying as you are no doubt concerned that they may be missing out on important key nutrients, such as iron, zinc and vitamin B.

● One of the reasons that many toddlers start to refuse protein is that once it goes from being served in a really puréed form to being sliced or diced, the texture and taste changes, and it is often served alone as opposed to being mixed up with vegetables. While it is very important that your toddler's food is no longer puréed, I have not found it a problem if parents continue to pulse the protein part of the recipe for a little longer so that it is soft and palatable. Using recipes such as spaghetti bolognaise, shepherd's pie and chicken meatballs, where the meat is more ground up, can also be a way of getting your toddler to eat protein.

● However if a toddler starts to refuse meat because of the flavour as opposed to the texture, I think it is important not to force him to eat it. I would advise that these particular foods should continue to be offered every couple of weeks, in the hope that they will eventually begin to accept small amounts, but never forced.

● In the meantime make certain that your toddler's diet includes eggs, nuts, and pulses, such as chickpeas, lentils and a variety of different beans. These foods have less iron than meat, so to ensure that your toddler's iron requirements are being met, it is important to serve them with foods high in vitamin C as this will help your toddler absorb more of the iron. Foods high in vitamin C include citrus fruits, kiwi fruit, blackcurrants, strawberries, and to a lesser degree, sweet potatoes.

CASE STUDY: Liam, aged 2 years and 10 months

Problem: Excessive night-time waking

Cause: Using commercially made meals

Serena contacted me a couple of months after the birth of her twin girls. Both babies were doing well on the Contented Little Baby routines, sleeping until 4am from their last feed at 10.30pm. However, since the birth of the twins, their older brother, Liam, had started to wake up two or three times a night, often staying awake for an hour or so at a time. Serena was at breaking point, trying to survive on two to three hours of broken sleep a night and to cope with two babies and a very irritable toddler during the day. Since the birth of the babies, Liam had gone from being an extremely placid, loving little boy to one who would get angry and aggressive, frequently having outbursts of uncontrollable behaviour. Her health visitor reassured Serena that Liam was probably feeling very insecure and jealous, suddenly finding that he had to share Mummy with not just one baby but two. She arranged for Serena to get some help with the twins twice a week from a government programme in her area called Sure Start so that she could give Liam some undivided attention. Things did improve slightly, but Liam still continued to wake up in the night and would settle back to sleep only when given a drink of fruit juice. He also continued to have uncontrollable outbursts once or twice a day. During one of these outbursts Liam scratched one baby's face so badly that she had to be taken to hospital to have the wound treated. It was at this point that Serena called me to see if I could offer any advice on how to deal with Liam's jealousy and rages.

Regardless of the type of problem a parent is experiencing and wants my help with, I always ask them to send me a feeding and sleeping diary. In my experience, a huge number of the varied problems that parents contact me about tend to be linked in some way to diet. Serena assured me that Liam had always eaten well and was given a wide variety of different foods. The only change in his diet was that she was unable to cook him as many fresh meals as she used to, and, more often than not, he would be given what she and her husband were having for lunch or dinner. In between meals he was only ever given fresh fruit and well-diluted juice.

At first glance it appeared that Liam was eating healthy food – plenty of bread, pasta and rice, along with a wide variety of different vegetables. Every day he would have chicken, fish or lamb at his main meal, and in the evening he would be given either a pasta dish or thick soup with sandwiches.

Serena assured me that this was the pattern of eating he had followed since reaching his first birthday. The only difference was that, following the birth of the twins, she did not have time to prepare as much of the food herself, but she always ensured that she did buy the best-quality commercially prepared food. She also admitted that she was allowing Liam to drink fruit squash, something that he had never had in the past.

I asked her to send me a list of the commercially prepared meals and food that she was using. I purchased everything that Serena mentioned on her list and spent a morning analysing the labels and the ingredients. Although experts are divided about the effect commercially prepared food can have on young children, I am convinced that excessive amounts of such foods can adversely affect their behaviour.

When I compared the commercial version with a home-made version of the same dish, I found additional starch fillers and sugars. While an occasional meal containing these things would not affect the behaviour of the majority of children, I believe that, given on a daily basis, they possibly could. This would apply particularly to a child such as Liam, who had always been given meals that consisted of pure, fresh food without fillers, additives and suchlike. Starch fillers, maltodextrin and sugars are of no nutritional benefit to young children, and the main reason they are used is to boost the calorie content of the meal. This means that a child who is fed exclusively on these types of meals would probably not be receiving a properly balanced diet. A well-balanced diet consisting of a variety of foods is essential for the healthy growth of both mind and body.

The food diary also showed that Liam was drinking several large cups of fruit squash and eating so-called healthy cereal and milk bars each day. There are many types of fruit drink on the market, which claim to be tooth-friendly and contain no added sugar or artificial colour, and many cereal bars make claims to have similar health benefits.

Once Serena had a clearer understanding of what was in the types of food that Liam was eating, I explained to her how the excessive amounts of refined carbohydrate and sugar in his diet were probably affecting his blood sugar balance, causing him to have erratic mood swings and excessive night-time waking. I explained to Serena that the problem could not be solved overnight as we would gradually have to wean Liam off all the highly refined food he was having back on to a well-balanced diet of complex carbohydrates, proteins and fats. His sugary snacks and fruit drinks needed to be replaced with healthier alternatives, such as well-diluted fruit juice and fresh fruit, whole grain rice cakes with a spread or home-made muffins or flapjacks.

The first thing I advised Serena to do was to replace all commercial snacks and drinks with healthier alternatives. Although Liam did have several tantrums about this, they were no worse than his behaviour before we started the change in his diet. By the end of the first week he was having only the fruit drink when he woke in the night, and all his daytime drinks were either water or very well-diluted juice. He was also happily eating healthier snacks and joining in the cooking of home-made treats such as muffins.

During the second week Serena started to replace the commercial meals with similar home-made recipes. Again Liam made a fuss at mealtimes, and on two occasions would not eat lunch. Serena was strong and did not give in to his demands, and by the end of the week he was having home-made meals at both lunch and tea. We then started to introduce healthier cereal options at breakfast, which proved difficult because Liam refused them. Serena did offer him alternatives of toast and spread, or fruit and yoghurt, but for five days Liam refused breakfast. Serena found this very difficult, as she was sure that not having breakfast was nutritionally damaging. I reassured her that she must not feel guilty as she was not starving Liam or refusing him food – she was giving him a choice of healthy options, and by giving in to his demands she could end up with him backtracking to a diet of unhealthy food, which in the long term would do him much more damage. It was a real battle of wills, but by the end of the week Liam was happy to eat one of the healthy breakfast cereals that he was offered.

He was now eating a very healthy diet, but was still prone to emotional outbursts, and although his number of wakings in the night reduced to only one a week, Serena was disappointed that she was still having problems. I explained to her that while Liam's diet was the main cause of his bad behaviour and night-time waking, these problems were also caused by habit, and it could take a long time for things to improve totally.

I suggested that she introduced a star chart to encourage Liam to sleep through the night without having the fruit drink, and for occasions when he behaved particularly well or performed tasks without a fuss.

Although it took a further three weeks to crack the nights, Liam did start to sleep right through the night and his behaviour saw a rapid improvement, with only the occasional temper tantrum (which is normal). He continues to be a very happy little boy who eats a really healthy diet. Serena and I went on to compile a healthy menu plan so that she could do a batch cook once a fortnight and combine healthy frozen meals with quick, fresh alternatives such as risotto, pasta and stir-fries.

Sleep

What to expect

Children of this age will still need at least 8 to 10 hours' sleep during the night and will cut right back on their daytime sleep. The length of time they nap can vary from day to day; sometimes they may sleep between one to two hours, other days they may only sleep one hour. By the time most children reach three years of age they have cut out the middle-of-the-day nap altogether. If your child is ready to cut his daytime nap, you should still make sure that you give your child some quiet time in the afternoon for him to wind down.

What to aim for

It is important to monitor your child's daytime sleep very closely during this stage, to ensure that, as the amount of sleep he needs decreases, the sleep he cuts back on is during the day and not at night. In my experience a sound night's sleep is essential if the child is to cope with the high demand on his energy levels during the day. Keeping a close eye on his daytime activities to ensure that he does not burn out at this stage is vital. Burn-out can happen when a toddler becomes exhausted with activities and play dates and doesn't have enough quiet time or rest to recharge his batteries. Maintaining a calm consistent bedtime routine is also a key factor in maintaining good-quality sleep at night.

Sleep Problems

Refusing to go to bed

Too much daytime sleep and overtiredness are two of the main causes of bedtime battles. As your toddler learns many new skills, in particular walking and talking, his confidence increases and he becomes much more assertive. His natural desire to take more responsibility and control of his own actions will often lead to him devising his own bedtime routine.

● While it is important to avoid confrontation and risking your toddler becoming upset at bedtime, it is essential that you remain consistent with his routine so that bedtime does not get increasingly later, which will result in him getting a second wind and fighting sleep.

● Not getting enough sleep during the day can also cause problems at bedtime, particularly with a child who has dropped his daytime nap. During this stage daytime activities have usually increased, demanding more of the child's mental and physical energy. Even the most easy-going of children can start to play up at bedtime, and overtiredness is one of the main reasons a child becomes difficult. A child you used to settle happily at around 7.30pm may need his bedtime routine brought forward so that he is in bed by 7pm, particularly if he has not had a nap that day.

Transferring your toddler from the cot to bed

In my experience, transferring a toddler to a big bed before he is ready can be a major cause of night-time waking. Many parents make this transfer between 18 months and two years of age, often prompted by the fact a new baby is on the way and the cot will be needed. Other parents listen to the advice of friends who say that their toddler sleeps much better now he is in a bed.

The majority of my clients leave their toddlers in a cot until they are nearly three years old. Because all of these toddlers are still sleeping in a sleeping bag, the possibility of them trying to climb out of the cot rarely arises. If a cot is needed for a second baby, many parents choose to buy a second cot, or a cot bed into which the toddler can be transferred before the new baby arrives. This can eventually be used as a first bed for the second baby. Before transferring your toddler to a bed consider the following points.

- A toddler who is transferred to a bed too early is more likely to wake up early or get up in the night. He is inclined to get more upset when parents try to settle him back to sleep in his own bed than an older child, and often ends up sleeping in his parents' bed.

- The arrival of a new baby often prompts the toddler to get out of bed if he hears the baby crying in the night. He quickly learns to demand the same attention as the baby in the night – feeds and a cuddle.

- A toddler who is potty-trained and sleeping in a bed will be more likely to take his nappy off in the night than a toddler sleeping in a cot with a sleeping bag. In the sleeping bag he won't have access to the nappy whereas in the bed he may be tempted to remove the nappy even if he is not able to get through the night without it.

- When the time comes to make the transfer from the cot to a bed, if you have not already done so I would recommend that you put a stair gate across your toddler's bedroom door, so that he is used to it being there before his move to the bed. Not having a gate in place will mean that should your toddler decide to get out of bed, he will more than likely have made it into your bedroom before you can get to him and return him to his bed. Once this happens a pattern can quickly emerge not only at bedtime but in the middle of the night, where the toddler will repeatedly get out of bed and come looking for you. Having a gate in place from the first night means that your toddler will realise that while he can get out of bed, he cannot get any further than the bedroom door.

- How quickly he will learn to stay in his bed will be very much determined by how you deal with the first few nights of him being put in his big bed. Each time he gets out of bed and comes to the gate you should promptly take him straight back to bed, without any discussion, apart from saying it is sleep time and everyone is in bed. Do not respond to requests for another drink or another story. By being consistent every time he gets up, not getting involved in conversation and taking him back to bed straight away, he will learn within a few nights that it is not worth the effort of him getting out of bed.

- When transferring a toddler to a big bed I would recommend doing it over a long weekend, so that any loss of sleep you may encounter the first few nights is easier to deal with during the day.

- It is also important that during the first few nights of your toddler going into the big bed, that you do not increase his daytime sleep to compensate for any sleep he may have lost in the night.

- Once your toddler goes from a cot to a bed, you may find that he will no longer sleep in the dark. This is perfectly normal and I certainly would not force a child of this age to sleep in the dark. Another reason for installing the stair gate is so that you can leave the door slightly ajar, with a small hall light on, or alternatively you can put a small socket light in his room, which gives off a dim glow.

Fear of the dark

During the third year even the most happy and confident child can develop a fear of the dark. A child who suddenly starts becoming fretful and frightened at bedtime and talking of monsters being in the room should be taken seriously. At this age he is still unable to comprehend the difference between what is real and what isn't, so telling him not to be silly and that monsters do not exist will be of no help.

- I think it can be very damaging to force a child of this age to try to face up to his fears and go to sleep in the dark. Many children of this age do develop certain fears and often are not really aware of what they are frightened of, using monsters as a reason for not wanting to be alone. Battling with your toddler to get him to go to sleep in the dark would create a sleeping problem which, if allowed to continue, would in the long term be much harder to resolve than his fear of the dark.

- Instead of dismissing your child's fears as silly, give him lots of reassurance that you are just next door. Leaving a small plug-in light on in his room until he goes to sleep can also be reassuring. If a child starts to wake up frightened in the night or have nightmares it would be advisable to leave it on all night. Or you can leave his room door slightly open with a dim light from the hall to reassure him. However, it would be better if he could be persuaded to settle for a night light in his room, as problems can often arise when a second baby comes along if the elder child is used to having the door open – he will be more inclined to get up in the night if he hears his mother attending to the baby.

- Using a star chart to reward him when he settles quickly and easily in the evening will also help.

- Dr Miriam Stoppard says, 'If your child is afraid of monsters or ghosts say that you are a parent who can do magical things to them. Say that you are able to blow them away and give a big blow.' I have found this sort of approach far more effective than trying to convince the child the monster doesn't exist; another idea is to fill a spray bottle with water to make a Monster Repellent.

- Giving your child a special magic toy that sits near the door to keep the monsters out can also be a successful way of eliminating a child's fears.

Nightmares

Although the majority of childcare experts say that nightmares are most common between the ages of three and six years, I personally believe that they can start much earlier, and when working as a maternity nurse I often had to deal with children as young as two years old who were experiencing nightmares.

Dr Richard Ferber says that children can experience dreams and nightmares from the second year of life, but at this age do not understand the difference between dreaming and reality. He says that nightmares are mainly a symptom of daytime emotional struggles. He believes that most nightmares do reflect emotional conflicts, but in most cases neither the nightmares nor the conflicts are 'abnormal'. Rather, the normal emotional struggles of growing up are at times significant enough to lead to occasional nightmares.

Nightmares usually occur during a REM sleep cycle, often referred to as the light sleep cycle.

- If your child has always slept well and suddenly wakes up screaming during the second half of the night, he is probably having a bad dream and should be comforted and reassured immediately. Because a child of this age is still not able to grasp the difference between dreaming and reality, it is pointless trying to convince him that the monster doesn't exist. In my experience parents who do this only cause the child to become more upset. I have found the best approach is to follow the advice of Dr John Pearce and Dr Miriam Stoppard and work out a plan for how best to deal with the monster, i.e. making the monster fall into a hole or saying a magical spell to make it disappear.

- Should your child repeatedly wake up crying – over several weeks, for example – it is advisable to look at what is happening during the day to see if there is a particular reason for the bad dreams. Keeping a detailed diary of his daytime activities and details of the nightmare will often help pinpoint something or someone that could be causing him distress. The following guidelines list the most common causes of frequent nightmares and how to deal with them:

  - Bedtime stories and videos that involve violence or have a frightening storyline can cause some children to have nightmares. A child under three years of age is unlikely to understand the difference between fantasy and reality, and stories and videos should be monitored to ensure that they are suitable for your child's age. If you have an older child it may be necessary to stagger the bedtimes for a short while so that the younger one is not subjected to anything frightening. Even a story such as Little Red Riding Hood or The Three Little Pigs is enough to trigger nightmares with a child under three years.

● Sometimes it is possible to pin down nightmares to a certain activity. Your child may feel threatened by an aggressive child at playgroup, or have developed a fear of certain animals or people such as a policeman, etc.

● A fear of the dark often contributes to a child having more frequent nightmares. Installing a low-voltage plug-in night light and buying a special new toy that will chase the monsters away often helps.

● Frequent late bedtimes, which usually result in a child getting overtired and irritable, are often a cause, particularly when parents get short-tempered and cross. The child ends up going to bed exhausted, fretful and feeling unloved. He will then often wake in the night and remember how cross his parents were, then get upset and cry out. Although he will blame a bad dream, often the real cause for him crying out is a need for reassurance that his parents are no longer angry with him.

Night terrors

Night terrors are very different from nightmares and need to be dealt with differently. Children who have night terrors will often wake up screaming with their eyes open. Whereas a child having a nightmare can be comforted, it can be very difficult to calm and comfort a child having a night terror and it is very distressing for parents to watch their child as he appears to be terrified, often sweating profusely and screaming as if he is experiencing something horrific. You may feel helpless, but it is best not to try to wake him but rather to stay close by and comfort him as he calms down. Some believe that night terrors may be caused by overtiredness, and most children do grow out of them.

- A child experiencing a night terror will usually wake up screaming during the earlier part of the night, usually within one to four hours of falling asleep. They occur during the non-REM sleep, often referred to as the deep sleep, and although a child having a night terror will scream, thrash around and have his eyes open, he is rarely awake. The majority of experts advise parents that unless the child shows signs of wanting to be held, it is better not to, as it often makes matters worse if the child becomes fully awake and is unaware of what has been happening.

- It is better to just stay close by so that if needed you can prevent him from injuring himself. A night terror usually lasts between 10 and 20 minutes and, provided the child is not woken up, he will settle back to sleep quickly once the terror is over. It is important not to mention the terror the following day, as your child may get very upset if questioned about something of which he has no recollection.

- In my experience night terrors are much more common among children who become overtired because they have inconsistent daytime and bedtime routines. Dr Richard Ferber shares my view and says in his book that in very young children overtiredness is the main cause of night terrors. He advises that parents should ensure their child gets sufficient sleep, and if necessary consider an earlier bedtime. He also emphasises the importance of a regular and consistent daytime routine.

● If your child is having regular night terrors and you are worried about this, you should consult your family doctor.

CASE STUDY: Zak, aged three years

Problem: Evening settling

Cause: Too much daytime sleep

From the age of six months Zak had always slept a solid 12 hours every night, from 7.30pm to 7.30am. At around two years he started to take longer to settle in the evening and Amber, his mother, reduced his lunchtime nap from one hour 30 minutes to one hour which quickly got him back to sleeping 12 hours. He slept well for a further three months when he started to resist bedtime again, Amber reduced his lunchtime nap again so that he was having only 40 minutes, which again resolved the problem. But within a few weeks the bedtime settling became a problem again. A pattern emerged where Zak would sleep well for two or three weeks, and then would need his lunchtime nap reduced again. By the time he reached two years and 10 months Zak had given up his daytime nap altogether. It was also around this time that Amber returned to work full time and Zak started attending nursery full time.

Amber would pick up Zak from nursery around 5.30pm and they would arrive home around 6pm. Although it was rushed trying to fit in tea and the bath and bedtime routine Amber would still aim to have Zak in bed by 7.30pm. However, it wasn't long before Zak was resisting bedtime again, crying and insisting on another story or more milk to drink. Sometimes he would get so upset that Amber would end up taking him into her bed until he fell asleep, and then transferring him back to his own bed. He then started to wake up crying around 5.30/6am and shouting for mummy. Amber would leave him for 10 to 15 minutes before going to him in the hope that he would settle back to sleep. However, this never happened and Amber would end up taking Zak into her bed to get him back to sleep, and then wake him up around 8.30am.

As the weeks went by Zak became more and more difficult to settle to sleep in the evening and more difficult to wake in the morning. His daily reports from nursery were regularly filled with comments about how tired and irritable Zak had been.

When Amber contacted me the first thing that I advised her was she would need to be more consistent with the settling at bedtime and the early morning waking. Taking Zak into her bed some of the time and not at others was not helping the situation, as it was sending mixed messages to Zak. I suggested that if in the early stages of the programme if she needed to assist Zak to sleep by being with him, either in the morning or the evening, that it should be done in his room and not hers. I also advised that when Zak woke in the morning, she should go to him immediately and help settle him back to sleep, even if it meant that she had to sit on the chair in his bedroom until he went to back to sleep. As Zak had never gone back to sleep, delaying going in to him only meant he became more awake and took longer to get back to sleep. I also said that she should start to wake Zak up around 7.30am, so that he was properly awake by 8am. Allowing Zak to sleep to nearer 8.30am meant that he was not tired enough to sleep at 7.30pm in the evening. Most children of Zak's age are capable of sleeping between 11 and 12 hours at night, so if Amber wanted Zak to settle well at 7.30pm and sleep consistently to 7/7.30am in the morning, she must start to wake him up earlier in the morning.

I also advised that for a few nights that Amber push the bedtime routine later by 30 minutes and spend a little more time with Zak, and then aim to have him in bed around 8pm. Putting him to bed too early before he was ready to sleep only resulted in him getting upset and bedtime becoming a battle of the wills. I explained that as we gradually brought Zak's morning waking-up time earlier and earlier, we would also gradually bring his bedtime earlier again until he was settling well at 7.30pm and sleeping to 7/7.30am.

Within a week Zak was sleeping to nearer 7am, which meant Amber was able to gradually bring his bedtime forward by 10 minutes every couple of nights until he was settling to sleep easily at 7.30pm.

PART 4

Helping Your Baby to Sleep

10

Teaching Your Baby to Self-Settle

The whole aim of my first book, *The Contented Little Baby Book*, and the nine routines within the book was to ensure that a baby's individual feeding and sleeping needs were met at all times, so that babies are never left to cry for lengthy periods and that babies happily and quickly learn to self-settle and gradually and naturally sleep a longer spell in the night, without the need for sleep training, which nearly always involves longer spells of crying. As I mention in all of my books, sleep training methods such as controlled crying/comforting should always be seen as a last resort and only when the habit of rocking, feeding and giving the baby a dummy to sleep have created such bad sleep associations that the night wakings are affecting the mental and physical development of the baby.

Of course, I do also accept that despite following my routines and being well fed and ready to sleep some babies simply do not fall asleep easily and will need help to learn to do so. The most common example of this is of babies who get overtired and fight sleep. An overtired baby rarely gives off the usual signals of tiredness and no matter how hard parents work at getting his feeding and sleeping times right, within a very short time of him being placed in his bed he will start to fight sleep. In this instance it really is important that you follow one of the methods below – appropriate for your baby's age – to help your baby get to sleep. To keep intervening and trying to settle an overtired baby will only result in the baby becoming more and more distressed and continuing to cry for a much longer period, than if allowed a short spell of crying down.

Crying down (for babies up to one year)

Crying down is a gentle method of assisting your baby to sleep that can be particularly helpful when feeding problems have been resolved and a baby has only mild sleep association problems or has difficulty falling asleep because he is overtired or overstimulated. Dr Brian Symon uses this term to describe the pattern of crying when an overtired baby is going to sleep. Crying down, he says, is the reverse of crying up; crying up being the description of a baby waking up from a good sleep and starting to demand a feed. Crying up starts with silence. The baby is asleep, then he wakes. His first sounds are soft, gentle and subtle. If not attended to straight away, the baby begins to cry. He will cry for a short spell, and then go quiet for a short spell, then crying starts again but louder. Crying gradually increases in volume, with the gaps between cries becoming shorter until the baby is emitting a continuous loud bellow.

Crying down is the reverse of that picture. The overtired baby will start to bellow loudly when put down to sleep and the reverse pattern begins. The process of crying down to sleep takes between 10 and 30 minutes. The more overtired the baby, the louder and longer he will cry.

Dr Symon stresses that this technique will only work if the baby is allowed to settle himself to sleep. Parents who find the crying difficult to ignore are advised to wait 10 minutes before going in to him. They can then enter and reassure the baby with a soothing touch or quiet voice. Reassurance must be kept to a maximum of one to two minutes and then the parent must leave the room. Parents should then wait a further 10–15 minutes before returning. For this technique to work it is essential that the baby is not picked up and that he is allowed to settle by himself in his cot. Dr Symon believes that parents who do not allow their overtired baby to get himself off to sleep are creating long-term sleep problems. His beliefs have recently been confirmed by research at Oxford University. They conclude that a 20-minute 'winding down' bedtime routine, coupled with ignoring crying for gradually-increasing intervals, is an effective way of dealing with babies and children who resist sleep.

Provided a baby has been well fed and is ready to sleep, I believe he should be allowed to settle himself. The above method works not only for overtired babies but also for babies who fight sleep. Although it is very difficult to listen to a young baby cry himself to sleep, it will prevent serious sleep problems in the future. Parents who are not prepared to leave their baby to cry for 10–20 minutes usually end up resorting to feeding, rocking or giving a dummy to induce sleep.

This can often take up to two hours, resulting in exhausted parents and the baby waking up when he comes into his light sleep looking for the same inducement to get back to sleep again.

I believe that, in the long term, allowing your baby to develop the wrong sleep associations and therefore denying him the sound night's sleep he needs in order to develop both mentally and physically is worse for him than hearing him cry for a short while. Allowing your baby to learn to go to sleep unassisted is your aim, and it is important to remember that this will prevent much greater upset and more crying if he is waking in the night because he is not able or does not know how to get himself back to sleep after having woken in light sleep. Babies who have learned the wrong sleep associations will be unable to get back to sleep unaided, and will need whatever methods the parents use to assist them to sleep, be it feeding, rocking or the dummy. Some babies may need all three comforts before dropping back off to sleep. These babies are very unlikely to learn to sleep through the night and usually continue to wake up several times a night for several months, or even years.

In my experience, if a baby under six weeks has been well fed and is ready to sleep, crying down usually lasts between five and 10 minutes, although with some babies who have become overtired and fight sleep it can last up to 20 minutes. Provided all the baby's needs have been met, he will normally learn how to settle himself to sleep within a few nights, although some babies do continue to cry down at bedtime for several weeks. However, the time they cry does usually get progressively less. The important thing to remember is that if crying down is working, the baby will settle to sleep after the short spell of crying down and then sleep well until his next feed is due. If you see a pattern evolving where your baby cries down, sleeps for 20 minutes, wakes up crying and then cries down again, and keeps repeating this pattern, then there is obviously another underlying problem, very possibly genuine hunger, that is causing this and this problem should be sorted out before continuing with crying down.

If you are breastfeeding, I would always advise that you offer your baby a top-up of expressed milk before attempting crying down to be 100 per cent sure that hunger is not the reason he is not settling.

Assisting to sleep (for babies from around one month to any age)

The assisting to sleep method is something I developed to help babies who have developed erratic sleeping and feeding patterns. It is a gentle method of assisting your baby to sleep and teaching him to self-settle, and the first step that I would recommend for parents of babies and toddlers of any age who have no consistent pattern of feeding and sleeping (and must only be used with babies who have regained their birth weight and are continuing to put on a good amount of weight each week).

The aim of this method is to get your baby used to sleeping at regular times during naps and in the evening, which will help him to sleep through the night as soon as he is physically able. After genuine hunger and the wrong sleep associations, I find that too much daytime sleep is the most common reason a baby does not settle in the evening, or wakes frequently during the night. When this happens a vicious circle soon emerges where the baby needs to sleep more during the day because they are not sleeping well at night. In my experience, the only way to reverse this with a small baby is to assist the baby to sleep. Once their sleep improves in the night, a baby becomes much easier to keep awake during the day, which in turn has a knock-on effect of them sleeping better in the evening and at night.

For this method to work it is important that it is done consistently and by one parent only. During stage one of the method, and for at least three days, do not attempt to put your baby in his bed at nap times or early evening. Instead, one parent should lie in a quiet room with him and cuddle him throughout the whole of the sleep time. Try to ensure that he is held in the crook of your arm, rather than lying across your chest. If he is older than two months and is no longer swaddled, it may help to use your right hand to hold both his hands across his chest; in this way, he will not wave his arms around and risk getting upset. It is important that the same person is with him during the allocated sleep time, and that you do not hand him back and forth, or walk from room to room.

Once he is sleeping soundly for three days in a row at the recommended times, you should then progress to the second stage and try to settle him in his bed. It is important to sit right next to his bed, so you can hold his hands across his chest and comfort him. On the fourth night, hold both his hands until he is asleep, and on the fifth night hold only one of his hands across his chest until he is asleep. By the sixth night you should find that you can put him down sleepy but awake in his bed, checking him every two or three minutes until he falls asleep. Do not try to settle him in his bed unless he has been sleeping soundly in your arms for at least three nights. Some babies may take longer than three days to sleep consistently at the recommended times.

When he reaches stage two, where he is settling within 10 minutes for several nights, you can progress to try leaving him to self-settle using the crying down method described on page 347. It will help your baby get used to being happy in his cot if you put him in it for short spells during the day, when he is fully awake, with a small book or toy to look at. For the lunchtime nap, if you prefer, you can take your baby out for a nap in his pram or buggy. The important thing is to try to be consistent; the lunchtime nap should be in the buggy or in the house, but do not switch from one to the other midway through the nap.

The core night (for babies over six weeks and weighing more than 4.5kg (10lb))

Sometimes a baby will follow a routine really well during the day and be feeding and sleeping at the right times, but will continue to wake up around the same time in the middle of the night, once or twice even, but not be interested in feeding. Provided your baby is feeding and sleeping at the right times during the day and you have eliminated too much daytime sleep and too small a late feed as the reason for the night waking, then the core night method can be used to help your baby sleep longer in the night. However, this method can only be used for a baby over six weeks who weighs more than

4.5kg (10lb) and is following the CLB routines to the letter, and provided he is putting on enough weight each week. You will know it is the right time to start thinking about this method when your baby is still waking in the night looking for a feed and either taking too big a feed in the night then not feeding well at 7am or taking too small a feed or not seeming interested when offered a feed.

The method can also be used to lengthen the time between feeds in babies over six weeks old who wake up at 2am out of habit, take only a small amount to eat, then wake again at 5am – provided they are achieving a good weight gain each week. The aim here is to eliminate one of the night feeds so that the baby feeds better at the second waking – it is not to push the baby through the night without any feed at all.

The 'core night' is a method that has been used for many years by some maternity nurses and parents who believe in routine. It works on the principle that once a baby sleeps for a few longer spells in the night – the 'core night' period – he should never again be fed during the hours slept in the course of that period. Once you have seen that your baby can last a certain length of time without a feed, you should see this moment as a sign and a window of opportunity to help him to continue to sleep longer. If he wakes during those hours, he should be left for a few minutes to settle himself back to sleep. If he refuses to settle, then without resorting to feeding you should try other ways to settle him. Hollyer and Smith, the authors of *Sleep: The Easy Way to Peaceful Nights*, recommend patting, offering him a dummy or giving him a sip of water (providing they are over 6 months old). Stimulation and eye contact should be kept to a minimum while reassuring the baby you are there. The authors claim that following this approach will, within days, have your baby sleeping at least the hours of his core night. It also teaches the baby the two most important sleeping skills: how to go to sleep and how to go back to sleep after surfacing from a non-REM (deep) sleep.

Dr Brian Symon recommends a similar approach for babies over six weeks. Babies who are putting on a good amount of weight each week, but who are still waking at 3am should be offered the dummy or some cool boiled water (providing they are over 6 months). If the baby refuses to settle, give him the shortest possible feed that will allow him to settle.

This method can also be used to try to reduce the number of times a demand-fed baby is fed in the night and to encourage a longer stretch between feeds. But, again, things should be done gradually, working towards eliminating one feed at a time. Attempting to eliminate two or three feeds in one night will lead to a very distressing night for both you and your baby. Before embarking on these methods, the following points should be read carefully to make sure that your baby really is capable of going for a longer spell in the night.

- It is important to ensure that your baby's last feed of the day is substantial enough to help him sleep for a longer stretch in the night. The majority of babies still need a fifth feed until they are weaned at six months old and some babies who are exclusively breastfed may not drop their fifth feed until nearer seven months.

- The main sign that a baby is ready to cut down and drop the middle-of-the-night feed is a regular weight gain and a reluctance to feed, or feeding less, at 7am.

The core night method can also work particularly well with babies under six months by getting them to feed less and less in the night, gradually dropping the middle-of-the-night feeding. It can also work well in getting rid of night-time feedings with older babies and toddlers, but with these some degree of controlled crying may be necessary if a sleep association problem has set in.

The method can also be used with babies over six months who are weaned and still waking up in the night looking for a milk feed. Older babies over 6 months and toddlers who are still feeding and waking in the night and have learned the wrong sleep associations can be prepared for controlled crying by using the core night method. Once they are down to one milk feed in the night, this can gradually be diluted until they are taking only water (see guidelines on page 364). Once the parents have arrived at this stage, they can then use controlled crying.

11

Sleep Training

Perhaps the most controversial area in parenting circles in recent years has been the different methods parents use to help their children to get to sleep, with questions about not only which are the most effective, but also apparently potential harmful effects in the longer term of any form of sleep training. I have never advocated controlled crying for babies under six months, but I do suggest using a method known as 'crying down' (see page 347) with overtired babies, which involves leaving them to settle themselves to sleep, as it is an effective way of helping an overtired child. This does not involve leaving a baby screaming for long periods, and in younger babies it generally only involves leaving them for a matter of minutes.

Over 30 years ago in the early stages of my career I worked with many different families. Some followed a strict feeding and sleeping routine while others would be led by their babies. With babies who were on strict four-hourly feeding routines, they were sometimes made to wait – often crying with genuine hunger – until it was the 'right time' to feed, then once they were fed, they became so overtired that they had to be left to cry for another lengthy period until they fell asleep through sheer exhaustion. With babies whose parents followed the baby-led approach and fed on demand, I would find that so often in the early days a baby would be sleepy and not demand to be fed. These babies would often go hours during the day not feeding and by the time they reached a month or two, they would be feeding several times a night through genuine hunger.

With both these approaches to parenting it was very common that after several months some form of sleep training was implemented to improve the babies' feeding and sleeping patterns. It was through working with hundreds of these parents that my first book – *The Contented Little Baby Book* – evolved. I was convinced that feeding and sleeping were so closely linked and over the years of observing the sleeping and feeding patterns of these babies I developed what is now known as the CLB routines. I knew from experience that one routine did not fit the individual needs of all babies, hence the reason there are nine routines in my first book, all of which can be adapted to suit the individual needs of each baby. Since the publication of my first book hundreds of thousands of parents have followed my routines, without having to resort to any form of sleep training. All of these parents can testify that if my advice is followed properly from the very early days, they have never had to leave their babies to cry for lengthy periods or embark on any form of sleep training methods. In my opinion sleep training should only be considered as a last resort, when all other attempts to improve a baby or toddler's sleep have been attempted. The aim of this book is to help parents pinpoint problems and give guidance on how to improve things *before* resorting to sleep training. However,

I do accept that there are times when sleep training may be the only option. Even then there are various methods of sleep training and I believe it is important to choose which form is used very carefully as different approaches are better for different problems and ages. The three most popular sleep training methods are controlled crying, sometimes known as controlled comforting, gradual withdrawal/ retreat or crying it out, sometimes known as CIO.

I would never recommend crying it out at any age regardless of the problem as I think it is too harsh and can result in a baby or toddler being traumatised. Crying it out involves settling the baby or toddler in their bed and basically leaving them to cry themselves to sleep, regardless of how long they take to go to sleep.

Controlled crying or comforting on the other hand involves checking and reassuring the baby at regular intervals, gradually increasing the intervals between checking, but never picking the baby up unless distressed. This usually works best with babies between six and 12 months who have a sleep association problem. With older children it can work, but it is more dependent on the child's nature and doesn't work so well with more sensitive toddlers and children. Controlled crying is what people often think of when discussing sleep training, but this is only one of many methods recommended for babies over six months, and is broadly based around the methods advocated by Dr Richard Ferber, where a child learns to soothe himself to sleep. These methods can be beneficial in helping to ensure children don't build up sleep associations which make it difficult for them to settle by themselves. Ferber's philosophy is often described as 'crying it out' but he also uses the phrase 'gradual extinction' to describe the idea of putting a baby to bed and returning at brief intervals to comfort him if he isn't settling. The intervals between returns are gradually increased and Ferber doesn't recommend leaving a baby to cry it out alone for long periods.

Another method for older babies and toddlers is gradual withdrawal, which is a more gentle approach to sleep training. Gradual withdrawal/retreat is in my experience the best approach for older babies and toddlers. It involves a parent initially staying in the room with the child who has been put to bed for a short spell and returning as and when necessary so that the child doesn't feel any sense of isolation when going to sleep.

Each of these methods is better suited to different babies and parents, depending on the age and temperament of the child, the family structure and the nature of the sleep problem.

Concerns about crying

If you are at that stage where things are so difficult that you are considering sleep training, you will possibly also have serious concerns about its impact, especially if you have read some of the huge amount of information available on how damaging sleep training can be.

Some parents worry about using any of these methods to help their child to sleep, fearing that they may be upsetting for the child or even that they could cause problems in the future. Critics who disapprove of any form of sleep training have argued that it may cause stress and trauma for a baby that could lead to long-term psychological difficulties further down the line.

In my experience if done properly implementing sleep training for a child with a serious sleep problem, should only result in a much happier, contented and confident child. Parents will also be reassured to know that a 2012 study published by a team from the Murdoch Children's Research Institute in Australia, led by researcher Dr Anna Price, which followed up the impact of early sleep training methods, found no evidence of any problems at all. The researchers followed children through to the age of six and the evidence suggests that sleep training made no difference at all to the children's mental health, stress levels, behaviour or relationships with their parents as they grew older. The reassuring results of the study suggest that the benefits for the whole family from getting a child settled into a regular sleep pattern outweigh any concerns.

To balance out the huge number of scaremongering reports, Dr Brian Symon, known as The Babysleep Doctor and author of *Silent Nights: Overcoming Sleep Problems in Babies and Children*, addresses some of the myths about sleep training methods and the damage they can cause, in his new book. He goes on to address the worries that many parents have about leaving a child to cry: 'Please remember that it is biologically impossible for a child to be damaged by protesting while settling to sleep. Universally, parents report to me that they and their children are happier once night-time sleep is complete. While the initial nights can be challenging, particularly on the mother, once a full night's sleep is achieved, parents consistently report to me that it was a small price to pay given the overwhelmingly important benefits.'

Dr Symon, who is a specialist medical practitioner and has conducted research into sleep training, explains that his views on the subject are backed up by evidence from other studies too: 'International research has failed to show any evidence of negative outcomes for the child or the mother from using these techniques. Critics of my and similar techniques, who work at a senior level, readily accept that there is no evidence anywhere in the published literature of damage to children or mothers. In the absence of evidence, new comments are put forward such as "damage may appear sometime in the future" or commentaries about the brain's stress hormone "cortisol" levels in the baby's saliva are used to imply risk of damage. My answer is quite straightforward. When working with children on a daily basis it becomes clear that if they sleep well, eat well and are in the care of a happy, confident mother, the child's emotional wellbeing is clearly and unambiguously improved.'

For anyone who has had concerns about sleep training, this combined with the scientific evidence from the Murdoch Institute's research should be reassuring, and should allow them to use the techniques which may not only help to improve children's sleep but also their parents' sleep too.

Night-time sleep may be one of the major issues that parents contact me about, but once I start looking into the causes of the problem, I often find that it is daytime sleep or feeding that must first be adjusted.

Some problems I outline in this book will best be solved by using a form of sleep training and I have listed it as an option where that is the case. For parents wishing to try a form of sleep training I hope the more detailed guide below will be of use in helping you prepare for and then resolve your baby's sleep problem.

Preparing for sleep training

The aim of my first book, *The Contented Little Baby Book*, was to ensure that a baby's feeding and sleeping needs were met in order that crying was kept to the minimum and the right sleep associations were established from day one, so that parents never had to sleep-train their babies. I have always maintained that sleep training is a last resort and should only ever be used with babies over six months who have learned the wrong sleep associations and are unable to settle themselves to sleep without assistance from their parents.

If your baby is over six months and not settling and sleeping well and you are considering sleep training because he has learned the wrong sleep associations, it is important that you eliminate hunger as the real cause of him not settling as opposed to him having learned the wrong associations. All too often I get parents coming to me with older babies they assume have a sleep association problem. The parents have been trying to sleep-train for weeks and without success, when in fact the reason for the disturbed sleep is genuine hunger. It is therefore essential that you double-check that your baby's feeding needs are being fully met, before you consider sleep training.

Parents are told their baby should manage to sleep through the night once they are six months, without night feeds. This is only true if a baby's needs are being fully met throughout the day.

Sleep training can be both mentally and emotionally draining for parents and it is not something that should be started without considerable thought. If you decide to sleep-train your baby or child, it is essential that your baby or child has a medical check-up with your doctor, so that he can confirm that there are no medical reasons why you should not attempt sleep training. It is also worthwhile seeking advice and support from your health visitor, who may be able to put you in touch with your nearest sleep clinic.

For sleep training to be successful it is important that you can commit at least two weeks of your time to resolving the problem. Sleep training should not be attempted under any of the following circumstances:

- Your baby is not gaining weight. A baby not gaining weight should always be seen by a doctor. Sleep training should only be used if your baby is over six months and is regularly gaining an average of 114–227g (4–8oz) each week.

- Your baby or toddler is just recovering from an illness, or any other member of the family is unwell.

- You are about to move home, go on holiday or have visitors to stay within the next two weeks.

- Any younger or older siblings are going through a difficult time either mentally, physically or emotionally, or about to start nursery or pre-school.

- Your baby or toddler has just started or is about to start nursery or pre-school.

● Either you or your partner is under pressure at work.

● It is also important that as much as is possible the same person deals with the baby throughout the sleep training. It can be very confusing for the baby or child when a different parent keeps appearing at different times during the night. At minimum you should aim that the one person does a full slot, for example one of you may do the 6pm to 10pm slot and the other the midnight to 6am slot.

Diluting feeds (for babies and toddlers over six months)

Before considering this method I urge parents to return to the preparation for sleep training section. It is important to note that this method should only be used if you have consulted a medical professional and your baby is over six months and has had his weight checked.

Diluting feeds is often recommended as a way of eliminating excessive night-time feeding with babies over six months and toddlers. The reason that many parents have problems stopping their baby taking night feeds is because a vicious circle has evolved in which the baby or toddler does not eat enough during the day and is therefore genuinely hungry in the night. When the parents attempt to dilute the feed each time the baby or toddler wakes, he will often settle at the first waking but not at the next or subsequent wakings. In my experience it works best if feeds are eliminated one at a time.

If you are considering diluting feeds in order to eliminate excessive night waking, it is essential that you discuss how best to do this with your health visitor or GP. It can be very dangerous for babies under a year to be given too much water, resulting in water intoxication and often death, so if feeds are to be diluted, then your health visitor needs to give you advice to ensure that the ratio of dilution is correct for your baby's weight and age.

Controlled crying (for babies over six months)

With babies between six months and one year of age, waking in the night is often due to a mixture of hunger and wrong associations, caused by a lack of structure in the baby's feeding and sleeping. If a baby or toddler has learned the wrong sleep associations and needs to be rocked, cuddled or fed to sleep, then it is inevitable that some degree of controlled crying will have to be implemented to address the problem. With toddlers and babies who have already got into seriously bad sleeping habits, the following sleep training techniques will need to be used along with the advice for sleeping and feeding requirements.

Controlled crying is always a last resort as a means of sleep training but for some babies it can be an effective way to train them between six months and a year. For babies over one year old I would be very cautious about using the controlled crying method and would recommend the gradual withdrawal method instead at this age (see page 370). However, if your baby is between six months and a year and still feeding in the night, I would advise implementing the core night method first so that you can be confident that your baby or toddler is not crying through genuine hunger (see page 352). One of the main reasons that controlled crying fails for so many parents is that a vicious circle has arisen in which the baby or toddler continues to feed in the night and does not eat enough during the day, so he is genuinely hungry in the night. The core night method and gradually reducing and diluting his milk feed in the night should see an increase in his appetite during the day. I would never recommend that a parent attempts controlled crying until they see an increase in the amount of food their child is eating during the day.

Dr Richard Ferber is widely recognised as America's leading authority in the field of children's sleep problems. His book *Solve Your Child's Sleep Problems* explains every aspect of children's sleep in great detail, as well as how problems evolve and how parents can resolve them. For older babies and children who are still feeding in the night, he advises gradually eliminating night feeds. If waking continues, he recommends controlled crying to break the habit. The controlled crying method is likely to be more successful if used at each of the baby's sleep times. While this method does teach a baby or child how to get to sleep on his own, it can be difficult to endure and can fail because parents get very distressed listening to their baby or child cry for lengthy periods of time. They resort to picking him up after 30–40 minutes and rocking him to sleep, which creates an even worse sleep problem. The baby soon learns that if he cries long enough and hard enough, he will be picked up. It can be very distressing to have to listen to your baby crying for any length of time; however, if done properly, this method will improve even the worst sleeping problems within days. In my experience, with babies between six and 12 months the problem is normally resolved within a week. For controlled crying to be successful it is essential that the baby or child learns to settle himself to sleep, no matter how long it takes.

The basic rules for controlled crying are as follows:

Day one

It is always best to start controlled crying in the evening on the first day. The following day it is important that you stick to your baby's usual routine and that you use the same procedure when settling him for daytime naps as you use in the evening.

- Decide on a regular time to start the bedtime routine and stick to it. Allow at least one hour for the bath, milk feed and settling. Ensure that your baby is calm and ready to sleep before you put him in his cot – don't try to put him in his cot if he is irritable or crying.

- Settle your baby in his bed before he gets too sleepy. Kiss him goodnight and leave the room.

- Decide on a checking time before returning to reassure him – most parents choose somewhere between three and five minutes the first night, increasing this to five to 10 minutes the second night. Reassurance should be kept to a minimum. You can stroke him or say 'Ssh ssh', but he must not be picked up. Leave the room after two minutes even if he continues to cry.

- After the first half hour of checking, the time between visits should be increased by five to 10 minutes each time.

- Continue with the checking plan until your baby falls asleep. Reassurance should still be kept to a minimum of no more than two minutes and he must not be lifted out of the cot.

- If your baby wakes in the night, continue to follow the same plan as for the evening, starting at five minutes and gradually increasing the time between visits to 10 minutes.

Day two

For daytime naps it is important that you start where you left off in the night. Wait at least 10 minutes before checking your baby or toddler and continue to keep visits to his room to a maximum of two minutes, with the minimum of reassurance.

If your baby does not fall asleep until nearer the time he normally wakes up from his nap, allow him 15 minutes of sleep at his morning nap and 45 minutes at his lunchtime nap; this way he will not end up sleeping after 3pm in the day. If your baby is very tired he may need a short nap of 15 or 20 minutes in the late afternoon if he is to get through until bedtime without becoming overtired.

- The second evening follow the same settling procedure as the first night, but this time wait 20–25 minutes before returning to his bedroom. During visits on the second night (which should last five to 10 minutes) you can reassure your baby by saying 'Ssh ssh', but do not stroke or touch him.

- If your baby is still crying after the first hour, the time between visits should be increased to 35–40 minutes.

- If he wakes in the night, you should wait 45 minutes before checking him, and you should not speak to him or stroke him. Reduce the time in the room to one minute.

Day three

By the third day, the majority of babies will be settling themselves at all sleep times within 20 minutes and there is no need to check on them.

- If your baby backtracks at one of the sleep times and you have to go back to checking him, start off with checking him every 15–20 minutes and increase the interval until you are back to 45–50 minutes.

- It is very important that by the third day you check your baby after no less than 15–20 minutes. Do not go back to checking every five to 10 minutes, as this usually results in the baby or toddler getting more upset by your visits.

● Once your baby has done a few days of settling within 20 minutes, you should be able to use the crying down method for getting him off to sleep at naps or in the evening. Within a couple of weeks the majority of babies and toddlers will be going to sleep without any fuss at all.

Gradual withdrawal (for babies from nine months to three years)

This method usually works best for toddlers between one and three years of age, particularly if they are sleeping in a bed and not a cot. It is generally seen as the gentlest approach to sleep training, so if parents of younger children want to avoid using the controlled crying method, they could consider this approach. However, I have not found this method to be very effective with younger babies as it seems to upset them even more when their parents potter around the room or sit by the bed. If this method is to be successful, the parents have to have the patience to be consistent for several weeks and be aware that it will take a lot longer than using controlled crying.

Though it takes longer than the controlled crying method, this approach is in my experience usually the best one for older babies and toddlers, especially those who have feeding problems or separation anxiety.

Dr Olwen Wilson, a chartered child psychologist, claims that the more gentle strategy she has devised will ease children into a good sleeping pattern within seven days, without stressing the child or the parents. It involves a parent initially staying in the room with the child who has been put to bed for a short spell and returning as and when necessary so that the child doesn't feel any sense of isolation when going to sleep. Every couple of nights the time spent out of the room is increased until the baby or toddler starts to fall asleep while the parent is out of the room.

She believes that children should be frequently supported while they are learning how to go to sleep without direct comfort from their parents. Dr Wilson stresses the importance of establishing the same rituals every night: bath, bedtime story and settling the child in his cot or bed. She also advises the parent to stay in the room but to be unobtrusive. She suggests moving around the room or sorting a drawer out before leaving the room for a short spell. The parents must be prepared to leave and re-enter the room many times during the first few nights of the programme. The maximum number of times a parent might have to enter the room could be as high as 300. She believes that this process gets the child used to being alone without making him feel isolated and fearful. By the third night she says that the child will become settled enough to be left on his own for a period of five minutes or longer. On the fifth night the child may backtrack and want to go back to his old, familiar pattern of settling. If parents are persistent at this stage and do not give in, she says that by the end of the week the problem of settling will be hugely improved and, within a further week or two, the child will be happy to go off to sleep on his own.

This method takes a lot of determination and patience on behalf of the parents, as it can take hours every evening of going in and out of the room before they reach a period when the child is calm enough for the withdrawal method to progress. I think this method works if the mother has the energy to spend perhaps two or even three weeks working at the plan without any other distractions. If your baby or toddler is suffering from seperation anxiety I would recommend that before starting the gradual withdrawal method you spend several nights where you actually stay in the room, sitting quietly until your baby or toddler is asleep. It is important not to get into lots of conversation with him, other than reassuring him now and again that Mummy is here, and it's sleepy time. Once he is used to settling to sleep without a fuss, you can then do the gradual withdrawal method. You would also need to follow the same approach at naptime

I have always believed that if the feeding and sleeping needs of young babies are properly met and the right sleep associations created from day one, then sleep training such as controlled crying should rarely be needed. Since the publication of my first book, *The Contented Little Baby Book*, in 1999 I have had phenomenal feedback from thousands of parents. The consensus from the majority of these parents is that following the routines without a doubt resulted in a happy contented baby who slept and fed well, who rarely cried.

It is important to stress that controlled crying is not part of the CLB philosophy, however I do appreciate that sometimes problems do arise where a baby's sleeping becomes so erratic that it can start to affect the health and well-being not only of the baby, but of the parents as well. When this happens, in certain circumstances and as a last resort, I would advise some form of sleep training may need to be implemented.

Index